I0160871

Fort Scott, Fort Hughes & Camp Recovery

Three 19th century military sites in Southwest Georgia

Dale Cox

2016

Copyright 2016 by Dale Cox
All Rights Reserved.

ISBN: 978-0692704011

Volume 1 in the Forts of the Forgotten Frontier Series

Visit the author online at:

www.exploresouthernhistory.com

Old Kitchen Books
An Old Kitchen Media Company
4523 Oak Grove Road
Bascom, Florida 32423

*"Greater love hath no man than this,
that a man lay down his life for his friends."*
John 15:13

*"And ye shall hear of wars and rumours of wars: see that ye be not
troubled: for all these things must come to pass, but the end is not yet."*
Matthew 24:6

This book is respectfully dedicated to the people of Decatur County, Georgia

Table of Contents

Maps

Introduction

I have dreamed of writing this book for many years. Fort Scott, Fort Hughes and Camp Recovery were known to me as far back as the days of my childhood. The Georgia branch of my family used to hold its reunions on the banks of the Flint River in Bainbridge and we would climb the bluff to the J.D. Chason Memorial Park to marvel at the size of the old cannon that marked the site of Fort Hughes. A second gun brought from the site of Fort Scott stood nearby and together these monuments fired our imaginations and filled us with childhood curiosity about what acts once took place on the grounds.

Somewhere along the way I met Mr. N.L. Sellers, now deceased, who owned and guarded the site of Camp Recovery. He could be tough on those caught trying to loo the site, but he was kind to me and guided me to the cemetery and the gun monument that marked it.

As I grew older I worked with a team of archaeologists who were working to document prehistoric and historic sites around Lake Seminole. One of the places we visited, although for a very limited amount of time, was Fort Scott. The narrative that follows will demonstrate the importance of this site in the history of United States. Few people know the actual location of the old fort, which is probably a good thing. The site was looted for many years. It is a sad place to visit, with memories of the scores of men who suffered and died there. Some lost their lives to battle wounds, but most died in the excruciating pain of yellow fever and malaria. Many of the deceased were first generation immigrants to the United States who joined the army because it offered a means of survival as they arrived from Europe with no money but filled with hope.

To walk the overgrown site today and think of these men is a moving experience. They rest there without so much as a piece of rock to mark the sites of their graves. A friend of mine once observed that Americans have very short memories. In the case of these dozens of servicemen, he was very right. Our memories have been short indeed.

Many people assisted in the writing of this book and I extend my thanks to them all. Special recognition must go to the staffs of the National Archives, Library of Congress, State Archives of Georgia, State Archives of Florida, Cleveland

Museum of Natural History and other repositories across the nation and in Europe. I would also be remiss if I did not note the help provided by the following key individuals:

Jack Wingate (deceased), Decatur County, Georgia.
N.L. Sellers (deceased), Decatur County, Georgia.
Hon. Frank S. Jones (deceased), Decatur County, Georgia.
E.W. Carswell (deceased), Washington County, Florida.
Dean DeBolt and Stephanie Johnson, University of West Florida.
Nancy White, Ph.D., University of South Florida.
Christopher Kimball, Seminole War Foundation, Inc.
Brian Rucker, Ph.D., Pensacola State College.
Robert Daffin, Jackson County, Florida.
Ashley Pollette, Jackson County, Florida.
Savannah Brininstool, who was serving her country this time.

My personal thanks are also extended to Pearl Cox, Rachael Conrad, Sue Tindel, Robert Earl Standland, Clayton Penhallegon, William Cox, Alan Cox, Chattahoochee Main Street and all of the friends who have assisted in one way or another through the many years that I spent assembling the documentation for this book.

May God bless and keep all of you.

Dale Cox
March 31, 2016

Fort Scott, Fort Hughes & Camp Recovery

Three 19th Century Military Sites in Southwest Georgia

Dale Cox

1

CHAPTER ONE

Trouble on the Forgotten Frontier

The early months of 1816 were particularly tense in the borderlands that separated the United States from Spanish Florida. The Treaty of Fort Jackson had been negotiated eighteen months earlier to bring the Creek War of 1813-1814 to a close, but the price it imposed on the Creeks – Red Stick and "friendly" alike – was severe. As indemnification for the cost of the war, Major General Andrew Jackson had exacted on the Creek Nation a land cession of 23 million acres. The new "public lands" completely separated the dwindling territory of the Creeks from the Gulf Coast and their former Spanish benefactors in Florida.

The cession was particularly shocking to Lower Creek chiefs living in Southwest Georgia and Southeast Alabama. Most of their towns had not taken part in the war neither had they been invited to participate in the treaty negotiations. Now, however, they were being told that they must give up lands that had belonged to their ancestors for as far back as memory could reach. As might be expected, many of these leaders were disgruntled. Similarly irate were the thousands of Red Stick warriors who had fled into Spanish Florida after the Battle of Horseshoe Bend. The Miccosukee and

1

Alachua Seminoles of Florida formed an alliance with them and together they began to accelerate a series of small raids across the Spanish border into Georgia and Alabama. The latter state was then part of the Mississippi Territory.

The situation began to achieve critical mass when U.S. surveyors tried to establish the lines marking the limits of the new cession. The Creeks were exhausted from war and desperately trying to recover from the cataclysmic destruction of their nation in 1813-1814. This was the likely reason that most of the chiefs, although they opposed the running of the lines, chose to resist with nonviolent methods. Most, but not all:

> The Indians, however, still adhere to their resolution not to permit their interpreters and hunters to go upon the line. This alone, considering the Indian Character, can not but be viewed as a strong indication of dissatisfaction, if not of hostility. But we have lately received unquestionable information of an outrage which leaves no doubt that a spirit of hostility exists in a part of the nation. A Colonel Powell, a Captain Daniel Johnston, and another person from the neighborhood of Fort Stoddert, were some 10 or 12 days ago fired on by a party of Indians near Fort Claiborne. Powell only escaped, three balls having passed through his clothes.[1]

The author of the above was Brevet Major General Edmund P. Gaines, a figure well known in the Mississippi Territory for his role in the 1807 arrest of former vice president Aaron Burr. He served on the Niagara frontier during the War of 1812 where he gained national acclaim for his role in the heroic defense of Fort Erie against a larger British army. Badly wounded in that engagement, he returned south and by January 1816 was in command of the Eastern Division of the Military Department of the South under Major General Andrew Jackson. Like frontiersman David Crockett, he later opposed Jackson's policy of Indian Removal.

Gaines soon learned that the victims of the attack had been exploring the new "public lands" obtained from the Creeks at Fort Jackson. He also began to refer to the incident as the Johnson & McGaskey murders, a reference to the men who lost their lives. The 1816 Census of what is now Baldwin County, Alabama, lists both Daniel Johnson and John McGaskey as residents of the fledgling seven-year-old county. Their presence so early on a frontier known for the 1813 attack on Fort Mims indicates they were likely hoping to improve their fortunes by seeking good lands on the leading edge of American expansion. They lost their lives by venturing into a region still frequented by Savannah Jack and other Red Stick chiefs and warriors, most if not all of whom were angry over the Treaty of Fort Jackson.[2]

The murders of Johnson and McGaskey brought the running of the survey to a temporary halt as Gaines ordered Lt. Col. Duncan Lamont Clinch's battalion of the 4th U.S. Infantry Regiment to march to Fort Mitchell on the Chattahoochee River from Fort Hawkins in Georgia. He also ordered the construction of flatboats to be used in transporting Clinch and his men down the Chattahoochee to the mouth of Cemochechobee Creek where the cession line struck the river.[3]

Gaines also had his eye on another potential target, the so-called "Negro Fort" at Prospect Bluff on the Apalachicola River. Built in 1814-1815 by British troops under Lt. Col. Edward Nicolls, the bastion had been left in the hands of a large force of African-American Colonial Marines and their Creek, Seminole and Choctaw allies when the colonel withdrew following the end of the War of 1812. The fort served as a beacon of freedom and American officers, politicians and planters feared the consequences of allowing it to exist so close to the plantation districts of the South. Slaveholders in both Spanish Florida and the Creek Nation agreed and all three nations were developing individual plans to deal with this perceived threat.

Gaines clearly had a military campaign against the fort at Prospect Bluff in mind when he told Jackson that the boats being built to carry Clinch's battalion to the cession line might also prove valuable should it prove "necessary to extend our operations lower down the river." There was no

3

way that Jackson would not recognize the hint, but Gaines left no doubt when he concluded his report with the latest intelligence about the fort.[4]

Attacks by Red Sticks and the believed threat from the fort on the Apalachicola were not the only issues facing the U.S. Army on the frontier. Settlers trying to squat on the new "public lands" represented a serious threat to the government's plans to sell the lands. Gaines evidenced this on February 22, just two days after his report on the Johnson and McGaskey murders, by publishing a warning from the War Department that potential settlers should stay off the treaty lands. Anyone remaining inside the limits of the Fort Jackson cession after March 10, 1816, would be removed by force and suffer the destruction of their homes and property.[5]

The warning also extended to those who might be disposed to trespass on the remaining lands of the Creek Indians as well:

> Intrusion upon the lands of the friendly Indian tribes, is not only a violation of the laws, but in direct opposition to the policy of the government towards its savage neighbors. Upon application of any Indian agent stating that intrusions of this nature have been committed, and are continued, the President requires that they shall be equally removed, and their habitations and improvements destroyed by military force, and that every attempt to return shall be repressed in the same manner.[6]

Communications of the time were slow but it did not take long for news of the troubling situation in the cession lands to reach the people of Georgia. The *Augusta Chronicle* reported on March 1st that Gaines had ordered U.S. troops to the frontier and then followed three days later with a more detailed article on Creek opposition to the running of the cession lines:

> *Creek Nation.* – A serious misunderstanding, which threatens the peace and tranquility of our frontiers, still exists between our commissioners for running the new

4

boundary line and the chiefs of that confederacy. A determined opposition has been made to their farther progress, and we understand they have suspended their operations until a sufficient military force arrives to protect them from indignity and injury. General Gaines, who is now in the nation, has ordered all the disposable military force of the United States, now at Fort Hawkins, among which is a company of light artillery, to march immediately to Fort Mitchell. This precautionary measure we hope will have its desired effect, and that the misguided savage will avert that destruction, which threatens the extinction of his nation.[7]

There is little doubt that the soldiers themselves believed they were going to war. An officer wrote to a friend in Richmond, Virginia, on March 20th that "we are going to have a Creek war to a certainty." The author noted that he was taking eight companies of infantry and one of artillery to the Creek Nation where Gen. Gaines was determined to run the line "PEACEABLY IF HE CAN, FORCIBLY IF HE MUST." The words were upper case in the original.[8]

Gaines reported to Jackson on the same day that Clinch's battalion had crossed the Flint River on the 16th and should be either at or near Fort Mitchell on the Chattahoochee. The general was less convinced than the anonymous letter writer that war was imminent, but was more than willing to spark one. After telling Jackson that he believed a military escort would allow the surveyors to complete their work in two weeks, he went on to suggest to Jackson the establishment of a new post lower down the Chattahoochee and the destruction of the fort at Prospect Bluff:

Should a post be established, its supplies, I am persuaded may be derived more conveniently and more economically from Mobile or New Orleans than any other source. If such an intercourse could be opened down the Appalachacola, it would enable us to keep an eye upon the Seminoles and the Negro Fort. This Negro establishment is, (I think justly,) considered as likely to produce much evil, among the blacks of Georgia & the eastern part of the Mississippi Territory. Will you permit me to break it up?[9]

Gaines was undoubtedly confident of Jackson's backing. He arrived at Fort Mitchell on March 21st to find Clinch and his men building the seven ordered flatboats. Ten days later on the 31st, without waiting for Gen. Jackson's response, he led Clinch's force down the river. In conjunction with this movement he sent word to Major David E. Twiggs of the 7th Infantry to establish a second fort on the Conecuh River at or near the Florida line. The latter post, to be named Fort Crawford, would prove more difficult to build but was in place on the high bluffs overlooking Murder Creek at what is now East Brewton, Alabama, by summer. Gaines and Clinch, meanwhile, reached their objective at the mouth of Cemochechobee Creek on April 2, 1816.[10]

The best location for the construction of a fort was clearly evident to the two officers. Just south of the confluence of the Cemochechobee with the Chattahoochee on the east bank stands an impressive bluff. Miles of the river are clearly visible from its crest, as is a remarkable expanse of cession lands along line dividing them from the Creek Nation in what is now Henry and Barbour Counties, Alabama.

Recognizing the military potential of the bluff, Gaines ordered Clinch to begin building a new fort. As a tribute to his commanding officer, the lieutenant colonel named it Fort Gaines:

> …The Lt. Colonel has commenced a small work, consisting of a square picketing and two block houses, to be defended by one company. The site is strong, handsome and apparently healthy. It is upon the left bank of the river on a hill or bluff 133 feet, nearly perpendicular from the edge of the water.[11]

The note that the fort could be defended by one company indicates it was small in size. A fort of similar design was built the following year on the Flint River in Georgia with exterior walls that measured 90 feet on each side. Fort Gaines probably was not much bigger, which indicates that most of the men in the seven companies present under Clinch camped outside the walls of the fort.

As their men worked to build the new post, Gaines and Clinch convened a council with the chiefs and leading men of the Creek towns in the vicinity:

> ...I explained to the Indians settled near Summochichoba the object of our movement – to complete the line according to the Treaty, and lay off the land, that our people may buy and settle it – That I brought the pipe of peace for our friends – and for our enemies the <u>cannon</u> & <u>bayonet</u>. They replied that they were too poor and too weak to oppose us, and therefore had determined to sit still and hold down their heads.[12]

The passive response of the chiefs not only reflected their recognition of the fact that they could not hope to oppose the United States, but also bade well for the running of the rest of the cession line. Gaines remained at the new fort only five days before leaving for Camp Montgomery on the Alabama River on April 7th. The name of the post first appeared in writing two days earlier on the 5th when Brevet Major Enos Cutler submitted Inspection Returns to the Adjutant and Inspector General for the seven companies present at "Fort Gaines, Chattohuche R."[13]

The council convened by Gaines and Clinch gave one officer from the 4th Infantry an intimate view of several of the leading figures in the Creek Nation:

> ...I had the opportunity of seeing the Indians in council, where the Big Warrior and Little Prince were both present. You no doubt will recollect that the Big Warrior was friendly to us during the late war. Let me tell you he does not conceal is disapprobation to our running the boundary line. However he received us courteously – not so the Little Prince, who showed us no mark of attention. The Big Warrior is the largest Indian known to us. He is dignified in his demeanor, affable and inviting in his manners; his enemies accuse him of cowardice, but I presume his inactivity of late years is to be ascribed to old age and an unwieldy person. The countenance of the Little Prince indicates him to be fierce and cruel, and I am told it does

8

not belie him. It is perhaps well for the United States, that he is now old and bigoted. There is also another very important personage in the nation – I mean the famous M'Intosh – the same to whom Congress gave a sword for services, &c. and to whom we are more indebted for our victories over the Indians in the late war than some persons would be willing to admit. He is a half breed, and but chief of a town. His figure would rival the Apollo, and such an air of majesty I never beheld. His every motion displays all that grace, dignity and elegance which you would imagine the Grecian model, when animated, to possess.[14]

While U.S. troops had gained military ascendency over the Creeks along the Chattahoochee River, things were not going so well on other fronts. Supply of Fort Gaines almost immediately became an issue when the contractor refused to deliver provisions and supplies to the post, claiming that his contract required him to deliver only to the populated areas of Georgia. Gaines referred the matter to the War Department while also requesting that Jackson push to supply the fort by way of the Apalachicola and Chattahoochee Rivers. Such a movement would save the government $2,000 per month he estimated. It also would require the passage of supply boats not only through Spanish Florida, but within range of the guns of the powerful fort at Prospect Bluff.[15]

The effort to capture the warriors responsible for killing Johnson and McGaskey likewise ended in failure. Gaines warned Jackson that he could not verify its source, but reported that intelligence had been received at Camp Montgomery that "they are gone to the Appalachacola, and that they carried McGlasky below the line, where they burned him alive by sticking lightwood splinters in his flesh."[16]

The method given for McGaskey's execution was a traditional Creek way of eliminating enemies. Lightwood, typically called "fat light'erd" by residents of the Deep South, comes from the dried stumps and trunks of fallen pines. It is so resinous that it will explode into flame almost instantaneously when it comes into contact with fire. Citizens of the region, like the Creeks and Seminoles before them, still use it as kindling for lighting their fireplaces. Using lightwood to burn a person to death after sticking splinters of it in their flesh was an excruciating form of execution that had its roots deep in the ancient traditions of the Creek Indians.

Gaines was at Fort Jackson near present-day Wetumpka, Alabama, by April 21st where he met with Col. Benjamin Hawkins, U.S. Agent for Indian Affairs. The aging Col. Hawkins, who would pass away just six weeks later, reported that the Creeks had decided not to oppose the running of the treaty lines, but neither would they provide any assistance to the survey party. He left little doubt, however, that officials already considered the fort at Prospect Bluff to be the looming issue of the moment:

> The Chiefs are making an effort of themselves, to aid the Seminolie Chiefs in destroying the negro establishment in that country, capturing and delivering up Negro's belonging to Citizens of the United States, to me, or some of our military establishment. The Little Prince and some warriors are by last report on the march for effecting this object. They have applied for some aid in corn which after conferring with the General is sent them 300 bushels.[17]

The view of the fort was the same among the officials of the Madison Administration in Washington, D.C. as well as in another town of the same name. Maj. Gen. Andrew Jackson was at Washington, the capital of the Mississippi Territory, when he penned a letter to Spanish governor Mauricio de Zuniga in Pensacola to inquire about the fort on the Apalachicola:

> I am charged by my Government to make known to you that a negro fort, erected during our late war with Britain, and at or near the junction of the Chatahoochee and Flint Rivers, has been strengthened since that period, and is now occupied by upwards of two hundred and fifty negroes, many of whom have been enticed from the service of their masters, citizens of the United States; all of whom are well clothed and disciplined. Secret practices to inveigle negroes from the citizens of Georgia, as well as from the Cherokee and Creek nations of Indians, are still continued by this banditti and the hostile Creeks. This is a state of things which cannot fail to produce much injury in the

10

neighboring settlements, and excite irritations which eventually may endanger the peace of the nation, and interrupt that good understanding which so happily exists between our Governments.[18]

The general was well known to Zuniga, who had been in command at Pensacola when U.S. troops seized the city in 1814 to drive out British forces under Lt. Col. Nicolls. The British had violated Spanish neutrality by using Pensacola as a base for their failed attack on Fort Bowyer at Mobile Point. Before they could regroup from that disaster, Jackson led his army across the line into Florida and took the city. The British evacuated ahead of his main attack and the American troops departed within a few days as well.

General Jackson clearly believed the fort on the Apalachicola to be a major threat to the national security of the United States and called on Spain to assure its destruction:

> …The principals of good faith, which always insure good neighborhood between nations, require the immediate and prompt interference of the Spanish authority to destroy or remove from our frontier this banditti, put an end to an evil of so serious a nature, and return to our citizens and friendly Indians inhabiting our territory those negroes now in said fort, and which have been stolen and enticed from them. I cannot permit myself to indulge a belief that the Governor of Pensacola, or the military commander at that place, will hesitate a moment in giving orders for this banditti to be dispersed, and the property of the citizens of the United States forthwith restored to them and our friendly Indians; particularly when I reflect that the conduct of this banditti is such as will not be tolerated by our Government, and, if not put down by Spanish authority, will compel us, in self-defence, to destroy them.[19]

Jackson's view of the fort as a threat to slavery is self-evident in his demand, as is his view of its garrison. He entrusted the letter to Capt.

Ferdinand Louis Amelung of the 1st U.S. Infantry, ordering him to deliver it in person and wait for the Governor's response.

An interesting individual, Amelung was from Germany, Louisiana. He had entered military service as a member of the Louisiana Volunteers during the War of 1812 before accepting rank as a captain in the 44th U.S. Infantry in March 1814. Capt. Amelung was among the Louisiana men called to defend their homes when the 44th formed part of Jackson's army. He remained with regiment until the reorganization of the army in 1815 when he was appointed to a similar post in the 1st U.S. Infantry. Amelung left the military in 1819 to serve as sheriff of Baton Rouge Parish but died from a head wound received in a duel with Captain Jones of the U.S. Army on August 7, 1821.[20]

It would take Amelung more than one month to reach Pensacola from the Mississippi River due to weather and problems obtaining transportation. On the Chattahoochee River, meanwhile, Creek chiefs learned that the U.S. was considering the construction of another fort, this one far down the river at its mouth with the Flint. The Little Prince (Tustunuggee Hopoi), speaker for the Lower Creeks, went to Fort Gaines to voice his concern. His remarks were interpreted for Lt. Col. Clinch by William Hambly, a former employee of the trading firm John Forbes & Company and one-time lieutenant in Nicolls' battalion of Colonial Marines at Prospect Bluff:

> ...Jackson and Hawkins spoke to us, and told us we were their children. At the Tuskeegee meeting you told us you would have the land as far down as the Summochichoba; but we chiefs did not agree to it. You did not tell us then you would build forts along the river bank down to the fork; but we heard, since, you issued orders to that effect. We do not think it friendly for one friend to take any thing from another forcibly. The commander and Hawkins did not tell us any thing about building these forts. We hear of your meeting at Tuskeegee. We hope you will detain the forces they are at present, and wait on the Indians, as I am sure they will be able to settle every thing; but all the chiefs are not yet met. You know that we are slow in our movements.[21]

The Little Prince asked that his talk be sent to Col. Hawkins and Gen. Jackson, requesting at the same time that they send him ink and paper so that he could continue to correspond.[22]

The Prince's objections did not deter Gaines and Clinch from the strategy they had developed for a move to the forks of the Chattahoochee and Flint Rivers. Writing to Clinch on the 28th of April, Gaines ordered him to collect as much beef as possible in order to save his barrels of salted pork for an emergency. He also advised Clinch to fortify his boats with higher sides before beginning his movement down to the forks and to exercise great caution in selecting site for the new fort.[23]

The post then envisioned would become a focal point for military activity in the Southeast over the next five years.

---

[1] Maj. Gen. Edmund P. Gaines to Maj. Gen. Andrew Jackson, February 20, 1816, Andrew Jackson Papers, Library of Congress.

[2] Dixie May Jones and Mary Elizabeth Scott, Citizens of Baldwin County, Mississippi Territory, in 1816 as enumerated in *Inhabitants of Alabama in 1816*, Broken Arrow Chapter, Daughters of the American Revolution, 1955.

[3] Gaines to Jackson, February 20, 1816.

[4] *Ibid.*

[5] Notice from Headquarters of Maj. Gen. Edmund P. Gaines, February 22, 1816, Spooner's Vermont Journal, April 15, 1816, p. 3.

[6] Orders of Hon. William Crawford, Secretary of War, included in Notice from Headquarters of Maj. Gen. Edmund P. Gaines, February 22, 1816, *Ibid.*

[7] *Augusta Chronicle*, March 6,1816.

[8] *Baltimore Patriot*, March 20, 1816, citing a letter from an officer to a friend in Richmond probably from February.

[9] Maj. Gen. Edmund P. Gaines to Maj. Gen. Andrew Jackson, March 20, 1816, Andrew Jackson papers, Library of Congress.

[10] Maj. Gen. Edmund P. Gaines to Maj. Gen. Andrew Jackson, April 18, 1816, Andrew Jackson papers, 1775-1874, Library of Congress.

[11] *Ibid.*

[12] *Ibid.*

[13] Bvt. Major Enos Cutler to the Adjutant and Inspector General, April 5, 1816, Adjutant General, Letters Received, NARA.

[14] Extract of a letter from an officer at Fort Gaines to a gentleman in Raleigh, April 16, 1816, appeared in the Massachusetts Salem Gazette, p. 2. On May 21, 1816.

[15] Gaines to Jackson, March 18, 1816.

[16] Maj. Gen. Edmund P. Gaines to Maj. Gen. Andrew Jackson, April 18, 1816, Andrew Jackson papers, 1775-1874, Library of Congress.

[17] Benjamin Hawkins to Maj. Gen. Andrew Jackson, April 21, 1816.

[18] Maj. Gen. Andrew Jackson to the Governor of Pensacola, April 23, 1816, American State Papers, Foreign Relations, Volume IV, p. 499.

[19] *Ibid.*

[20] *Historical Register and Dictionary of the United States Army: 1789 – 1903*; Report dated Baton Rouge, August 11, 1821, from the *New York Gazette*, September 4, 1821, p. 3.

[21] Talk from the Little Prince, Tustunnuggee Hopoi, to the Commander of the United States forces in the Indian nation, April 27, 1816, *American State Papers*, Foreign Relations, Volume IV, p. 558.

[22] *Ibid.*

[23] Maj. Gen. Edmund P. Gaines to Lt. Col. Duncan L. Clinch, April 28, 1816, Andrew Jackson papers, Library of Congress.

CHAPTER TWO

Establishment of Fort Scott

By the end of April 1816 the U.S. Army had its sights on the fort at Prospect Bluff. The planned movement against the fort by the Creeks had been delayed by a paperwork snafu. The ailing Col. Benjamin Hawkins had failed to send a written requisition for the 300 bushels of corn needed by the warriors for their expedition into Spanish Florida. As Clinch and Gaines worked to correct this bureaucratic logjam, they also prepared for a movement of their own.[1]

On the 28th Gaines approved a plan proposed by Clinch to descend the Chattahoochee to its confluence with the Flint River and build a new post directly on the Spanish border:

> Until you are perfectly satisfied as to the strength and healthiness of the position which you may select for a permanent post, you may limit yourself to a temporary work, as I have before suggested, to be thrown up at a convenient point for the present security of your command, until you have it in your power to select a proper site for the

intended fort. You will probably find a handsome and suitable bluff on the left or East side of the junction of the rivers. Examine and report to me the situation of the Country at, and for eight or ten miles above the junction, - upon and adjacent to the rivers – noting the different sites which appear to you most eligible – the distance of each from the river, & from the junction of the two.[2]

Implied but not actually stated in the general's letter was a belief that the new post would be an excellent base for operations against the fort at Prospect Bluff. The confluence of the Chattahoochee and Flint Rivers is the head of the Apalachicola River on which the targeted fort was located.

The Apalachicola stretches from the confluence to Apalachicola Bay on the Gulf of Mexico. It is 112 miles long from top to bottom and drains a vast floodplain that reaches as far north as the base of Brasstown Bald, the highest mountain in Georgia. It was the technical dividing line between the Spanish colonies of East and West Florida, although the Spanish fort of San Marcos de Apalache at St. Marks, Florida, operated under the control of the garrison at Pensacola for logistical reasons. The Spanish governor in the West Florida capital was likewise faced with the problem of the fort at Prospect Bluff, even though its location on the east bank of the Apalachicola technically placed it in East Florida and the jurisdiction of the governor in St. Augustine. The original forks of the Chattahoochee and Flint at the head of the river is now inundated by the waters of Lake Seminole, a 37,500-acre manmade reservoir.

General Gaines warned Lt. Col. Clinch to be extremely careful as he made his way down the Chattahoochee. If the Creeks and Seminoles appeared ready to oppose the construction of the new fort with force, Clinch was to halt his movement until an additional battalion of the 4th Infantry could arrive from Charleston. He was then to lead his force down the Chattahoochee while the other battalion made its way down the Flint. The two wings of the regiment would meet at the forks.[3]

Gaines cautioned Clinch to be on his guard. "He who acts otherwise, among savages," the general wrote, "not only places himself at the disposal of fortune, but invites insult and disaster."[4]

Even as Gaines and Clinch were working to put a military force in place at the head of the Apalachicola, the Creeks continued their effort to field an expedition of their own. Gen. Gaines informed the Secretary of War on April 30th that the Little Prince had gone down to visit the chiefs living near the Florida line:

> The ostensible object of the visit was to adopt measures to take the negro fort; and as Colonel Hawkins had confidence in the promises of the Indians to effect this object, I sanctioned a requisition for supplying them with three hundred bushels of corn, to serve as rations. That I have little faith in their promises, I will not deny; but it seemed to me proper to encourage them in the prosecution of a measure which I felt persuaded would, if successful, be attended with great benefit to our southern frontier inhabitants, as well as the Indians themselves.[5]

The Prince was less than successful in his mission. Although the towns on the lower river appear to have agreed not oppose his expedition, they also declined to support and take part in it. One exception was Lafarka or John Blunt, a refugee chief from Alabama who had established himself on the west side of the Apalachicola in what is now Calhoun County, Florida. Blunt had allied himself with the British during Nicolls' stay on the river during the War of 1812 but now saw the writing on the wall and agreed to help any force that might go against the fort at Prospect Bluff.

An officer at Fort Gaines soon provided more information on the climactic end of the Little Prince's mission. So alarming was the news brought back by the Lower Creek leader that the soldiers expected an attack at any minute:

...The Little Prince, and all the chiefs of the friendly party,
have been below endeavoring to make friends of the hostile
party, but without effect; the night before last a chief of the
Seminoles made his appearance at the council house with
200 warriors, and dissolved their meeting, firing and
threatening to put the friendly chiefs to death if they did not
leave there immediately; some of the friendly chiefs passed
here to-day on their way home.[6]

The same officer reported that a serious incident had taken place just
two miles from Fort Gaines on May 1st. Several supply wagons had left the
post on their way back to Fort Hawkins when they were stopped by a small
party of warriors. One of the wagon drivers escaped and ran back to Fort
Gaines to sound the alarm. The officer, whose name remains unknown, led
out thirty volunteers from the 4th Regiment to save the wagons. They were
successful and the lives of the other drivers were saved. He went on with his
men to escort the wagons to Fort Hawkins, but the warriors continued to
hover in the area:

...[D]uring my absence, the same party was guilty of one
of the most daring outrages I ever heard of; while two men,
belonging to my company, were attending 30 cattle
belonging to us, within half a mile of camp, about 12
o'clock, at noon, they were driven off along with two public
horses; we sent a small party in pursuit, but without coming
up with them; they took the road on to St. Marks, crossing
Flint river about 20 miles from its mouth. I have no doubt
but that it is a small party of Seminoles or [Mc]Queens
party. I regret the loss of the two poor fellows, as I have no
doubt they are scalped before this, it being unusual for the
Indians to keep prisoners.[7]

The McQueen referenced in the letter was Peter McQueen, a major
leader of Red Stick forces during the Creek War of 1813-1814. He had

18

escaped into Florida following the destruction of a key Red Stick army at the Battle of Horseshoe Bend. He quickly allied his warriors with the British forces of Lt. Col. Edward Nicolls and served with the British until the end of the War of 1812. He was still in Florida and commanded a force of several hundred warriors. Jackson, Gaines and other U.S. leaders considered him to be an absolute threat.[8]

Rumors reached Fort Gaines that another 250 Red Stick and Seminole warriors had gathered about 40 miles below the post. An attack was expected and the anonymous officer warned that "you may expect to hear of some scalping in this quarter very soon." There were fewer than 300 effective men at the fort, although he noted that his company – apparently of artillery – had three good field pieces, "2 six pounders and a 4."[9]

The issue of the captured soldiers was a major one to American officers, as was the loss of so much beef. Clinch informed Gaines on May 7th that a spy he had sent in pursuit of them had returned on the 5th with word that the warriors and their captives had crossed the Flint "at Burges's old place," a reference to the site of the former trading post of James Burges at what is now Bainbridge, Georgia. The two soldiers were still alive at that time but the spy warned that they would be killed if they became too tired to keep up with the movements of their captors. They were being taken to the fort at Prospect Bluff.[10]

The spy reported that war was imminent:

> …He further states that he understood from some of his friends in that quarter, that the Semilones, all the Towns on the Flint near the Confluence of the two rivers, and most of those on the Chattohoochee were preparing for war – that they had been dancing and drinking their war Physic for several days that they had determined to divide themselves into two parties, one party to go against Hartford (Georgia) and the other to come up and attack the Troops under my Command. This rumour has been confirmed by an Indian just from Flint, who arrived at the Town of the Oketeyocannes last evening, the Chief of which town sent

W. Hardridge who lives near him to me this morning, to inform me that such were the reports but that he did not know what to think of them.[11]

The "W. Hardridge" mentioned by Clinch was William Hardridge, a white trader and sometimes assistant Indian agent who lived near Fort Gaines. He told the lieutenant colonel that a major division was taking place in the lower towns. Those who wished to remain at peace with the United States were preparing to relocate upriver to within the new limits of the Creek Nation. The rest, with a force of 1,500 to 2,000 warriors, were determined on war. William Hambly reported that the British had organized a force of 3,000 Creeks, Seminoles and Choctaws during their sojourn on the Apalachicola. "I they are determined on a fight," wrote Clinch, "I feel every disposition to gratify them."[12]

The Little Prince reached Fort Gaines on his return home from his mission to the lower towns and brought similar news. His effort to obtain support there had failed, he told Clinch, because "they were crazy, and would not listen to him." The chief, William Hambly and their escort had been pursued by a party of warriors from Tuttolossee Talofa ("Fowl Town" and had been forced to flee to save themselves from being burned alive.[13]

> …The Tuttolosees and Miccosookus, are the principal instigators, but he thinks most of the Towns on the Flint, below Barnetts, and several towns on the East Bank of the Chattohoochie will join them. Several of the chiefs below and near me have come in and begged protection, they state that they have their crops in the ground, and unless I will let them stay at home and till them, their women and children must starve. I have told them to stay at home and make their corn, that when I approached their towns, the Chiefs must meet me with their warriors without arms, that I would take a list of them, and if any of them joined the hostile party, they were never to suffer them to return again, on pain on having their towns destroyed.[14]

The chiefs agreed to Clinch's terms and the Little Prince reported that he had ordered the leaders of all towns that wished to remain friendly to report themselves to Fort Gaines at once.

From all indications, Lt. Col. Clinch was as eager to go to war as his Red Stick and Seminole counterparts. He proposed that two companies of the battalion from the 4th Infantry on the march from Charleston be sent to reinforce him:

> ...I then propose leaving all my heavy baggage, and a sufficient number of men to man the boats at this post, and move the balance of my command down the river by rapid marches, and destroy every hostile town between this and the Confluence of the two rivers, after which my boats can drop down with ease and safety in two days. I will then select a strong position on the Flint, fortify my Camp, move up that river, and destroy all the Towns to Burgess old place, and order the Command left at the Agency to descend the Flint with our supplies, and if my force will admit of it; I will pursue the enemy further, and strike a blow in another quarter.[15]

Clinch's vague reference to striking a blow in "another quarter" likely referred to the fort at Prospect Bluff. The "Negro Fort," as the Americans called it, was definitely on the minds of Edmund Gaines and Andrew Jackson. Writing to Jackson on May 14th, Gaines informed Jackson that he had "reconnoitering parties" operating from each post along the frontier looking for the murderers of Johnson and McGaskey. Meanwhile, the first movement of the campaign to take the fort on the Apalachicola had begun:

> The Little Prince with other chiefs and Warriors have engaged to take the Negro Fort on the Apa'la'cha'co'la and deliver the negroes at 50$ each. Col. Hawkins is of the opinion they will succeed, and although I have little faith in

21

Indian promises, it seems to me proper to encourage the undertaking and wait a reasonable time for the result. I have sanctioned Col. Hawkins requisition for 300 bushels of corn for the subsistence of the Indians. They are not however to be considered as in our service or entitled to Pay. Should they fail, I shall then avail myself of the discretionary power which you have been pleased to confide to me and shall adopt such measures as may appear best Calculated to Counteract Indian hostility and at the same time to break up the Negro establishment, which I have reason to believe is acquiring strength and additional numbers.[16]

On the border north of Pensacola, Major David E. Twiggs had finally begun his march to establish the long awaited post near the Conecuh, while in Charleston, South Carolina, Captain Alex Cummings started his forced march for Fort Hawkins with the final battalion of the 4th Infantry. Two companies of light artillery were preparing to march as well.[17]

General Gaines, meanwhile, took action to put the U.S. operation against the fort at Prospect Bluff into operation. Writing from Fort Montgomery in Alabama on May 22nd, he explained the situation to Commodore Daniel Patterson of the U.S. Navy. Patterson was the senior naval officer at New Orleans and his approval would be necessary for U.S. warships to escort supply vessels to the Apalachicola. Gaines detailed both the capture of the two soldiers at Fort Gaines and the murders of Johnson and McGaskey then mentioned his plans for Clinch to establish a new fort near the head of the Apalachicola. He concluded by asking for help from the navy:

> …I have determined upon an experiment by water, and for this purpose have to request your co-operation; should you feel authorized to detach a small gun-vessel or two as a convoy to the boats charged with our supplies up the Appalachicola, I am persuaded that, in doing so, you will contribute much to the benefit of the service, and the accommodation of my immediate command in this quarter. The transports will be under the direction of the officer of

the gun-vessel, and the whole should be provided against an attack by small arms from shore. To guard against accidents, I will direct Lieutenant Colonel Clinch to have in readiness a boat sufficient to carry fifty men, to meet the vessels on the river and assist them up.[18]

The general included as much information as he could on the construction and armament of the Prospect Bluff establishment and told the commodore that if the passage of the ships was greeted with opposition from the inhabitants of the fort, "it shall be destroyed."[19]

On the following day, General Gaines ordered Lieutenant Colonel Clinch to begin his descent of the Chattahoochee River. "If your supplies of provisions and ammunition have reached you," Gaines wrote from Camp Montgomery near the former site of Fort Mims, "let your detachment move as directed in my letter of the 28th of last month." The soldiers were to carry with them twenty-five days' rations with more provisions to follow via boat from Fort Gaines. Clinch was to move with caution, but the time to move had come:

> ...The force of the whole nation cannot arrest your movement down the river on board the boats, if secured up the sides with two-inch plank, and covered over with clapboards; nor could all the nation prevent your landing and constructing a stockade work, sufficient to secure you, unless they should previously know the spot at which you intended to land, and had actually assembled at that place previous to or within four hours of your landing; but your force is not sufficient to warrant your march to the different villages, as suggested, by land. The whole of your force (except about forty men, or one company, for the defence of Fort Gaines) should be kept near your boats and supplies until the new post shall be established. You may then strike at any hostile party near you, with all your disposable force; but even then you should not go more than one or two days' march from your fort.[20]

Gaines cautioned his subordinate to be wary of William Hambly. Future events would show that the interpreter had indeed transferred his allegiance to the United States, but the general was not yet over the fact that Hambly had served as a lieutenant in the British forces during the War of 1812 and worried that he might still be a spy or agent for Colonel Nicolls.[21]

The general provided Clinch with information on the movement of the ships being sent to supply him and further informed him that heavy guns were being sent to help in the reduction of the fort at Prospect Bluff:

> ...Should the boats meet with opposition at what is called the Negro fort, arrangements will immediately be made for its destruction; and for that purpose you will be supplied with two eighteen-pounders and one howitzer, with fixed ammunition and implements complete, to be sent in a vessel to accompany the provisions. I have, likewise, ordered fifty thousand musket cartridges, some rifles, swords, &c. Should you be compelled to go against the negro fort, you will land at a convenient point above it, and force a communication with the commanding officer of the vessels below, and arrange with him your plan of attack. Upon this subject you shall hear from me again, as soon as I am notified of the time at which the vessels will sail from New Orleans.[22]

The first step, of course, was the establishment of the new fort at the head of the Apalachicola. "The post near the junction of the rivers, to which I called your attention last month," Gaines wrote, "must be established speedily." This was to be done, he continued, "even if we have to fight our way through the ranks of the whole nation."[23]

It would take some time for the general's orders to travel across the modern state of Alabama from Camp Montgomery to Fort Gaines. As the courier made his way forward, undoubtedly with a military escort, other events continued to develop. Captain Amelung had finally reached Pensacola to deliver Jackson's communique to Mauricio de Zuniga. The Spanish governor replied on May 26th giving Jackson basic information about the location and history of the fort at Prospect Bluff and explaining that Spanish citizens were also aggrieved by its existence. Nicolls and Woodbine, he continued, had carried away many slaves belonging to Spanish subjects in Florida. Zuniga was willing to move against the fort if properly supplied and reinforced, he explained to Jackson, and had sought authority from the Captain General of Cuba for such a movement. His thinking, he told the American commander, "exactly corresponds with yours as to the dislodging of the negroes from the fort, the occupying it with Spanish troops, or destroying it, and delivering the negroes who may be collected to their lawful owners."[24]

The proposed Spanish expedition would be approved and assembled, but events were now outpacing both Jackson and Zuniga. Gaines' orders reached Lt. Col. Clinch at Fort Gaines and he began final preparations for his move down the Chattahoochee. There was a bit of good news to report in the midst of the preparations for war. The two soldiers taken with the herd of beef cattle survived their ordeal and were released by their Red Stick captors. Part of the herd was also sent back. A group of Upper Creeks, meanwhile, located the killers of Johnson and McGaskey. Two of the Red Sticks were captured and had been jailed at Fort Jackson by June 3, 1816.[25]

General Gaines rescinded a request that Georgia call out is militia to protect the frontier, but made no changes to his plans for a movement against the fort at Prospect Bluff. This first step in this expedition was made on June 7, 1816, when Lt. Col. Clinch began his long awaited trip down the Chattahoochee River from Fort Gaines. Five days later he was able to report on his efforts to find a site for the construction of a fort near the confluence of the Chattahoochee and Flint Rivers:

> ...I was very desirous to have found a suitable site for a fortification nearer the Confluence of the two rivers, than the one I have selected, but the situation of the country would not admit of it. The land near the Confluence is very low and subject to inundation for several miles up, on the west side of the Flint, on the east side, there is a range of hills that runs between a half and a quarter of a mile from the river, but the intervening space is of a low, swampy cast and also subject to inundation. I had learnt before leaving Fort Gaines that there was a considerable pine bluff about seven miles up on the east side of the river. On reaching it

> I was disappointed in the site, but determined at once on landing my command, and on reconnoitering the country on both sides the river as the labour and fatigue in ascending in our heavy boats was very great.[26]

The number of potential sites for a post at the head of the Apalachicola was severely limited because the territory both south and west of the actual confluence belonged to Spain. This eliminated the high bluffs at present-day Chattahoochee from consideration. Colonel Nicolls had built a fort atop one of the prehistoric mounds at River Landing Park during the War of 1812, but like the towering bluffs that overlooked the site, this location too was off limits.[27]

The actual point of land formed by the joining of the Chattahoochee and Flint Rivers was unsuitable for other reasons. As Clinch observed, the narrow peninsula was only "three or four feet wide" for several hundred yards before it began to gradually broaden. The Spanish had once established the mission of La Encarnacion a la Santa Cruz de Sabacola on the southernmost heights of this peninsula in 1675 and the Apalachicoli Creeks had built a stockade there in 1716, but the site was not suitable for the U.S. military's purposes due to the expanse of swamp that surrounded it and separated it from either of the rivers.[28]

Likewise disappointed by the bluff seven miles up the Flint that he mentioned in the quote above, Clinch now focused on looking for potential sites further up that river. He led his men through the swamps to the foot of a high range of hills on the south or east side. The river here runs in a generally northeast to southwest direction, which leads to some variance in the directional terms used to describe its banks. The hills to which he was referring, however, are those which now form the southern shore of the Flint River arm of Lake Seminole nearly opposite the mouth of Spring Creek. To Clinch's disappointment, however, they also proved unsuitable for his planned fort:

> ...[T]he distance from the river, the difficulty of ascending it and the want of water, induced me to take a small party of men in a Canoe and explore the river until I could find a more eligible site, and to my great satisfaction I had not proceeded more than a mile before I discovered a high pine bluff on the west side of the river and on examining

determined at once on occupying it. The bluff is not more
than half as high as the one at Fort Gaines, but the site is
rather a more military one in as much as it commands the
country round it.[29]

The bluff selected by Lt. Col. Clinch today rises only about seven feet
above the normal surface level of Lake Seminole, but in 1816 formed an
impressive elevation that soared 35-40 feet above the Flint River. Its surface
formed a broad plateau of more than 12-acres that offered plenty of room
for a military encampment. The location of the bluff on a sharp bend of the
river combined with its height would allow cannon placed there to command
both the water approaches to the site and the low-lying swamps on the
opposite shore. The availability of good water was a key consideration in
the selection of military sites during Clinch's time and the bluff was in close
proximity to several freshwater springs:

> …On examining for water we have discovered two of the
> most extraordinary springs (if they may be so called) that I
> have ever seen, within less than half a mile of the site. They
> are at least 90 feet in circumference and twenty or thirty
> deep, the water cool, well tastes, and I have no doubt will
> prove healthy which is the most important consideration (in
> my opinion) in selecting a military site.[30]

These springs are now inundated by Lake Seminole, but archaeological
research shows that they attracted human settlement for thousands of years.
In fact, the bluff selected by Clinch has revealed evidence of prior habitation
during the Creek (1763-1816), Mississippian (900-1540), Woodland (400-
900) and earlier time periods. Archaeologists found no evidence of burial or
ceremonial mounds at the site, but believe that it was long used as a
habitation or village site before the arrival of the military in 1816.[31]

Clinch's initial orders were to select a site for a fortified encampment,
but there is little doubt that both he and Gaines considered the need for a
permanent fort to be obvious. The site selected, the lieutenant colonel
believed, would function well in either eventuality. He soon notified
General Gaines that he was in place and would soon make contact with the
gunboats and supply ships being sent to the mouth of the Apalachicola:

I have thrown up a pretty strong temporary work, erected a store house and have my command under shelter and comfortable in a few days, and feel confident we can repel the whole Creek Nation were they to attack us. I shall send a confidential Indian down the river to the bay with a letter to the Commanding officer of the Gun Boats, in the course of two days, with instructions to remain in sight of the bay until the Gun boats [arrive], deliver the letter and return to me as soon as possible. If the vessels do not arrive with some supplies very soon we shall be entirely destitute of provisions before we can get them up the river.[32]

The temporary fort was named Camp Crawford, likely to honor then Secretary of War William Crawford of Georgia. The name remained in use only three or four months before the post was given its permanent designation, Fort Scott.

----

[1] Maj. Gen. Edmund P. Gaines to Lt. Col. Duncan L. Clinch, April 28, 1816, Andrew Jackson papers, Library of Congress.
[2] *Ibid.*
[3] *Ibid.*
[4] *Ibid.*
[5] Maj. Gen. Edmund P. Gaines to Hon. William Crawford, April 30, 1816, *American State Papers*, Foreign Relations, Volume IV, pp. 557-558.
[6] Officer at Fort Gaines to Editors of the Baltimore Patriot, May 5, 1816 (Appeared in the Virginia American Beacon, p. 3., on June 10, 1816).
[7] *Ibid.*
[8] For an account of McQueen's escape into Florida and his subsequent alliance with the British, please see *Nicolls' Outpost*, Old Kitchen Books, 2015, by this author.
[9] Officer at Fort Gaines to Editors of the Baltimore Patriot, May 5, 1816.
[10] Lt. Col. Duncan L. Clinch to Maj. Gen. Edmund P. Gaines, May 7, 1816, Andrew Jackson papers, Library of Congress.
[11] *Ibid.*
[12] *Ibid.*
[13] Lt. Col. Duncan L. Clinch to Maj. Gen. Edmund P. Gaines, May 9, 1816, Andrew Jackson papers, Library of Congress.

[14] *Ibid.*

[15] Lt. Col. Duncan L. Clinch to Maj. Gen. Edmund P. Gaines, May 9, 1816, Andrew Jackson papers, Library of Congress.

[16] Maj.Gen. Edmund P. Gaines to Maj. Gen. Andrew Jackson, May 14, 1816, Andrew Jackson papers, Library of Congress.

[17] *Ibid.*, *North Carolina Star*, May 31, 1816, p. 2.

[18] Maj. Gen. Edmund P. Gaines to Commodore Daniel T. Patterson, May 22, 1816, American State Papers, Foreign Affairs, Volume IV, p. 559.

[19] *Ibid.*

[20] Maj. Gen. Edmund P. Gaines to Lt. Col. Duncan L. Clinch, May 23, 1816, American State Papers, Foreign Affairs, Volume IV, p. 558.

[21] *Ibid.*

[22] *Ibid.*

[23] *Ibid.*

[24] Gov. Mauricio de Zuniga to Maj. Gen. Andrew Jackson, May 26, 1816, American State Papers, Foreign Affairs, Volume IV, pp. 499-500.

[25] Maj. Gen. Edmund P. Gaines to Maj. Gen. Andrew Jackson, June 3, 1816, Andrew Jackson Papers, Library of Congress.

[26] Lt. Col. Duncan L. Clinch to Maj. Gen. Edmund P. Gaines, June 12, 1816, Andrew Jackson Papers, Library of Congress.

[27] For a history of this little known fort, please see *Nicolls' Outpost*, Old Kitchen Books, 2015, by this author.

[28] Clinch to Gaines, June 12, 1816.

[29] *Ibid.*

[30] *Ibid.*

[31] Nancy Marie White *et. al.*, "Archaeology at Lake Seminole," Cleveland Museum of Natural History.

[32] Clinch to Gaines, June 12, 1816.

CHAPTER THREE

The Apalachicola Fort Expedition

Camp Crawford, as Fort Scott was first known, is perhaps best remembered in American history as the base from which U.S. troops launched their attack on the fort at Prospect Bluff. When Gen. Gaines approved Lt. Col. Clinch's move down the Chattahoochee to establish the new fort, he knew that the occupants of the "Negro Fort" would likely block U.S. supply vessels from moving up the Apalachicola River. This, the American officers knew, would create a food crisis at Camp Crawford and justify their destruction of the African American establishment.

By the time he settled his men into their new situation at Camp Crawford, Clinch had made contact with two important chiefs living on the Apalachicola River but willing to help the American troops. The first of these was John Yellow Hair, who lived on the west bank of the Apalachicola about two miles below the confluence. The other was John Blunt, sometimes called Lafarka, who lived on the west side of the river in present-day Calhoun County, Florida. Yellow Hair was a mestizo Lower Creek of long familiarity to the region. Blunt, however, was an Upper Creek who had fled south to Spanish Florida near the end of the Creek War of 1813-1814. Both men had been allied with Col. Nicolls during the War of 1812 and both recognized the need to improve relations with the United States following the departure of the British from the Apalachicola in 1815.

Clinch probably met both chiefs through the interpreter William Hambly. It is known that he conferred extensively with Hambly prior to the movement down the Chattahoochee and some writers have claimed that Hambly was a participant in the expedition. While this is certainly possible, it cannot be confirmed through the surviving documentation. He was on the scene after the destruction of the fort, but could have arrived on a Spanish expedition. The names of Blunt and Yellow Hair do appear in Clinch's reports and he appears to have been familiar with both by the time of his arrival at the confluence. Yellow Hair assisted the lieutenant colonel in making contacts with other local chiefs while Blunt served as a courier to and from naval forces in the Gulf.

Writing again from Camp Crawford on June 14th, Clinch informed Gen. Gaines of his plans to send a "friendly Indian" (i.e. Blunt) on the next morning to make contact with the supply ships at Apalachicola Bay. He had already dispatched Yellow Hair to request a meeting with the Fowltown chief Neamathla.[1]

The lieutenant colonel also told Gaines that he had come into possession of an enigmatic letter from the commanders of the fort at Prospect Bluff:

> I think the best plan I can adapt will be to take about eighty men, drop down the river and take the Fort at once as they will certainly oppose our passing it. The rascals have sent over to England to inform them that we are coming down to take their fort as appears from a letter in my possession written by one of them.[2]

Clinch's belief that he could take the fort with only eighty men shows surprising naivety on his part. He had met in person with William Hardridge, William Hambly, Yellow Hair, John Blunt and others who had been to Prospect Bluff and knew from their accounts the strength and armament of the fortifications there. No further details about the intercepted letter have been found nor has a copy of it surfaced to date. It apparently included an appeal for help from the British, but little else can be said of its contents with certainty.

Chief Blunt left Camp Crawford for Apalachicola Bay on June 17, 1816, well ahead of the departure of the naval flotilla from Louisiana and Mississippi. It was not until the 24th that Commodore Daniel T. Patterson sent orders instructing Sailing Master Jairus Loomis at Bay St. Louis, Mississippi, to provide an armed escort for the supply schooners *Semelante* and *General Pike*. Loomis sailed from Bay St. Louis on board Gunboat #149 in the company of Sailing Master James Bassett's Gunboat #154.[3]

The little gunboats of the early 19th century U.S. Navy originated from the defensive policies of President Thomas Jefferson. Normally around 50 feet long, they carried crews of around 20 men and normally mounted no more than two or three guns. Normally powered by their sails, the vessels could also be rowed in battle or when the winds were calm. The boats were built in a variety of styles, but most had two masts. Their heaviest cannon, 18-pounders in the cases of Gunboats #149 and #154, were mounted forward of the front mast and could be pivoted to aim in various directions.

Sailing east in company with the *Semelante* and *General Pike*, Loomis and Bassett headed for Apalachicola Bay. It was an impressive journey for the low-decked gunboats but passed without incident. At roughly the same time, an editorial from Milledgeville, Georgia, spread northward through the nation's newspapers. Included was a clarion call for the destruction of the fort at Prospect Bluff:

> It has long been known, that the British station at Appalachicola bay, within the Spanish territory, where Nicolls concentrated his force and erected a fort, has, since he evacuated it, been held by runaway negroes and hostile Indians, who have done and continue to do mischief to the whites, as occasion and opportunity offer. It was not to have been expected, that an establishment so pernicious to the southern states, holding out to a part of their population temptations to insubordination, would have been suffered

to exist after the close of the war. In the course of the last winter several slaves from this neighborhood fled to that fort; others have lately gone from Tennessee and the Mississippi territory. How long shall this evil, requiring immediate remedy, be permitted to exist? If the Spaniards connive at this nuisance, shall we out of respect to them (suffering from its present ills and anticipating greater) continue to tolerate it? True, it is within their territorial limits, and as good neighbors, they should disperse this horde of ruffians, and deliver up the slaves to their owners. But if they decline to do so or are dilatory about it, we can discover no reason why the regular troops, of them there are more than enough in the nation, should not be ordered on that service with the least possible delay.[4]

How much the writer knew about the plans then unfolding on the Apalachicola is not clear. His proposed method of destroying the targeted fort, however, was so similar to the plan being implemented by Gaines and Clinch that it seems likely he was at least familiar with their expedition. "A few hundred men sent down the river and some gun boats up the bay," he wrote by way of example, "would readily effect the object."[5]

With Loomis and his flotilla finally closing in on Apalachicola Bay, word also reached the settled areas of Georgia that the long-discussed expedition by the Lower Creeks against Prospect Bluff had also moved forward:

We learn by gentlemen from the westward, that a party of the Creek warriors, from 500 to 1000 strong, under their gallant chief M'Intosh, contemplated marching early this month against the hostile Indians in Florida, (the Seminoles) and had given assurance that they would capture and destroy the obnoxious Fort on Appalachicola Bay – most of the hostile Indians were said to be on a visit at Pensacola, where 600 Spanish troops had lately arrived.[6]

34

The timing of the movement of the Creeks under Maj. William McIntosh was a remarkable coincidence. Military reports indicate that the warriors moved out on their own without prior coordination with Lt. Col. Clinch. McIntosh and other chiefs undoubtedly knew that U.S. troops had dropped down the Chattahoochee to the confluence, but they do not appear to have known the exact nature of Clinch's plans. The launch of the Creek expedition, however, meant that three strong forces – two by land and one by sea – were closing in on the lower Apalachicola at virtually the same time.

The gunboats and their charges reached Apalachicola Bay on July 10, 1816. There he found John Blunt waiting with dispatches from Clinch, who requested that the vessels wait off the mouth of the river until troops could be brought down to assist the supply ships in passing the "Negro Fort." Clinch also asked Loomis to intercept and hold any vessel that might attempt to escape via the mouth of the Apalachicola.[7]

The first opportunity for Loomis to do so came five days after his arrival in the bay when a small boat was spotted off the site of today's city of Apalachicola:

> On the 15th, I discovered a boat pulling out of the river, and being anxious to ascertain whether we should be permitted peaceably to pass the fort above us, I despatched a boat with an officer to gain the necessary information; on nearing her, she fired a volley of musketry into my boat, and immediately pulled in for the river; I immediately opened a fire on them from the gun vessels, but with no effect.[8]

No one was injured in this first exchange of fire but it was now obvious that U.S. vessels would not be allowed to pass the fort at Prospect Bluff. Loomis clearly considered the opening of musketry on the boat from his vessel to be a hostile act. No records exist to explain the reaction of the occupants of the vessel that had pulled from the river, but it is certainly that they similarly considered the approach of sailors in a small boat to be a hostile act and had fired in self-defense. Either way, it was now clear that the U.S. vessels would not be allowed to pass the fort at Prospect Bluff. That conclusion was punctuated by the thunder of Loomis' cannon as he tried unsuccessfully to sink the vessel that quickly disappeared from sight back into the mouth of the river.[9]

Chief Blunt reached Camp Crawford on the same day with news of the arrival of the ships in Apalachicola Bay. Lt. Col. Clinch immediately sent the chief back down to let Sailing Master Loomis know that the soldiers were coming, while his men prepared for an active campaign on the Apalachicola. They spent July 16th loading supplies aboard their flatboats and equipping themselves with rations, arms and ammunition. Major Enos Cutler was put in command of the small force being left to hold the fort during the absence of Clinch's main force, which was ready to go by the following morning:

> …On the 17th I left this place with one hundred and sixteen chosen men in boats and commenced descending the river. The Detachment was divided in two companies commanded by B. Major Muhlenberg and Capt. Taylor. On the same evening I was joined by Major McIntosh with one hundred and fifty Indians, and on the 18th day by an old chief called Capt. Isaacs and the celebrated Chief Kotcha-hajo or Mad Tiger at the head of a large body of Indians many of whom were without arms. My junction with these Chiefs was accidental their expedition having been long since projected. Their object was to capture the negroes within the Fort, and return them to their proper owners.[10]

At about the same time that Clinch and his men left Camp Crawford, a disaster took place near the mouth of the Apalachicola River. Gunboats #149 and #154 had been at sea for more than twenty days and the supply schooners for even longer. Fresh water was running short and Loomis found it necessary to send a boat into the mouth of the river for a new supply. He did his best to secure the boat against attack but it was not enough:

> On the 17th, at 5 A.M. I manned and armed a boat with a swivel and musketry and four men, and gave her in charge of midshipman Luffborough, for the purpose of procuring fresh water, having run short of that article. At 11 A.M. sailing master Bassett, who had been on a similar expedition, came alongside with the body of John Burgess, O.S. [i.e. ordinary seaman] who had been sent in the boat with midshipman Luffborough; his body was found near the mouth of the river, shot through the heart; at 4 P.M. discovered a man at the mouth of the river on a sand bar, sent a boat and brought him on board, he proved to be John Lopaz, O.S. the only survivor of the boats crew, sent with midshipman Luffborough.[11]

Lopaz (or Lopez) told Loomis that Luffborough's boat had entered the mouth of the river as ordered when they "discovered a negro on the beach, near a plantation." The word "plantation" on the Gulf Coast of 1816 referred as often to a farm as to the large cotton plantations of the later antebellum era and the establishment described by Lopaz undoubtedly fit the former description. The presence of a farm so near to the mouth of the river shows how extensive the colony of free African Americans had become in just the two years since it was established. Other reports indicate that the fields of the settlement extended for 50 miles above and below the fort at Prospect Bluff and the existence of a farm nearly 15 miles downstream by the mouth of the Apalachicola adds substantiation to this claim.[12]

It is odd that Luffborough was not more on his guard after the incident two days earlier when the mysterious boat opened fire on sailors in Apalachicola Bay:

> ...Mr. Luffborough ordered the boat to be pulled directly for him; that on touching the shore he spoke to the negro,

and directly received a volley of musketry from two divisions of negroes and Indians who lay concealed in the bushes on the margin of the river; Mr. Luffborough, Robert Maitland, and John Burgess, were killed on the spot; Lopaz made his escape by swimming, and states that he saw the other seaman, Edward Daniels made prisoner, Lopaz supposed there must have been forty negroes and Indians in the capture of the boat.[13]

It was a sad end for Midshipman Luffborough and his men. At least some of the unfortunate sailors were scalped and the prisoner, Edward Daniels, was carried back to Prospect Bluff where he was "tarred and burnt alive."[14]

The attack on the watering party was carried out by detachment from the fort at Prospect Bluff and led in person by Garcon, the commandant of the post. A party of Choctaw warriors also took part. They were the last survivors of a group that had fled its own nation in 1813 to follow the Creek Prophet Josiah Francis. With their wives and children and led by a chief of their own, they comprised about 20-30 of the estimated 300 people living at the "Negro Fort." Garcon had led the allied groups down to reconnoiter after learning that unidentified ships had appeared in Apalachicola Bay. Whether the party involved in the attack was the same that exchanged fire with sailors in the bay two days earlier is not known.

Lt. Col. Clinch, meanwhile, continued his movement down the Apalachicola River. A council was held with the chiefs McIntosh, Mad Tiger and Captain Isaacs on the 18th and an agreement was struck for the Creek and U.S. forces to cooperate in their attack on the fort. Lt. Kendal Lewis of McIntosh's command served as interpreter and the resulting document was necessarily to the point. It included only three articles:

Art. 1 We agree to unite in reducing the Negro Fort.
Art. 2 In case the Fort should be taken the Indians are to have all the Powder (cannon excepted) small arms,

> clothing &c. & Fifty Dollars for every ground Negro taken by them, not the property of the Creek Nation.
>
> Art. 3   Lt. Col. D.L. Clinch is to take possession in the name of the U. States of all the Cannon, Ordnance Stores &c. & all the property the Indians cannot carry from the Fort.[15]

Clinch ordered the Creeks to keep advance parties moving ahead of their main columns and the slow-moving flatboats as the now combined forces continued to move down the river. At Prospect Bluff, meanwhile, Garcon dispatched couriers to seek reinforcements from Fowltown, Miccosukee and other groups of Seminoles and Red Sticks. One of these messengers was snapped up by a Creek scouting party on the evening of the 18th:

> …On the 19th they brought in a prisoner taken the evening before. He had a scalp which he said he was carrying to the Seminoles. – He further stated that the Black Commandant and the Choctaw Chief had returned to the Fort from the Bay the day before, with a party of men, with information that they had killed several Americans and taken a Boat from them. I was met the same day by Lafarka who informed me that he had not been able to deliver my second letter to the officer commanding the Gun Vessels.[16]

By nightfall on the 19th the allied force was approaching its objective. Continuing to move through the darkness, the boats landed just north of the fort two hours after midnight:

> …At two o'clock on the morning of the 20th we landed within cannon shot of the Fort, but protected by a skirt of woods. I again sent Lafarka with a letter notifying the officer commanding the convoy of my arrival. My plan of attack was communicated to the Chiefs, and a party of

Indians under Major McIntosh were directed to surround the Fort. Finding it impossible to carry my plans into execution without the assistance of Artillery, I ordered Major McIntosh to keep one third of his men constantly hovering around the fort and to keep up an irregular fire – this had the desired effect as it induced the enemy to amuse us with an incessant roar of Artillery without any other effect than that of striking terror into the souls of most of our red friends.[17]

The landing place described by Clinch was probably at or near the mouth of Brickyard Creek at the northern end of Prospect Bluff. The fort stood near the southern end of the low bluff, just above the mouth of Fort Gadsden Creek. The long 24-pounders at the installation were the largest cannon on the scene and had an accurate range of around 3,600 yards (4,800 feet). The elevation of the guns on the ramparts of the fort extended that range somewhat, so it is reasonable that a landing point at Brickyard Creek would be considered "within cannon shot" of the works. Any closer and the men would have been in the exposed field of fire that surrounded the fort. Any further back and they would not have been numerous enough to completely seal off the garrison.

One look at the fort was all it took for Lt. Col. Clinch to realize that is plan of taking it with 80 men was absolutely impossible. Even with the much larger force now at his disposal he realized that the fort was too strong to be taken without artillery. Although Prospect Bluff was not the soaring height described by some authors, it was extremely well fortified. Natural creeks, branches and swamps ringed its landward sides and the defenses themselves were designed to present a layered system of moats, trenches, breastworks, stockades and heavy walls to any attacking force. A wide field of fire had been cleared around the works and strong bastions allowed for musket and cannon fire to sweep the approaches to all three of its land faces. Inside the bastioned outer line were additional stockade lines, a moat and finally an octagonal citadel built of earth and logs. An earthwork water battery faced the river. Three magazines were positioned at strategic points in the complex, the largest being in the central octagon which also contained storehouses for weapons, offices and other rooms.

Although accounts of the battle often list a garrison of 300-320 men for the fort, that number actually contains women and children as well. The total strength of the male garrison was 80-100 men, including Choctaw warriors. This figure is perhaps a bit deceptive as it is clear that women and undoubtedly some of the older children also took part in the defense. While 80 men could not have defended the extensive outer entrenchments as infantry, the plentiful cannon in the fort altered the equation and made it extremely hazardous for Clinch's soldiers or the Creek warriors to approach too close.

John Blunt (Lafarka) traveled downriver by canoe with four other Creeks and reached the flotilla on the same day. How they passed the fort is not clear, but they may have taken the shallow channel behind Forbes Island to shield their passage from the battery. They also could have passed around the land side of the installation and found a canoe somewhere below. Either way, they soon made contact with Sailing Master Loomis and handed over new dispatches from Clinch. The naval officer had been tricked twice by the occupants of the Prospect Bluff fort, however, and was not willing to be tricked again. His vessels remained in the bay.[18]

Loomis could hear heavy cannonading from the direction of the fort on the 22nd and on the following day received a second party of messengers, this time composed of an unidentified white man and two Creek warriors who brought word from the lieutenant colonel that he wished the gunboats to come up to a "certain bluff" south of the fort. Once again Loomis refused to move:

> ...Considering that by doing so in a narrow and crooked river, from both sides of which my decks could be commanded and exposed to the fire of musketry, without enabling me to act in my own defence, and also, that something like treachery might be on foot from the nature of the message, I declined acting, retaining the white man

and one of the Indians as hostages, and despatched the other with my reason for doing so to colonel Clinch; that his views and communications to me in the future must be made in writing, and by an officer of the army.[19]

Clinch now responded by sending down Lt. Wilson of the 4th Infantry with a detachment of thirteen men. Wilson confirmed that the previous parties had come from the lieutenant colonel and also brought a written response from Clinch that offered assurances that the garrison of the fort was pinned down and could not oppose the movement of the vessels.[20]

Thus reassured, Loomis began to warp his vessels up the river and reached what he called "Duelling Bluff" about four miles below Prospect Bluff on the 25th. This was probably the low elevation known today as Bloody Bluff. It has been speculated that the name originated from the attack on Luffborough's watering party, but its distance from the mouth of the river renders this doubtful. The sailing master's use of the name "Duelling Bluff" suggests that it might have been considered bloody because it was a site where duels were conducted. [21]

Loomis found Clinch waiting for him at this bluff and welcomed him aboard Gunboat #149:

> …[H]e informed me that in attempting to pass within gun shot of the fortifications, he had been fired upon by the negroes, and that he had also been fired upon for the last four or five days, whenever any of his troops appeared in view; we immediately reconnoitered the fort, and determined on a site to erect a small battery of two eighteen pounders, to assist the gun vessels to force the navigation of the river, as it was evident from their hostility, we should be obliged to do.[22]

Lt. Col. Clinch reported that he and his officers had previously selected a spot for the battery in rear of the fort. Upon inspecting the two 18-pounders brought by the supply schooners, however, he discovered that they were mounted on heavy garrison carriages. It would be virtually impossible for his men to drag them through the thick cypress swamp to the site of his proposed battery.[23]

Disappointed, he conducted a joint reconnaissance with Sailing Master Loomis and the two selected a new battery site on the west side of the river below the fort. Brevet Major Peter Muhlenberg and Capt. William Taylor were instructed to move their companies to the proposed site while Lt. McGavock stayed behind with a detachment to help coordinate and support the Creek forces surrounding the land sides of the fort.[24]

The siege had now been underway for five days. All of the key forces of both sides were now on the scene. Casualties had thus far been light, considering the nature of the fighting. Known U.S. losses were Midshipman Luffborough and three sailors killed. Losses inside the fort to this point cannot be determined, although it is entirely possible there had been none at all.

The final attack on the fort took place on the morning of July 27, 1816. Clinch and his men had spent the previous day preparing the site of their intended battery. Loomis had planned to convey the *Semelante* up to the position under cover of darkness to land the guns on the night of the 26th. Before he could do so however, he found himself embroiled in a debate with the lieutenant colonel over whether it was worth the effort:

> ...[H]e however stated to me, that he was not acquainted with artillery, but that he thought the distance was too great to do execution; on this subject we unfortunately differed totally in opinion, as we were within point blank range, he however ordered his men to desist from further operations; I then told him that the gun vessels would attempt the passage of the fort, in the morning *without his aid*.[25]

Lt. Col. Clinch did not explain in his own report why he thought his artillery could do no damage to the fort. He had already decided the position was too strong to assault without first battering down its walls with cannon fire. Now he had given up the attempt to use 18-pounders for that purpose without having fired a single shot in the effort. Whether Clinch had decided that the siege was useless is not clear nor is it clear what he intended to do next.

Frustrated by the army's failure to follow through on the joint plan of attack, Sailing Master Loomis took matters into his own hands:

> …At 4 A.M. on the morning of the 27th, we began warping the gun vessels to a proper position; at 5, getting within gun shot, the fort opened upon us, which we returned; and after ascertaining our real distance with cold shot, we commenced with hot (having cleared away our coppers for that purpose) the *first* one of which entering their magazine, blew up, and completely destroyed the fort.[26]

Clinch described the attack in similar terms, but with one exception. He claimed in his report to Col. Robert Butler that he had ordered the naval attack. This was probably an embellishment as Army officers have no authority over the operations of naval vessels:

> …About six in the morning they came up in handsome stile and made fast along side of the intended battery. In a few minutes they received a shot from a thirty two pounder which was returned in a gallant manner. The contest was but momentary, the fifth discharge a hot shot from Gun Vessel 154 commanded by sailing Master Bassett entered the magazine and blew up the Fort.[27]

The explosion of the fort at Prospect Bluff had a lasting impact on most if not all of those who witnessed it. Clinch himself was clearly shocked by the aftermath:

> …The explosion was awful and the scene horrible beyond description. Our first care on arriving at the scene of

destruction was to rescue and relieve the unfortunate beings that survived the explosion. The war yells of the Indians, the cries and lamentations of the wounded compelled the soldier to pause in the midst of victory and to drop a tear for the sufferings of his fellow beings, and to acknowledge that the Great Ruler of the Universe must have used us as his instrument in chastising the blood-thirsty and murderous wretches that defended the Fort.[28]

Other officers gave similar accounts. Dr. Marcus Buck, a surgeon from the 4th Infantry who was acting as a staff member to Clinch during the expedition, was credited later for his role in trying to alleviate the sufferings of the wounded. He gave his own thoughts in a letter to his father:

> …You cannot conceive, nor I describe the horrors of the scene. In an instant, hundreds of lifeless bodies were stretched upon the plain, buried in sand and rubbish, or suspended from the tops of the surrounding pines. Here lay an innocent babe, there a helpless mother; on the one side a sturdy warrior, on the other a bleeding squaw. Piles of bodies, large heaps of sand, broken guns, accoutrements, &c. covered the scite of the fort. The brave soldier was disarmed of his resentment, and checked his victorious career, to drop a tear on the distressing scene.[29]

It is telling that both Lt. Col. Clinch and Dr. Buck described soldiers shedding tears at the scene of the explosion. Buck went on to describe how the troops rushed to extinguish the flames spreading from the destroyed magazine to prevent the explosion of a second magazine "between the picquets and parapet." This achieved, the men turned their attention to the wounded.[30]

An estimated 270 men, women and children died in the explosion. Of the surviving 50, most were injured and a number died of their wounds. Both Garcon and the Choctaw chief, remarkably, survived the blast although the former was blinded. Garcon was interviewed briefly by American officers and then executed by the Creeks, as was the Choctaw leader. Prior to being shot, the African American leader told his captors that he had been operating under orders from Lt. Col. Edward Nicolls to defend his post against any and all threats. This and the fact that the occupants of the fort fought beneath the flag of Great Britain leaves little doubt that in their minds they were still carrying out the charge given to them by the British to defend the post until Nicolls or other officers could return.

Only seven of the survivors of the explosion were found to have come from the United States. The others told officers that they had come from the environs of Pensacola and St. Augustine or had previously lived in the Seminole and Creek towns. At least one was from Jamaica.[31]

It was said at the time that the explosion was felt as far away as Pensacola.

---

[1] Lt. Col. Duncan L. Clinch to Maj. Gen. Edmund P. Gaines, June 14, 1816, Andrew Jackson papers, Library of Congress.
[2] *Ibid.*
[3] Sailing Master Jairus Loomis to Commodore Daniel T. Patterson, August 13, 1816.
[4] *Georgia Journal*, quoted in the South Carolina *City Gazette*, July 4, 1816, p. 2.
[5] *Ibid.*
[6] *Georgia Journal*, July 10, 1816, p. 3.
[7] Sailing Master Jairus Loomis to Commodore Daniel T. Patterson, August 15, 1816.
[8] *Ibid.*
[9] *Ibid.*
[10] Lt. Col. Duncan L. Clinch to Col. Robert Butler, Adjutant General, August 2, 1816, Andrew Jackson Papers, Library of Congress.
[11] Sailing Master Jairus Loomis to Commodore Daniel T. Patterson, August 15, 1816.
[12] *Ibid.*
[13] *Ibid.*
[14] *Ibid.*
[15] Articles of Agreement entered into on the 18th July 1816 by Lt. Col. D.L. Clinch on the part of the U.States & the Chiefs Capt. Isaacs, Kotcha harja, & Majr.

McIntosh on the part of the Creek Nation, enclosed in Lt. Col. Duncan L. Clinch to Col. Robert Butler, Adjutant General, August 2, 1816.

[16] Lt. Col. Duncan L. Clinch to Col. Robert Butler, Adjutant General, August 2, 1816.

[17] *Ibid.*

[18] Sailing Master Jairus Loomis to Commodore Daniel T. Patterson, August 15, 1816.

[19] *Ibid.*

[20] *Ibid.*

[21] *Ibid.*

[22] *Ibid.*

[23] Lt. Col. Duncan L. Clinch to Col. Robert Butler, Adjutant General, August 2, 1816.

[24] *Ibid.*

[25] Sailing Master Jairus Loomis to Commodore Daniel T. Patterson, August 15, 1816.

[26] *Ibid.*

[27] Lt. Col. Duncan L. Clinch to Col. Robert Butler, Adjutant General, August 2, 1816.

[28] *Ibid.*

[29] Dr. Marcus C. Buck to his father, August 4, 1816, included in "General Clinch and the Indians," *Army and Navy Chronicle*, Volume 2 (New Series), 1836, pp. 114-116.

[30] *Ibid.*

[31] For a detailed history of the attack and destruction of the fort on the Apalachicola, please see *The Fort at Prospect Bluff* by this author, scheduled for release in the summer of 2016 by Old Kitchen Books.

CHAPTER FOUR

Fort Scott on the Flint

The destruction of the fort at Prospect Bluff led to the capture of a stunning arsenal of military hardware and supplies. American authorities had long known that Col. Nicolls had left his former allies in possession of a large stock of ammunition and weaponry, but the volume of material found in the surviving magazines and storehouses of the ruined fort exceeded anything they had imagined.

An inventory of the material that could be salvaged was taken in the days following the explosion by men detached for that purpose. The U.S. Navy contingent was headed by Sailing Master James Bassett of Gunboat #154, while the U.S. Army detachment was placed under the command of Lt. Henry Wilson. In addition to a wide variety of tools, shoes, uniforms, etc., they reported being able to collect 550 muskets and twelve pieces of artillery. Another 2,500 or so muskets could not be salvaged. Cannon shot was so plentiful and so scattered that the officers were unable to collect and inventory it. They did succeed in saving 163 barrels of powder, all of which was claimed by the Creeks per their prior agreement with Lt. Col. Clinch.[1]

Also captured at the fort were a number of boats. These included three flatboats, one gig, one cutter and one schooner. The troops additionally captured 23,500 gunflints as well as cavalry equipment, 1,852 cartridge boxes, ammunition carriages and a limber for field guns.[2]

As Wilson, Bassett and their men were working to collect and catalog the captured inventory of the fort, other soldiers transferred the cargo of the *General Pike* to Clinch's flatboats for the trip up to Camp Crawford. Some of the cargo of the *Semelante* was also removed in order to lighten the schooner enough for it to make the trip upriver. Also placed aboard the flatboats was a number of shovels, pick axes and other tools from the fort along with the 5 ½ inch British howitzer, two casks of gunflints, 50 muskets and a variety of other items. The rest of the captured artillery and supplies was loaded aboard the three remaining vessels of Loomis's flotilla.[3]

Clinch's command began its return to Camp Crawford on July 30, 1816. On the evening of August 1st, as they neared the confluence, the soldiers were warned that an attack by outraged Seminole warriors might be looming:

> ...I received information that a large body of Seminole Indians were within a day's march of us, and in a few hours the report was confirmed by a letter from Major Cutler left in command at Camp Crawford informing me that a large body of Seminoles were descending the Appalachicola. I immediately ordered Major Muhlenburgh to keep the boats together, and to be in readiness to receive them, and directed one hundred Indians to keep with the Boats, and to act in concert if necessary. I advanced with two hundred Cowetas under the gallant Major McIntosh to meet them, but the cowardly wretches dispersed without our being able to get a view of them.[4]

Dr. Marcus C. Buck reported that the Seminoles had assembled in order to attack the rear of Clinch's force and break the siege of the fort at Prospect Bluff. The destruction of the fort had taken place so quickly, however, that they had not had time to act. He noted on August 4th that they had withdrawn from the river and had "since sent word that they wished to make peace."[5]

The soldiers reached Camp Crawford on August 2, 1816, completing an expedition that had been both strenuous and horrific. The supplies, artillery and captured material was unloaded and the eight captured African American men were placed in confinement. Clinch prepared a list of his prisoners on August 4th, enclosing it in his letters to Col. Robert Butler, adjutant for the troops in the South, and Gov. David B. Mitchell of Georgia:

Names	Owners	
Lamb	Col. B. Hawkins	
Elijah	Mr. Lewis	Georgia
Abraham	W.B. Howell	do.
Jo	Capt. Bowen	do.
Bature	Owned by a Frenchman living at the bay of St. Louis, M.T.	
Jacob	William Margart	
William	Dulendo a "Jew King" Jamaica	
Charles	Said he belongs to John Tharp, but it is supposed he is owned by some gentlemen in Virginia, as he arrived at Pensacola in the English Vessel Sea Horse.[6]	

It is telling that here were no women or children on Clinch's list. The vast majority of the individuals killed in the explosion fell within this category. The lieutenant colonel also reported that most of the former slaves from the United States had escaped to the Suwannee River ahead of his advance.

Of particular interest is the appearance of the name Abraham on the list. The noted Black Seminole chief Abraham was a member of the British Colonial Marines at Prospect Bluff and remained behind when Nicolls evacuated the majority of his troops. He remained in custody only a short time and within the next two years wound up in the Black Seminole settlement on the Suwannee River. Abraham played a critical role during the Second Seminole War, but was shipped west to what is now Oklahoma on February 25, 1839. His party reached Fort Gibson on April 13, 1839, and he lived out the rest of his life on the Little River. He was still alive there as late as 1870.[7]

The return of the troops to their base on the Flint River marked the beginning of a new phase in the history of the fort. The need for a more permanent occupancy of the site was recognized and Lt. Col. Clinch and his men soon initiated the construction of a new cantonment or post at the site. The original stockade erected by the 4th Infantry continued to stand as work went forward on this new facility. Major J.M. Davis visited the fort on an inspection tour during the fall of 1816 and reported during the spring regarding the original fort that it was "nothing more than a temporary work of logs, with a small magazine." Two 24-pounders, mounted on sea coast carriages, along with some smaller guns provided extra security to the site.[8]

Davis was much more impressed with the new "elegant cantonment" then under construction at the site:

> This cantonment was built on the bank of the river, which is so high & perpendicular that it would be impossible for an enemy to approach or do any injury on that part. The mens barracks are built of squared logs, laid lose together; all in one line parrallel with the river, at a distance of about one hundred yards from it; they were put up in such a manner as, by closing the doors & windows, would make them secure in front from small arms; and by losing the flanks with a picket work (which was their intention) would secure three hundred men from any body of Indians or small arms, - As long as their supplies of provisions & amunition would hold out. – The Officers Quarters was built between the line of mens barracks & the river – This place I conceive to be perfectly healthy, altho.' there were a number of men Sick at that post last Summer, which I believe was owing more to a severe campaign the

Regiment had in the early part of the summer on the Appalachicola than to any other cause.[9]

Major Davis also made note of the large springs adjacent to the site that were first described by Lt. Col. Clinch earlier in the year. The most impressive of these, he wrote, was "about one hundred & fifty yards from the cantonment, appears to be about forty feet deep and as much as one hundred & fifty feet in circumference." Its run was eight or ten inches deep and ten to twelve feet wide. The current was sufficient "to turn any water works."[10]

This was probably the "Little 'Ish" spring remembered by local residents as a popular swimming hole from the days before the completion of the Jim Woodruff Dam and flooding of Lake Seminole in 1958.

The effects of the recent campaign on the Apalachicola, however, continued to be felt at the post. Major Davis noted that sickness had been a problem during the summer and enlistment records show that at least one soldier died there shortly after returning from Prospect Bluff. Sylvannus Atwood, a fifer in Brevet Maj. Muhlenberg's company, died on August 19, 1816 and is believed to have been the first person buried at the post.[11]

Col. Clinch, meanwhile, was faced with the resignations of a number of his officers. Dr. Buck and Dr. Hall resigned almost immediately after the return of the expedition to Camp Crawford. Lt. Pendleton of the 4th Regiment resigned while on furlough to Washington D.C. Capt. William Taylor likewise announced his intention to resign.[12]

Exactly when the name of the post was changed from Camp Crawford to Fort Scott is not known. The similarly named Fort Crawford had been established on Murder Creek near the Conecuh River in Alabama during the summer and confusion between the two installations could have been the impetus for the change, but this cannot be proved using the available documentation. It is known that Lt. Col. Clinch continued to use the name Camp Crawford in his correspondence as late October 26, 1816. Not long after that date, however, he began calling his post Fort Scott.

The name probably was selected to honor Maj. Gen. Winfield T. Scott, a hero of the War of 1812 and future commanding general of the U.S. Army. Although there is no evidence that Scott himself ever visited the fort, he was a rising star in the army the other great heroes of the War of 1812 – Andrew

Jackson, Edmund Pendleton Gaines and William Henry Harrison – had already been honored by having military installations named for them. Suggestions that it instead honored Lt. Richard W. Scott who was killed in action on November 30, 1817, are unlikely as he was an unknown figure on the frontier at the time of the name change.

The timing of the renaming of the fort coincided closely with the near completion of the new cantonment. U.S. officials then believed that the destruction of the fort at Prospect Bluff would sufficiently intimidate the Red Sticks and Seminoles and prevent them from further resisting plans to survey and settle the lands taken from the Creek Nation by the Treaty of Fort Jackson. Col. William King of the 4th Infantry was consequently ordered to direct the evacuation of the fort and the movement of Lt. Col. Clinch's troops to Fort (Camp) Montgomery by way of Fort Mitchell. Slow communications hindered the delivery of these orders and they did not arrive until November 22, 1816:

> This movement at this season of the year is as strange as to me unaccountable. The troops had just got into their winter quarters when I left them for F.H. [Fort Hawkins] where I expected to have had the pleasure of seeing you, but on my arrival found a letter from Colo. King informing me that the order for the movement of the Regt. would be sent to me from F. Montgomery, on his arrival at that place, which order did not come until the 22d. Ult.[13]

Clinch was greatly alarmed by both the timing and nature of the orders to evacuate Fort Scott. Moving a large body of troops from new winter quarters and across a long stretch of unsettled frontier just as the coldest weather of the year settled in was problematic at best. He was even more concerned by Col. King's instructions that he should completely abandon Fort Gaines but leave a subaltern and 24 enlisted men at Fort Scott. The lieutenant colonel was well aware of the growing anger among the Seminoles and Red Sticks over the destruction of the Prospect Bluff establishment and clearly believed that leaving only 25 men to hold a fort designed for four companies was to invite their massacre. In a December letter to General Gaines, Clinch wrote that "it would have been better to have them shot at once."[14]

After he failed in an effort to locate and speak with Gen. Gaines in person, Lt. Col. Clinch deviated from his orders by carrying out the complete evacuation of Fort Scott but leaving a full company at Fort Gaines. The latter post was much smaller and could be held safely by one company. He also had as much of the government property as possible moved to that fort. Clinch arranged for George Perryman to move with his wife and children into one of the buildings at Fort Scott so that he could watch over the supplies being left behind. The last of the troops then evacuated the post and began their journey upriver to Fort Mitchell. The exact date on which the troops departed was not recorded, but appears to have been in mid-December.

By the time the evacuation took place, however, U.S. authorities were already beginning to change their minds about the wisdom of abandoning the fort. George Graham, the acting Secretary of War, wrote to Gen. Jackson on Nov. 5, 1816, noting that the Governor of Georgia had informed him of the presence of "a party of negroes and Indians" on the river below Fort Scott. If the information was correct, he suggested, "it would perhaps be advisable not to remove all the troops from that post."[15]

Concerns over the evacuation of Fort Scott were magnified in early January when news reached Gov. David B. Mitchell in Milledgeville that Maj. George Woodbine, the former second-in-command to Lt. Col. Edward Nicolls, was back in Florida:

> Mr. Kingsley of East Florida has this day informed me that Woodbine has returned to Bowlegs Town at Swaney and has been telling the Negroes that freedom had been granted the blacks at the neighboring Islands; that theirs was withheld by the villany of the white people – this he was told at St. Augustine last week by Mr. Popall and by Mr. Dexter. – at Swaney there are (he says) a great many run-away negroes from Georgia who receive and protect all that go to them, and prevent all those that wish to return to their masters from doing so. All those belonging to Mr. Popall and the most part of his wished to return, but were hindered by them from doing so. – He says that it is reported that Woodbine has gone to Havanah and left a white man there as an agent until his return. This information I

conceived it to be my duty to make known to your excellency without delay.[16]

Gov. Mitchell relayed the information to Acting-Secretary Graham without delay. He had previously protested the removal of the 4th Infantry from Georgia and now reiterated his concerns in letters to both the Secretary and Gen. Gaines. Any news of a return to Florida by Nicolls or Woodbine was alarming to residents of the frontier and such rumors often spread but were disproved by subsequent events. This time, however, there seems to have been some truth behind the alarm. Woodbine, no longer a British officer, had engaged in a shadowy plot to seize some or all of Florida from Spain. The identity of the agent or assistant left behind at Suwannee is not known, but it could have been either Alexander Arbuthnot or former Lt. Robert Ambrister of the Colonial Marines. Both men soon involved themselves in the affairs of the Seminoles and Red Sticks. "I think the information communicated may be relied upon as true," Mitchell wrote, "and furnishes a strong additional reason against the removal of the troops."[17]

The evacuation of Fort Scott also raised concerns across the line in Spanish Florida. John Forbes & Company had reestablished its trading post at Prospect Bluff following the destruction of the former British post. The departure of the troops from the lower Flint led to a surge in threats against company employee Edmund Doyle who had been assigned to rebuild the store:

> …Since the evacuation of the Camp on Flint River we have had very trying times here. I never suffered more uneasiness from various sources. I think now everything is safe and we shall have quiet times in the Nation: On the 23rd Inst four negroes came here from the Mikasukkys and demanded of me protection which of course was offered; they returned same day to bring the rest of their party there, they belong to a Mr. Kingsley of St. John's River.[18]

Doyle's hope that tensions were calming proved to be premature. Within days of his report a large force of Red Stick warriors arrived at Fort

Scott to demonstrate their opinion of the United States and the recently evacuated post on the Flint River.

---

[1] Inventory of Military Stores captured at the Negro Fort East Florida, July 28, 1816, enclosed in Lt. Col. Duncan L. Clinch to Col. Robert Butler, August 2, 1816, Andrew Jackson Papers, Library of Congress; Lt. Col. Duncan L. Clinch to Col. Robert Butler, Adjutant, August 2, 1816, Andrew Jackson Papers, Library of Congress; Articles of Agreement, July 18, 1816, enclosed in Lt. Col. Duncan L. Clinch to Col. Robert Butler, August 2, 1816, Andrew Jackson Papers, Library of Congress.

[2] *Ibid.*

[3] Inventory of Military Stores captured at the Negro Fort East Florida, July 28, 1816, enclosed in Lt. Col. Duncan L. Clinch to Col. Robert Butler, August 2, 1816, Andrew Jackson Papers, Library of Congress.

[4] Lt Col. Duncan L. Clinch to Col. Robert Butler, Adjutant, August 2, 1816.

[5] Dr. Marcus C. Buck to his father, August 4, 1816, in "Colonel Clinch and the Indians," *Army and Navy Chronicle,* Volume 2 (New Edition), 1836.

[6] "List of Negroes in Confinement at this Post," August 4, 1816, enclosed in Lt. Col. Duncan L. Clinch to Col. Robert Butler, August 2, 1816, Andrew Jackson Papers, Library of Congress.

[7] Kenneth W. Porter, "The Negro Abraham."

[8] Major J.M. Davis to Col. Arthur P. Hayne, April 30, 1817,

[9] *Ibid.*

[10] *Ibid.*

[11] *Ibid.*; Enlistment Registers.

[12] Lt. Col. Duncan L. Clinch to Brig. Gen. Daniel Parker, September 6, 1816, Adjutant General, Letters Received, NARA; Lt. Col. Duncan L. Clinch to Brig. Gen. Daniel Parker, October 5, 1816, Adjutant General, Letters Received, NARA.

[13] Lt. Col. Duncan L. Clinch to Maj. Gen. Edmund P. Gaines, December 26, 1817, Adjutant General, Letters Received, NARA.

[14] *Ibid.*

[15] Hon. George Graham to Maj. Gen. Andrew Jackson, November 5, 1816, Library of Congress.

[16] William Gibson to Gov. David B. Mitchell, January 4, 1817, Andrew Jackson Papers, Library of Congress.

[17] Gov. David B. Mitchell to George Graham, Acting Secretary of War, January 13, 1817, Andrew Jackson Papers, Library of Congress.

[18] Edmund Doyle to John Innerarity, January 28, 1817; FHQ, XVIII, October 1939, No. 2. pp. 312-313.

CHAPTER FIVE

Reoccupation of Fort Scott

The evacuation of Fort Scott was perceived as a victory by the Red Stick warriors in the vicinity who, far from being convinced of the superiority of U.S. troops, were just recovering from the shock caused by the destruction of the Prospect Bluff fort. Anger was now surging emotion and they soon vented it by arriving at the fort with torches in hand:

> When the colonel with the troops left Fort Scott, he gave the buildings in charge of one of the Perrymans, from whom I have just received a letter, handed me by his brother, who arrived here after I had commenced writing this.
>
> Perryman states in his letter that the Red Sticks, (or hostiles) after we had left the fort, came in companies and carried off every thing we had left with him, and what he had purchased of Butler; burnt three houses, and threatened, if he did not leave the place, to burn it over his head. He got

what few articles he could, with his family, in a canoe, and came to his brother's, who informs me that there are at present about 300 Indians embodied at the forks, and others constantly joining them. He does not know their intentions, but understood a party was going out to steal horses &c. &c.[1]

The Perrymans were members of an extensive mestizo family that lived along the lower Chattahoochee River. The grandsons of the English trader Theophilus Perryman, they included William, George, Ben and others. Their father, Thomas Perryman, had been in important leader of the Lower Creek/Seminole towns on the Apalachicola and lower Chattahoochee Rivers and a colonel of British auxiliaries during both the American Revolution and War of 1812. He is also noted in American history as the father-in-law of the noted adventurer and pirate William Augustus Bowles. Thomas Perryman, however, had died between the time of Lt. Col. Edward Nicolls' withdrawal from the region in May 1814 and the date of the destruction of the fort at Prospect Bluff fourteen months later. William Perryman, himself a captain in the British auxiliaries during the American Revolution and War of 1812, ascended to the leadership of the primary Perryman towns. His father's town site, on the east side of the Chattahoochee in what is now Seminole County, Georgia, was abandoned and the inhabitants crossed over the river to live with William's people at Tellmochesses on the west bank in today's Jackson County, Florida.

Since George Perryman was the caretaker left behind at Fort Scott, William Perryman was the brother to whom he fled for safety. William carried news of the partial burning of Fort Scott up to Fort Gaines where he met with Lt. Richard M. Sands and discussed the growing turbulence in the borderlands. The Red Sticks were not far behind and by the next morning had made their presence known:

This morning [February 3 1817] one of the settlers waited on me to advise in what manner to act, as eight or ten Indians had been at his house and ordered him off;

telling him that in six days they would come back, and, if he was not gone, they would drive him away.

Let their intentions be what they will I feel perfectly safe with my small command (32) & can contend with safety against 500 Indians if we had but five minutes notice of their approach. I have three 5 8/10 inch Howitzers, 2 Sixes & 1 four pounder and ammunition in abundance.[2]

General Gaines was by this point in Milledgeville where on February 5th he learned from Gov. Mitchell of a raid by a different group in Wayne County, Georgia. A party of warriors had entered the county and stolen two horses and a few head of cattle. The local residents quickly took up arms and went in pursuit. Coming up with the Indians, they demanded the return of the stolen property. The warriors, however, "immediately fired upon the whites, who retired without returning a shot. One of the whites was mortally wounded.[3]

The general promised "immediate and particular" attention:

> …I am not authorized to change the destination of the 4th infantry; but, should I receive no authority to recall a part of that corps, I shall order one or two companies of artillery (to do duty as infantry) from Charleston to the southern frontier of this State, with instructions to check Indian hostilities, and at the same time to remove from Indian land such intruders as may remain after being duly notified to remove.[4]

It was now evident that the decision to evacuate Fort Scott was a mistake. The need for a strong force on the Florida border became even more apparent when news reached Gaines at Fort Hawkins that efforts were underway by citizens in the Mississippi Territory, including present-day Alabama, to launch a filibustering expedition against the Spanish capital of Pensacola:

I am informed by a letter from Colonel King under date the 28 of last month that from information he has received from various sources he has reason to believe that the "Spanish Patriots" are about to get possession of Pensacola – that the expedition destined for this service was to rendezvous at the mouth of the Perdido on the 4th instant where they expected to be joined by a considerable force from the Mississippi Territory – that their agent, have been for some time actively employed in that quarter engaging men; and that he has been indirectly applied to for the loan of arms to equip them, which he has very properly disregarded.[5]

Attempts by American civilians to change the allegiance of Florida by force of arms were not knew. A party of revolutionaries had seized control of West Florida from the Mississippi River nearly to Mobile in 1810, capturing the capital city of Baton Rouge and announcing the establishment of the Republic of West Florida. The United States ultimately invaded the fledgling republic and seized control under a questionable claim that the territory was included in the Louisiana Purchase. U.S. troops then seized control of Mobile from the Spanish in 1813 and had pushed their country's territorial limits to the Perdido. A "Patriot Rebellion" in East Florida had surged to the gates of St. Augustine as a force of "revolutionaries" seized control of much of the colony and quickly turned it over to troops of the United States. Spain formed a military alliance with the Alachua Seminole, however, and drove back the so-called "Patriots," handing a major embarrassment to the Madison Administration in the process.

News of another such attempt was not pleasant to Gen. Gaines, who had ended perhaps the best known filibustering attempt in American history by arresting former Vice President Aaron Burr on February 19, 1807. President Thomas Jefferson had accused Burr of threatening the security of the United States by planning an unsanctioned conquest of Spanish territory. Gaines was still a young officer when he came up with Burr at a ferry over the Tombigbee River about 14 miles north of Fort Stoddert, Alabama (then the

Mississippi Territory). He had been tipped to the movements of the former Vice President by Nicholas Perkins, a resident of the area who had been asked for directions by Burr's traveling companion.[6]

One of very few men who would dare to lecture Andrew Jackson, Gaines warned his expansionist-minded commanding officer about the dangers that could come from U.S. involvement in such activities as the planned filibustering raid on Pensacola:

> However anxious an American officer witnessing a struggle of this sort may feel to take an active part and to throw his weight into the scale of national liberty against legitimate despotism; yet he who knows what is due to himself and to the country [torn] him with power and honoring him with trust and confidence can only stand aloof and look on as a passive neutral; so long at least as the belligerents confine their operations within the limits chalked out by national law. With this view of the subject I heartily approve of the stand taken by Colonel King.[7]

Gaines also reported that the Red Sticks had "given some recent indications of a hostile disposition towards the little settlement upon the Chattahoochie" and enclosed a copy of Lt. Sands' report of February 2-3, 1817.[8]

The general also notified Gov. Mitchell of the developing situation on the frontier, suggesting that militia troops might be called out to protect against any eventuality. Mitchell responded on February 16th with news that "as of yet I do not feel authorized to order out any militia." He did feel that militia troops could soon be provided to "punish the Seminolies," but doubted they could reach the field before the "expected conflict at Pensacola will either have taken place or become as less probable than at present."[9]

The rumored attack on Pensacola never took place, possibly due to the military's refusal to supply arms, but news soon arrived of surging activity among the Seminoles and Red Sticks in Florida. George Perryman, the former caretaker, wrote to Lt. Sands at Fort Gaines on February 24th with considerable new detail. The following excerpts have been edited for clarity:

> …There was a friend of mine not long since in the lower town on Flint [i.e. Fowltown] & he saw many horses, cattle and hogs that had came immediately from the State [of] Georgia and they are bringing them away continually. They speak in the most contemptuous manner of Americans and threat to have satisfaction for what has been done, meaning the destruction of the Negro fort. There is another of my acquaintances returned immediately from the Seminolie Towns, and saw the negroes there on parade. He counted about six hundred that bore arms. They have chosen officers of every description and endeavor to keep up a regular discipline and is very strict in punishing violators of their Military orders.[10]

The Perrymans were former allies of the alliance of Seminole and Red Stick towns and maintained many contacts with them. Consequently, they were able to provide consider intelligence to U.S. authorities. Kenhajo [Cappachimico] of Miccosukee was resisting war, but otherwise the talk among the Seminoles and Red Sticks was for conflict with either "the Americans or McIntosh's troops." Perryman went on to tell Sands that the warriors were promising a much more severe fight for U.S. forces "than they had at Appalachicola."[11]

He also reported the growing role of a chief named Boleck (or Bowlegs). A leader of the Alachua Seminoles, he had been driven from his home and his town destroyed at the time his brother, Payne, was killed in battle with American forces that had invaded East Florida in 1812. The infuriated chief had relocated to the Suwannee where he had joined the alliance put together by Lt. Col. Edward Nicolls and Maj. George Woodbine in 1814-1815. The destruction of the fort at Prospect Bluff had deprived him of a source for arms and ammunition, but the arrival of a Scottish trader named Alexander Arbuthnot on the Suwannee had replenished his supply.

The Red Sticks and many of the Seminoles had now chosen him as their leader, Perryman reported, nominated him king and were paying him "all kind of Monarchial Respect almost to Idolatry." They also were keeping a picket guard at a distance of five miles from their towns.[12]

The descriptions provided by Perryman are undoubtedly of the co-located Seminole and Black Seminole towns on the Suwannee and as such provide an extremely rare contemporary glimpse of the activities going on there. These towns were located at present-day Old Town in Dixie County, Florida. Boleck's people lived adjacent to but under separate leadership from the Black Seminole town that shared their fields and resources. Many of the warriors from the latter place had served in Nicolls' Colonial Marines and were well trained in light infantry tactics. Their presence in growing numbers on the Suwannee had almost immediately replaced the fort at Prospect Bluff as a point of fixation in the minds of U.S. slave holders.

The political and social complications at play in the developing Seminole Nation were utterly incomprehensible to American settlers and officials. The one authority who might have been able to understand them, longtime Agent for Indian Affairs Benjamin Hawkins, had died the previous year. The various groups had formed a formal alliance on March 15, 1815, when Lt. Col. Nicolls convened a council at the British outpost immediately below the Chattahoochee and Flint Rivers. This little known fort was a sister post to the British Post at Prospect Bluff. The council included representatives from towns or groups of Lower Creeks, Red Sticks, Miccosukee, Alachua, Yuchi and Choctaw. Languages spoken included Hitchiti, Muscogee, Yuchi and Choctaw. In short, a wide range of cultures was combining into the group that we know today as Seminoles.

U.S. officials did not realize the fierce independence that many of these bands maintained, even after the signing of the treaty at Nicolls' Outpost in 1815. The council and document began the process of concentration, but it would continue for many years and there are stark differences in culture and language between many of the different Seminole bands even today. The lack of central authority that existed in 1817 was extremely difficult for the United States military to understand. At various times they tried to make

Boleck of Suwannee, the Prophet Francis of the Red Sticks, or Cappachimico (Kenhajo) of Miccosukee the preeminent leader of the Seminoles. In reality, though, there was no central leader or figure who could exert control and power over the various bands. The Seminoles were a nation in progress during the era that Fort Scott stood on the Flint River.

The situation on the frontier worsened on February 24, 1817, when a party of warriors struck the Garrett farm in Camden County, Georgia:

> On the 24th instant the house of Mr. Garrett, residing in the upper part of this county, near the boundary of Wayne Co. was attacked, during his absence near the middle of the day, by this party consisting of about fifteen, who shot Mrs. Garrett in two places, and then dispatched her by stabbing and scalping. Her two children, one about three years & the other two months, were also murdered, and the eldest scalped; the house was then plundered of every article of value, and set on fire – a young man in the neighbourhood at work hearing the report of guns went immediately towards the house where he discovered the murdered family. The family having only commenced were soon extinguished – and he spread the alarm.[13]

Archibald Clark, the Intendant of St. Marys and author of the above, reported that workmen from his mills assembled with a few others of the neighborhood assembled to give pursuit but they had few arms. They followed the tracks of the raiding party down the western branch of Spanish Creek but soon gave up the chase.[14]

A second report from William Gibson indicated that Mr. Garrett was the foreman of William Barber and lived on his plantation. One of the slaves, a man named Abram, went to Clark's mills and reported the attack:

> …[He] told the people that he saw six or seven Indians at his master's place at Spanish Creek (about three miles

above the mills), that the Indians went to the door of the Overseer's House, who was in the woods cutting timber, that the wife of the overseer came to the door, and on seeing them screamed, that two of them shot her in the forehead and shoulder, he does not know what happened afterwards, as he ran to his house, took his child and carried it to the mill.[15]

Gibson reported that the men of the neighborhood went immediately to the Barber place where they found Mrs. Garrett and her two children dead. "Herself and the eldest child had been scalped and stripped of everything but their linen," he reported, "the youngest child was not stripped." The house was set afire but the volunteers managed to extinguish the blaze before it could be destroyed. He went on to note that the houses of the slaves had also been plundered, but reported no other casualties.[16]

A group of the frontier citizens went to Mr. Clark at St. Marys and asked him to send their call for help to Governor Mitchell and the army:

> To you Sir, therefore, the inhabitants on the Frontier as well as others, thro me appeal for some protection – a small detachment of troops, upon the head of the St. Mary's, would serve a most valuable purpose by at once checking the inroads of the savage and preventing our abandoned and unprincipled citizens from adventuring into the Indian Country and stealing herds of Cattle.[17]

Clark believed that the warriors were "Lower Creeks," but the Miccosukees were later blamed for the attack. The murders at the Garrett home heightened tensions on the frontier but a letter that arrived at Fort Gaines a few days later sent them soaring. Datelined from Okolokne (Ochlockonee) Sound, the unexpected missive was signed by Alexander Arbuthnot who claimed to be representing the Red Stick chief Peter McQueen:

> When McQueen left Tucky Batche his property was considerable both in negroes and cattle; of the former, ten

grown negroes were taken by a half breed man named
Barney, nine of which he believes were sold & one a girl is
still in possession of said Barney: Twenty able negroes
were taken by a Chief named Colonel, or Auche Hatcho –
who acts also as an interpreter; and as he never had
possession of any of those persons' property, nor ever did
them an injury to his knowledge; he claims as farther proof
of your friendship, that you will use your influence in
procuring those Negroes for them; And, should they be
given up by the persons holding them, there is one faithful
Negro among them named Charles who will bring them to
him at Okolockne River.[18]

Arbuthnot described McQueen as "an unfortunate Indian chief" who
had been forced to flee his home at Tuckabatchee during the Creek War of
1813-1814. He sought the help of the military in returning to him an African
American man named Joe.

The request stunned U.S. officers. McQueen was, to the best of their
knowledge, a bitter enemy and one of the principal leaders of the Red Stick
movement. Even more concerning was the sudden emergence of a new
British "agent" in Spanish Florida. The letter confirmed rumors that had
been reaching the frontier posts since January of a renewed British presence
among the Seminoles and Red Sticks. The Americans were particularly
alarmed by the fact that the Scottish trader appeared to be speaking on behalf
of the Indians in a manner that far exceed those of a businessman seeking to
trade among them. In addition, the letter included a claim that an important
British official was on his way to the region:

I hold in my possession a letter received from the
Governor of New Providence, addressed to him by His
Britannic Majesty's chief secretary, informing of the orders
given to the British ambassador at Washington to watch
over the interests of the Indian nations, and see that their
rights are faithfully attended to and protected, agreeably to
the treaty of peace made between the British and
Americans.

> I am in hopes that ere this there is arrived at New
> Providence a person from Great Britain with authority to
> act as agent for the Indian nations; and, if so, it will devolve
> on him to see that boundary lines, as marked out by the
> treaty, are not infringed upon.[19]

Such statements, regardless of Arbuthnot's intent, did not go over well in the United States. The letter was similar to the missives that Lt. Col. Nicolls had sent to Col. Benjamin Hawkins following the end of the War of 1812 and the very thought of British agents on the border was enough to inspire the ire of military commanders including Andrew Jackson and Edmund P. Gaines.

More information came on March 15, 1817, when Lt. Sands at Fort Gaines informed Col. William King of the 4th Infantry that William Perryman had arrived with reports of the looming arrival of a British force on the Gulf Coast:

> …Yesterday, William Perryman, accompanied by two
> of the lower chiefs, arrived here. He informs me that
> McQueen, the chief mentioned in one of the enclosed
> letters, is at present one of the heads of the hostiles; that
> they are anxious for war, and have lately murdered a
> woman and two children.
>
> He likewise says he expects the news in George
> Perryman's letter is true; for there are talks going through
> the towns that the English are to be at Ochlochnee river in
> three months.
>
> I have sent an Indian runner to Ochlochnee to ascertain
> what preparations the hostiles are making.[20]

General Gaines had heard enough. Pursuant to the directions of Gen. Jackson, orders were given on March 24th for a company of artillery to move from Charleston to Fort Scott. On the same day the Federal contractor in Georgia was told to begin delivering rations to the post:

> You are hereby required to keep up a supply of rations
> for one hundred men at Fort Scott near the confluence of

Flint and Chatahoochie rivers, for Four Months always in advance. This supply to consist of Flour and Bacon or such Pickled Pork as may have been preserved for safe keeping through the summer, together with the small parts of the ration required by the contract – the whole to be kept in store, independent of the casual supplies of fresh beef &c., depending upon the thing settlements in the vicinity of that post. The above supply for the first four months maybe deposited and issued at Fort Gaines, until ordered by the Commanding Officer at that Post to Fort Scott.[21]

Gaines told the contractor that the troops from Charleston could escort the first shipment of provisions as they passed from Fort Hawkins down to the frontier.

The general clearly believed that attacks against the frontier were coming and that Fort Gaines would be a particular target. He instructed Lt. Sands to be on the alert for any danger and to summon the settlers of the neighborhood to the fort where the men could assist in its defense while the women and children were safe under the protection of its guns. He further promised that Maj. William McIntosh would be instructed to go down with some of his best warriors if the situation became critical. Sands, meanwhile, was to prepare boats to help the artillery company reach Fort Scott.[22]

Reports from the frontier continued to arrive. Timothy Barnard, who had married a Yuchi woman and lived with his extensive family on the Flint River, reported on March 29th that the Red Sticks had begun dancing the Dance of the Indians of the Lakes. The evacuation of Fort Scott, he reported, had convinced the warriors that the troops of the United States were afraid to continue there.

Governor Mitchell, the recipient of Barnard's letter, had resigned his office on the 4th of the same month to accept the appointment as the new Agent for Indian Affairs. He pointed out to the Secretary of War that Timothy Barnard had lived among the Creek Indians for more than 50 years and was extremely well-informed due to his long residence and many family connections in the Nation. The new Agent went on to report that Barnard's account was supported by others from the frontier:

As an additional inducement to this measure, I will further state that I have received information from other persons at or near Fort Gaines that a British agent is now among these hostile Indians, and that he has been sending insolent messages to the friendly Indians and white men settled above the Spanish line: he is also charged with stimulating the Indians to their present hostile aspect; but whether he is an acknowledged agent of any foreign Power, or a mere adventurer, I do not pretend to determine, but am disposed to believe him the latter; but, be that as it may, and let the hostile disposition of the Indians proceed from what it may, a moderate regular force stationed at Camp Crawford, or any other suitable position in that quarter, will, I am confident, keep all quiet; and, without it, some serious mischief will result.[23]

Gaines updated Gen. Jackson from Camp Montgomery on April 2nd, confirming that Red Stick looting at Fort Scott had ended with the burning of the new barracks. He gave Jackson the latest information on the Garrett attack and then addressed the presence of Arbuthnot in Spanish Florida. Calling the Scottish trader "one of those self-styled Philanthropists who have long infested our neighboring Indian villages, in the character of British Agents," Gaines went on to accuse Arbuthnot and his ilk of "fomenting a spirit of discord" that would lead to the "destruction of these wretched savages."[24]

General Gaines also requested Maj. William McIntosh to take a company of his best warriors down to Fort Gaines. He informed Lt. Sands of this in a letter that urged him to "store up every bushel of corn and every point of meat you can obtain" and to be ready for war:

If you should have war your command will be a perilous one; but I am sure it will not on that account be the less desirable to you. He who would woo the sweet goddess of Military fame, must calculate upon finding her only in the midst of dangers.[25]

On the same day, April 2nd, Gaines received a letter from a settler named Alexander McCulloh who was living near Fort Gaines. The document was undated but clearly had been written in March. McCulloh, whose name has incorrectly been given as Culloh by some writers, told the general that he and other settlers had gathered under the safety of the cannon of Fort Gaines and were unable to make a crop or safely evacuate to more populated areas:

> We are hourly told, by every source of information, by the friendly Indians, by letters from Wm. Hambly and Edmund Doyle, who resides low down on the Appalachicola, that all the lower tribes of Indians are embodied, and are drying their meats to come on to the attack of this post. The British agent at Oakclocking Sound is giving presents to the Indians. We have amongst us Indians who have been down and received powder, lead, tomahawks, knives, and a drum for each town, with the Royal Coat-of-Arms painted on it. We have, at this time, at least five hundred Indians skulking in this neighborhood, within three or four miles of us, who will not act for themselves and who are evidently waiting the signal to strike an effectual blow. They have stolen almost every horse belonging to the citizens, they have scared them from the fields which they have cleared and have taken possession of their houses.[26]

McCulloh begged Gaines to send more troops, pleading that a strong force was the only way to protect the frontier and its residents. The general responded two weeks later by ordering the commanding officer at Charleston to detach another company of artillery and have it moved down the coast by water to St. Marys. The troops were then to move up the St. Marys River to Camp Pinckney where they were to build a small fort with two blockhouses for the protection Camden and Wayne Counties. The soldiers were to carry muskets and bayonets so they could serve as infantry, but were also to take along two 6-pounder field guns. The captain of the company was to "take the most effectual measures in his power to protect the defenceless inhabitants from Indian depredation" and was to arrest or destroy "any hostile party of Indians found lurking about that frontier."[27]

The first concrete step for the reestablishment of Fort Scott took place on April 27, 1817. Capt. Sanders Donoho left Charleston with a company from the 4th Artillery drawn from the "different garrisons in this harbor." Units from the 4th and 7th Infantry Regiments would soon follow. Donoho's orders called for him to proceed to Fort Scott by way of Forts Hawkins and Gaines. Boats would be waiting at the latter post to carry his men and supplies down the Chattahoochee. Artillery would be provided from the guns then housed at Fort Gaines.[28]

An inspection report filed about the same time by Maj. J.M. Davis showed that the troops on the frontier were well-trained and ready to fight:

> Special Report of the first Brigade composed of the 4th and 7th Regiments of Infantry. –
>
> 1st. This brigade is under excellent discipline in General and particularly in the knowledge of the evolutions prescribed for the practice of the Troops, - They are in habits of Obedience, the prescribed uniform is strictly adhered to – and the rules of interior economy appears to be their greatest care – notwithstanding all the economy that can possibly be used the expenditures may appear great, yet I cannot well see how they could in any way be curtailed.
>
> 2d. The field and Company officers respectively know their duty, and are willing to perform it – The Adjutants, Quartermasters, and Pay-masters, are competant to the duties assigned them. –
>
> 3d. The meat & Bread furnished by the contractor is of good quality and regularly Issued.
>
> 4th. The forage which has been issued to the officers of this Brigade has not been of the best quality and the quantity has been very deficient – Hay there is none – Fodder has

been so scarce, and will have to draw from Government for the Hay or Fodder part of the Forage.

5th. Hospital Supplies have been sufficient and regularly dispensed. –

6th. There has been no irregularity in the proceedings of Courts Martial, or in the execution of Sentences pronounced by them in this section.

7th. The Ordnance & Ordnance Stores are generally good & in good order – Lieut: C. Keiser is the only officer with whom I am acquainted of the ordnance department in this Section; he is an attentive and vigilent Officer, and has that Department so far as he regulates in good order & well regulated.[29]

The only problem noted by Davis was that ammunition stocks were insufficient. There were fewer than 30,000 musket cartridges in store at the time, or only around 30 rounds for each man in the 4th and 7th Regiments.[30]

The movement of Donoho's company to Fort Scott can be traced in the pages of the newspapers of the time. The unit had left Charleston on April 27th and by the evening of Monday, May 5th, was at Augusta, Georgia. The company moved on via Fort Hawkins to Fort Gaines and finally by mid-June was in place at Fort Scott. The first word from the captain to Gen. Gaines about the situation there went out on June 23rd:

I have placed this post in a state of defence capable of repelling a thousand Indians, with the force under my command. But from all the information I have been able to collect respecting the intentions of the lower creeks, they seem to me to be more disposed to massacre and plunder the defenceless and helpless, than to attack military posts. For the purpose however of ascertaining their final intentions, I despatched an Indian into Florida, whose report as soon as he returns, shall be communicated to you.

74

I am sorry to inform you that what with desertions, and discharges that are soon to take place, I shall scarcely have an artificer left.[31]

Fort Scott was again a post of the U.S. Army and would remain such for the next four years. The arrival of Capt. Donoho's men saved the works from further destruction. As the soldiers busied themselves with the rebuilding of the burned barracks and improvement of the defenses, anger grew in the nearby Lower Creek village of Fowltown over their return to the fort. The principal chief of the town was Neamathla (Eneah Emathla) and his determination to give up no more of his peoples' land soon put him at odds with the offers at Fort Scott and the full might and power of the United States.

---

[1] Lt. Richard M. Sands to Commanding Officer Fort Hawkins, February 2, 1817, Andrew Jackson Papers, Library of Congress.
[2] *Ibid.*
[3] Gov. David B. Mitchell to Maj. Gen. Edmund P. Gaines, February 5, 1817, *American State Papers*, Indian Affairs, Volume II, p. 155.
[4] Maj. Gen. Edmund P. Gaines to Gov. David B. Mitchell, February 5, 1817, *American State Papers*, Indian Affairs, Volume II, p. 155.
[5] Maj. Gen. Edmund P. Gaines to Maj. Gen. Andrew Jackson, February 14, 1817, Andrew Jackson Papers, Library of Congress.
[6] Samuel P. Menefee, "Aaron Burr's Arrest," Encyclopedia of Alabama, online article at www.encyclopediaofalabama.org/article/h-2039, February 23, 2009.
[7] Maj. Gen. Edmund P. Gaines to Maj. Gen. Andrew Jackson, February 14, 1817.
[8] *Ibid.*
[9] Gov. David B. Mitchell to Maj. Gen. Edmund P. Gaines, February 16, 1817, Adjutant General, Letters Received, NARA.
[10] George Perryman to Lt. Richard M. Sands, February 24, 1816, Andrew Jackson Papers, Library of Congress. Edited for clarity by the author.
[11] *Ibid.*
[12] *Ibid.*
[13] Archibald Clark to Maj. Gen. Edmund P. Gaines, February 26, 1817, Andrew Jackson Papers, Library of Congress. (Similar letter sent to Hon. David B. Mitchell, Agent for Indian Affairs, on the same date.)
[14] *Ibid.*
[15] William Gibson to Hon. David B. Mitchell, Governor of Georgia, February 26, 1817, Andrew Jackson Papers, Library of Congress.

[16] *Ibid.*

[17] Archibald Clark to Maj. Gen. Edmund P. Gaines, February 26, 1817.

[18] Alexander Arbuthnot to the Officer Commanding at Fort Gaines, March 3, 1817, Andrew Jackson Papers, Library of Congress.

[19] *Ibid.*

[20] Lt. Richard M. Sands to Col. William King, March 15, 1817, *American State Papers*, Indian Affairs, Volume II, p. 156.

[21] Maj. Gen. Edmund P. Gaines to the Contractor for the State of Georgia, March 24, 1817, Andrew Jackson Papers, Library of Congress.

[22] Maj. Gen. Edmund P. Gaines to Lt. Richard M. Sands, March 26, 1817, Andrew Jackson Papers, Library of Congress.

[23] Hon. David B. Mitchell to the Secretary of War, March 30, 1817, *American State Papers*, Indian Affairs, Volume II, pp. 156-157.

[24] Maj. Gen. Edmund P. Gaines to Maj. Gen. Andrew Jackson, April 2, 1817.

[25] Maj. Gen. Edmund P. Gaines to Lt. Richard M. Sands, April 2, 1817, Andrew Jackson Papers, Library of Congress.

[26] Alexander McCulloh to Maj. Gen. Edmund P. Gaines, n.d. (apparently late March 1817 and received at Camp Montgomery on April 2, 1817), Andrew Jackson Papers, Library of Congress. An edited version of this letter has appeared in numerous print sources incorrectly giving McCulloh's name as "A. Culloh" and with numerous other transcription errors.

[27] Maj. Gen. Edmund P. Gaines to Commanding Officer, Harbor of Charleston, April 16, 1817, Office of the Adjutant General, Letters Received, 1805-1821.

[28] *Georgia Journal*, May 6, 1817, p. 3.

[29] Major J.N. Davis to Col. A.P. Hayne, April 30, 1817, Carter, Territorial Papers of the Unites States: Alabama, pp. 92-96.

[30] *Ibid.*

[31] Capt. Sanders Donoho to Maj. Gen. Edmund P. Gaines, June 23, 1817, Andrew Jackson papers, Library of Congress.

CHAPTER SIX

The Summer of 1817

The summer of 1817 was a critical time in the history of Fort Scott. Capt. Sanders Donoho's artillery company arrived on the Flint by mid-June and started the backbreaking labor of rebuilding the burned barracks. A reinforcement of 73 men from the 7th Infantry started overland from Fort Crawford under Maj. David E. Twiggs, who had been ordered to take command of the post.

Later nicknamed the "Bengal Tiger," Twiggs was a particularly stern disciplinarian. He was 27-year-old veteran of the War of 1812 at the time of his march through the ceded territory from Fort Crawford to Fort Scott and reported that his men were exposed to rain on each day of their journey. As he moved through what is now South Alabama during the last two weeks of June, he ordered blockhouses built on the Yellow Water and Choctawhatchee Rivers. A miniscule force of one corporal and four privates was left to garrison each, far away from support of any kind. The major estimated the total distance from Fort Crawford to Fort Gaines to be around 130 miles and believed that it would take 100 soldiers on pioneer duty one month to build a useable road along his route of march.[1]

From Fort Gaines, where he arrived on June 29th, Twiggs and his command moved by boat down the Chattahoochee River to the confluence and Fort Scott. When he left the former post on July 1st, there were only forty days of flour rations left on hand. Beef, however, was available "in almost any quantity." The Seminoles and Red Sticks, he reported, had been largely quiet for the last several weeks.[2]

Twiggs likely reached Fort Scott by Independence Day of 1817. The addition of his command to the small 39-man unit of Captain Donoho raised the total strength at the post to around 112 men. With the artillery carried down from Fort Gaines, this was a sufficient force to make a good account of itself should the fort fall under attack. This garrison, however, was but the tip of the spear that Gen. Gaines intended to plant on the Flint River. Writing to Gov. William Rabun of Georgia on July 20th, he noted that he had been ordered by Gen. Jackson to demand that the Seminoles turn over the warriors responsible for the murders of Mrs. Garrett and her two children near St. Marys. An attempt was made to meet with Cappachimico (Kenhajo) and other chiefs in May, but none had responded to the invitation:

> ...I have ascertained that a strong spirit of hostility towards us still exists among them; I have therefore made arrangements for assembling at Fort Scott, near the head of the Appalachicola river, in next month, the whole of my disposable force, in order to settle our differences with the Indians, and put a stop to the predatory war, carried on for some time past at the expense of the lives and property of unoffending and helpless settlers.[3]

The general informed Gov. Rabun that he believed the 4th and 7th Infantry Regiments fielded sufficient firepower to deal with warriors living in the vicinity of the Apalachicola River, he would need additional forces if his attempt to arrest the murder suspects led to a general outbreak. He requested that the governor order one battalion of riflemen and one battalion of light or mounted infantry to be ready to assemble at Fort Hawkins in

August for two months' service. The units were to be armed, clothed and equipped. Supplies, he reported, were being sent to Fort Scott by water:

> I have ordered a supply of provisions and other military stores to the Appalachicola by water, to be delivered at Fort Scott by the 30th of next month – at which time I wish to be in readiness to adjust our difference with the Indians. – Should they be disposed to continue in a state of war, they shall receive a full portion of its evils; but, should they desire peace, and yield to the demands of justice, they shall be gratified. In this case the troops will be occupied in completing a road which I have commenced from this place, via Fort Crawford on the Conaka, to cross the Chattahoochie about midway between Forts Scott and Gaines, and thence to Hartford in Georgia. – By this route the distance from Georgia to this place and Mobile will be considerably shortened.[4]

Through some quirk of the mails, however, Gaines' request did not reach Milledgeville for two full months. By the time it reached Rabun's hands the time period by which the militia battalions were to have rendezvoused had already passed. The governor did order men from Irwin's Blackshear's, Hamilton's and Scott's Brigades to be ready to march should the word come.[5]

At Fort Scott, meanwhile, William Perryman and several other chiefs from the vicinity arranged to meet with Maj. Twiggs at the post on August 4th. The meeting was ostensibly scheduled to allow the local towns to express their allegiance to the United States, but subsequent events revealed that Perryman actually planned to flog the chief of Fowltown for the rudeness he had shown the troops.

The story of Neamathla (Eneah Emathla) is one of the more intriguing in American history. He had been living with his people higher up the Flint River when the Creek War erupted in 1813. Despite the remoteness of his town from the territory of the Upper Creeks, the chief had become interested in the teachings of the Prophet Josiah Francis. In late 1813 he crossed the Chattahoochee River with warriors from his own town and from Miccosukee to join with a party of Yuchi who were planning a march to join the Prophet's forces on the Alabama River. They were intercepted at the Battle of Uchee Creek by forces under William McIntosh and handed a disastrous defeat. McIntosh and his warriors pursued the Neamathla's Tuttalossees back to the Flint River and destroyed their town and stock.[6]

Deciding to remove his people to safety, Neamathla withdrew down the Flint River to the vicinity of the confluence. He quickly made contact with Thomas Perryman, the principal chief in the area, and was among the first key leaders to affiliate with the British when they arrived on the Apalachicola in the summer of 1814. The chief and two others of the same title signed the treaty at Nicolls' Outpost on March 10, 1815, and he was among those promised access to the arms, ammunition and other supplies that the British left behind in the magazines of the post at Prospect Bluff. His warriors were accused of involvement in the capture of two soldiers and a herd of cattle at Fort Gaines in May 1816 and of participating in other raids against the Georgia frontier.

By the time of Lt. Col. Duncan L. Clinch's descent of the Chattahoochee River to build Camp Crawford in June 1816 it appears that at least some of Neamathla's people had settled in the open fields on the former site of Thomas Perryman's town as well as at a site south of the Flint River about 12 miles east of Fort Scott. The former location is now mostly inundated beneath Lake Seminole but was off the shoreline of today's Fairchild Park area in Seminole County, Georgia. The second site was about four miles south of today's Bainbridge, Georgia, on the southwest edge of Fowltown Swamp.

On his way down to the forks, Clinch stopped at Perryman's old town – which he called Fowltown – and demanded an interview with Neamathla:

> ... Our movements were so rapid the Indians had no knowledge of our being on the river until they saw our boats as soon as we approached Fowl Town. The Cowardly

rascals hoisted a white flag and appeared to be much alarmed. I [ordered] their chief on board, but was informed by the Indian that came on board that he had not returned from the N.F. where he had been for the purpose of procuring ammunition. I learnt last evening that he has since returned and have ordered him to be here in two days & shall be governed in my future operations by circumstances.[7]

The chief tried to avoid a confrontation with Clinch by next responding that he was busy with his corn fields and could not come to Camp Crawford within the time specified. The lieutenant colonel responded by sending Yellow Hair to tell Neamathla – or "Ene emartler" as Clinch spelled his title – that unless he came immediately, the army would treat him as an enemy and take him by force. The Tuttalossees had not threatened the troops at Camp Crawford and the harsh response from Lt. Col. Clinch surprised the chief. He agreed to meet with Clinch but expressed great apprehension about going into the American camp. The U.S. commander mocked Neamathla in his report to Gen. Gaines about their meeting:

… On arriving on the opposite side of the river his heart failed him and he told the chief that he could not come into the fort (as he called it) but wished me to cross over and see him. I directed the Adjutant to go over with the Interpreter and Chief and to tell him that unless he came over immediately that he had orders to compel him to come on which he came over and I never saw a poor devil manifest as much fear as he did. I had several friendly chiefs with me and they all informed me that they never saw him so completely cut down before. He consented to every demand I made of him and informed me that King Hago [i.e. Kenhajo/Cappachimico] would come and see me in a short time and that everything should be settled as I wished it.[8]

Neamathla's response, if described accurately by Clinch, was atypical for the chief. His forcefulness as a leader was described in grudging but admiring terms by numerous American officials over the next twenty years. The rapidity with which so many U.S. troops had arrived at their new position on the Flint and directly between two of his towns undoubtedly surprised the chief and he may have reflected this in his meeting with the lieutenant colonel. His first view of the construction underway at Camp Crawford probably also surprised him as the military advantages of the high bluff then being fortified were evident. It is also possible that he was simply stalling to give him time to see Cappachimico (Kenhajo) with whom he was closely allied.

It is worth recalling that the courier captured by Clinch's forces as they made their way down the Apalachicola for the attack on Prospect Bluff was on his way to deliver the scalp of one of Luffborough's sailors to Fowltown and Miccosukee. During the siege of the fort, Garcon even told Mad Tiger and Captain Isaacs that he could not surrender the post without first meeting with the chiefs of Fowltown and Miccosukee.

Neamathla's attitude about American troops was much more apparent by the time they returned to Fort Scott in 1817. During the intervening months he had evacuated the portion of his people settled on the old Perryman town site to his primary village east of the fort. In a meeting with Major Twiggs on August 3rd he made clear that U.S. soldiers should not cross the Flint:

> ... the Chief of Fowl town near this who is very frequently among the Seminolas told me eight days ago that the Flint river was the line between us & I must not cut another stick of timber on the opposite side from this, the land was his & he was directed by the Powers above to protect & defend it & he should do so & I would see that talking could not frighten him since which I have not seen one of his town. The Indians on the east of the Flint will in my opinion in the event of a movement on that side of the river commence

82

hostilities. It is possible I may be mistaken but I shall think so till the contrary is proved.[9]

The chief's sentiments were well known to the Lower Creeks living in the vicinity of the confluence and William Perryman called for a council to convene at Fort Scott on the 4th of August. It was later learned that Perryman and the others planned to flog Neamathla in Clinch's presence because they believed he was instigating hostilities with the United States. The meeting convened as planned, but the Fowltown chief did not come, sending word instead that he had already spoken.[10]

Neither did Kenhajo (Cappachimico) of Miccosukee appear, also sending word that he saw no point in discussions:

> ... Kenhagees last message to the Commandant at Fort Scott Flint River was rather insulting – he said he had no talks for him – that he expected shortly an English agent who would settle the affairs of the Indians, and drive the Americans back – another fellow the Fowl Town Chief ordered them not to cut trees on the east of Flint river – and is otherwise high crested they have also refused to give an audience to one of the officers sent to them by General Gaines.[11]

The public contractor in Georgia, meanwhile, failed to deliver expected supplies to Fort Scott and by early August the stock of provisions both there and at Fort Gaines was dwindling. Major Twiggs notified Gen. Gaines on the 11th that he had been forced to evacuate the blockhouse on the Choctawhatchee because Lt. Sands at Fort Gaines could no longer supply the five men there. The blockhouse on the Yellow Water was probably being supplied through Fort Crawford and Twiggs made no mention of its fate.[12]

Let down by the contractor, Army officers turned to the Pensacola firm of John Forbes & Company for help in getting provisions to Fort Scott and Fort Gaines. Storekeeper Edmund Doyle reported from Prospect Bluff on August 17th that 125,000 rations ordered by Gen. Gaines were either at the bluff or on their way up to the forts. Another 125,000 rations were still expected. He also requested more goods and noted that he was buying corn for the sutler at Fort Scott at a price of no more than 6 reals per bushel. In Spanish silver coinage, this was about the equivalent of 75 cents. He had also sold the sutler $190 worth of sugar and coffee at 19 and 17 cents per pound respectively.[13]

As July turned to August, the army focused more on finding and punishing the murderers of Mrs. Garrett and her children. General Gaines sent a written "talk" to Fort Scott with instructions for Maj. Twiggs to have it read to the principal chiefs at Miccosukee. The major sent an interpreter named Gregory to the massive village on September 6, 1817:

> … The interpreter informed me that the principal warriors were not present when he was there, but those who were present said they had never heard of Indians being given up to be punished by the whites; that they had heard of their being sometimes killed by themselves for offences committed, but seemed to think that giving them up was out of the question, but said they would have a meeting, and would answer the letter in a few days. As they have not done so, I think but one construction can be put on their conduct. The young men seemed to dislike the communication very much, and when Gregory was about leaving the town he offered his hand to an Indian, who held out his with a knife in it, and refused to shake hands with him; he staid so short a time among them that it was impossible for him to give much information respecting them.[14]

Twiggs reported to Gen. Gaines that the chiefs had promised an answer within ten days. He also noted that Capt. Donoho, who had been sick in Hartford, Georgia, was harassed by warriors on his way back down to Fort Scott. "The Indians were very rude to him, and frequently threatened his guide," the major wrote, "and once caught hold of the captain's bridle in a threatening manner."[15]

Kenhajo (Cappachimico) did respond to Gaines' talk within the time promised, but sent his reply to the commanding officer at Fort Hawkins instead of Maj. Twiggs at Fort Scott. The reason for this is unclear, but it slightly delayed receipt of the chief's talk by the general. Because the document would prove critical to future events at Fort Scott and on the frontier, it is given in its entirety here:

> Since the last war, after you sent word we must quit the war, we, the red people, have come over to this side. The white people have carried all the red people's cattle off. After the war I sent to all my people to let the white people alone, and stay on this side of the river, and they did so; but the white people still continue to carry off their cattle. Barnard's son was here, and I inquired of him what was to be done, and he said we must go to the headman of the white people and complain. I did so, and there was no white headman, and there was no law in this case. The whites first began, and there is nothing said about that, but great complaint made about what the Indians do. This is now three years since the white people killed three Indians; since that they have killed three other Indians, and taken their horses and what they had; and this summer they killed three more, and very lately they killed one more. We sent word to the white people that these murders were done, and the answer was that they were people that were outlaws, and we ought to go and kill them. The white people killed our people first, and the Indians then took satisfaction. There are yet three men that the red people have never taken satisfaction for. You have written that there were houses burnt, but we know of no such thing being done; the truth in such cases ought to be told, but this appears otherwise. On that side of the river the white people have killed five

Indians, but there is nothing said about that; and all that the Indians have done is brought up. All the mischief the white people have done ought to be told to their headman. When there is any thing done, you write to us, but never write to your headman what the white people do. When the red people send talks, or write, they always send the truth. You have sent to us for your horses, and we send all that we could find; but there were some dead. It appears that all the mischief is laid on this town; but all the mischief that has been done by this town is two horses – one of them is dead, and the other was sent back. The cattle that we are accused of taking were cattle that the white people took from us. Our young men went and brought them back, with the same marks and brands. There were some of our young men out hunting, and they were killed. Others went to take satisfaction, and the kettle of the en that were killed was found in the house where the woman and two children were killed; and they supposed it had been her husband who had killed the Indians, and took their satisfaction there. We are accused of killing up Americans, and so on; but since the word was sent to us that peace was made, we stay steady at home and meddle with no person. You have sent to us respecting the black people on the Suwanee river. We have nothing to do with them; they were put there by the English, and to them you ought to apply for any thing about them. We do not wish our country desolated by an army passing through it for the concern of other people. The Indians have slaves there, also – a great many of them. When we have an opportunity, we shall apply to the English for them, but we cannot get them now.

That is what we have to say at present.

Sir, I conclude by subscribing myself your humble servant, &c.

N.B. There are ten towns that have read this letter, and this is the answer.[16]

The reply was probably written by Alexander Arbuthnot but undoubtedly expressed the sentiments of the Miccosukee chiefs. General Gaines was not pleased:

> By this communication it appears that instead of a compliance, the Chiefs have set up a claim against us for the lives of three Indians, for whom they allege they have not yet taken satisfaction. They charge us with having killed ten of their warriors – and allowing a balance of three to be due them, they consequently admit, that they have killed seven of our Citizens. They acknowledge the murder of a woman (Mrs. Garret) and her two children – but justify the act upon the ground that the Warriors who committed this outrage had lost friends, had entered our Settlements to take satisfaction, found at the house of Garret a kettle belonging to the Indians that had been killed, and therefore "Supposing the murder had been committed by the husband of the woman," killed her and her children.[17]

Gaines went on to inform Gen. Jackson that he had decided that "nothing but the application of force, will be sufficient to ensure a permanent adjustment of this affair." He reported that he was ordering the movement of the First Brigade, which consisted of the 4th and 7th Infantry Regiments, to Fort Scott and believed it would reach the post by the 20th or 25th of October. He also explained that he would send his heavy supplies by water with an escort force and promised to finish the new road across the ceded lands in South Alabama in the process.[18]

In Georgia, Gov. Rabun ordered a squadron of cavalry and ten companies of infantry to prepare to march on short notice from their home counties of Hancock, Washington, Baldwin, Putnam, Morgan, Twiggs, Pulaski, Jones and Jasper. Arms and accoutrements would be provided at

Fort Hawkins. The *Georgia Journal* in Milledgeville reported, however, that the troops would probably not be needed:

> We learn by a gentleman from Head Quarters, (Fort Montgomery) that Gen. Gaines, who was then at St. Stephens, intends visiting Georgia in a few days; and that but little expectation appeared to be entertained in that part of the country, of an approaching rupture with the Indians. It is probable, therefore, the troops from this State will not be called into service.[19]

Whether or not the soldiers of the 4th and 7th Infantry Regiments knew it, they were marching into a hornets' nest. The "rupture" that the editor of the *Georgia Journal* did not think would take place was now looming on the near horizon.

---

[1] Maj. David E. Twiggs to Maj. Gen. Edmund P. Gaines, June 29, 1817, Andrew Jackson Papers, Library of Congress.
[2] *Ibid.*
[3] Maj. Gen. Edmund P. Gaines to the Governor of Georgia, July 20, 1817, included in Georgia Journal, September 15, 1817.
[4] *Ibid.*
[5] *Ibid.*
[6] Col. Benjamin Hawkins to ----------, 1813.
[7] Lt. Col. Duncan L. Clinch to Maj. Gen. Edmund P. Gaines, June 12, 1816, Andrew Jackson Papers, Library of Congress.
[8] Lt. Col. Duncan L. Clinch to Maj. Gen. Edmund P. Gaines, June 14, 1816, Andrew Jackson Papers, Library of Congress.
[9] Maj. David E. Twiggs to Hon. David B. Mitchell, August 11, 1817, from the Easton Gazette, April 5, 1819, p. 1.
[10] *Ibid.*
[11] Edmund Doyle to James Innerarity, August 17, 1817, FHQ, XVIII, October 1939, No. 2, p. 139.
[12] Maj. David E. Twiggs to Maj. Gen. Edmund P. Gaines, August 11, 1817, Andrew Jackson Papers, Library of Congress.
[13] Edmund Doyle to James Innerarity, August 17, 1817, FHQ, XVIII, October 1939, No. 2, p. 139.

[14] Maj. David E. Twiggs to Maj. Gen. Edmund P. Gaines, September 17, 1817, American State Papers.

[15] *Ibid.*

[16] Kenhago to the commanding officer of Fort Hawkins, September 11, 1817, enclosed in Maj. David E. Twiggs to Maj. Gen. Edmund P. Gaines, Sept. 18, 1817, *American State Papers*, Indian Affairs, Volume II, p. 159.

[17] Maj. Gen. Edmund P. Gaines to Maj. Gen. Andrew Jackson, October 1, 1817.

[18] Maj. Gen. Edmund P. Gaines to Maj. Gen. Andrew Jackson, October 1, 1817.

[19] *Georgia Journal*, September 30, 1817.

CHAPTER SEVEN

The Battle of Fowltown

The movement of the 4th and 7th Infantry Regiments to Fort Scott signaled the beginning of a dramatic new phase in the troubled relationship between the United States and the Seminole and Creek bands living in Spanish Florida. The Battle of Fowltown would soon follow.

General Gaines was aware that the movement of the troops from their posts at Camps Montgomery and Montpelier as well as Fort Crawford on Murder Creek might expose the settlers on that frontier to attack. To prevent raids in the region he wrote to the Commanding Officer of the 8th Military Department which comprised territory west of the Alabama River to request that he help on a temporary basis:

> I am in possession of no information tending to excite any apprehension of danger upon this frontier, never the less possible that the absence of the First Brigade may embolden the Indians in the vicinity of Pensacola, or other evil disposed persons, to renew the scenes of massacre and

plunder by which this ill fated settlement has, some time past, suffered and bled. You will therefore take measures to keep yourself necessarily informed of the prospect of danger or invasion; and counteract or repel the same in the most effectual [manner] the means and disposable force under your control will enable you.[1]

Troops from the 8th District were sent to reinforce the posts along the Spanish line from the Perdido to the Conecuh, particularly Fort Crawford. This arranged, Gen. Gaines moved forward with plans for the movement of the brigade to Fort Scott. Brevet Major Peter Muhlenberg was assigned to escort two supply ships from Mobile, Alabama, to Fort Scott by way of the Gulf of Mexico and Apalachicola River. The ships would carry ordnance stores, the baggage of the troops and rations. An advance shipment had already left Mobile with an escort detachment of soldiers under the command of Lt. Richard W. Scott of the 7th Infantry. Gaines was clear about the dangers of the assignment:

> The unfriendly character of the Seminole Indians and other persons inhabiting the country south and east of Fort Scott, and the possibility of your falling in with some pirates with which the coast upon the Gulph of Mexico has been infested, render it proper that your men should be kept upon the alert, and always ready for action in defence of the vessels and cargo. Any hostile movements or outrage towards, either will be repelled with a prompt effort of the skill and prowess of your command.[2]

The general promised that boats would be sent down from Fort Scott once Muhlenburg reached the Apalachicola and would help him ascend the river to the fort.[3]

Gaines had put his operation into action before receiving formal approval from the Secretary of War. He may have anticipated that the Secretary would agree with his actions and if so he was not disappointed.

Acting Secretary George Graham wrote to Gaines from Washington, D.C., on October 30th to approve the movement of the First Brigade to Fort Scott:

> ...I am instructed by [the President] to inform you that he approves of the movement of the troops from Fort Montgomery to Fort Scott. The appearance of this additional force, he flatters himself, will at least have the effect of restraining the Seminoles from committing further depredations, and, perhaps, of inducing them to make reparation for the murders which they have committed. Should they, however, persevere in their refusal to make such reparation, it is the wish of the President that you should not on that account pass the line and make an attack upon them within the limits of Florida, until you shall have received instructions from this Department.[4]

The orders from Washington were an authorization for war. This fact was made more clear by the second part of the Secretary's letter, which gave Gen. Gaines approval for movements to expel such villages as Fowltown from the ceded lands:

> You are authorized to remove the Indians still remaining on the lands ceded by the treaty made by General Jackson with the Creeks; and, in doing so, it may be proper to retain some of them as hostages until reparation may have been made for the depredations which have been committed. McIntosh and the other chiefs of the Creek nation, who were here some time since, expressed then, decidedly, their unwillingness to permit any of the hostile Indians to return to their nation.[5]

Graham cautioned Gaines not to disturb any Creeks with claims to reservations of land under the provisions of the Treaty of Fort Jackson. His authorization to take hostages, however, was particularly blunt. Whether he understood the "eye for an eye" culture of the Creek and Seminole Indians is not clear.[6]

The Creeks and Seminoles in Florida also recognized that war was imminent. Rumors reached Fort Scott in late September that a mass meeting of chiefs and warriors had been held at Miccosukee:

> ...I have a character in confinement, who was present at the meeting at the Mikasuka town the last of September. The determination of the Indians is, to give up no murderers or others to the whites, and as soon as we cross Flint River to attack us. The chiefs counted the number present at the meeting – there were 2700 warriors."[7]

General Gaines and other U.S. officers would question the claim that the Seminoles and Red Sticks could muster 2,700 warriors, but the number was consistent with British reports of the strength of their allies on the Apalachicola during the War of 1812. Twiggs believed that troops would be attacked as soon as they crossed the Flint River.

Gaines reacted to this latest report from Fort Scott with a direct message to the chiefs and warriors aligned to oppose the United States:

> The president of the United States has been informed of the murders and thefts committed by the hostile Indians in this part of the country. He has authorized General Jackson to arrest the offenders, and cause justice to be done. The Indians have been required to deliver up the murderers of our citizens, and the stolen property, but they refused to deliver either; they have had a council at Mickasukee, in which they determined upon war; they have been at war against helpless women and children, let them now calculate upon fighting men.[8]

The general explained that he knew the United States enemies across the Flint, but also remembered that the country had friends among the Seminoles and Lower Creeks. "The President," he wrote, "wishing to do justice to his red friends and children, has given orders for the bad to be separated from the good." He challenged the bands for war against the United States to assemble at Miccosukee and Suwannee while at the same time urging those who wished peace to stay home and help supply the army. He then alluded to rumors that the British were coming to join the fray:

> ...The hostile party pretend to calculate upon help from the British! They may as well look for soldiers from the moon to help them. Their warriors were beaten, and driven from our country by American troops. The English are not able to help themselves: how, then, should they help the old "Red Sticks," whom they have ruined by pretended friendship?[9]

Through all of this the troops were on the move. Led in person by Gen. Gaines, the main bodies of the 4th and 7th Infantries left their barracks and began the long march from the Conecuh to the Chattahoochee. The general left Camp Montgomery on October 27, 1817, and reached Fort Gaines on November 9th. He reported to General Jackson from that post that he had learned of the presence of a band of 30-35 Yuchi warriors near the mouth of the Yellow Water River. Among them were believed to be some of the murderers of the settlers Johnson and McGaskey and a third man named Mr. Glass who had been killed near Murder Creek. The band had stolen some horses and "declared their determination to be always hostile towards our citizens."[10]

With Gaines still on the march and near Fort Gaines, officials of the Monroe Administration in Washington, D.C., suddenly made a dramatic shift of plans. Acting Secretary Graham wrote to the general on November 12th ordering him to a new front:

> I am instructed by the President to direct you to repair immediately to Point Petre. The enclosed copies of letters addressed to Lt. Colo. Bankhead and to the Governor of Georgia, will advise you of the object of this order, and the necessity of a prompt execution of it.
>
> If previously to reaching point Petre, you should be advised of the abandonment, or surrender of Amelia Island, you will then exercise your discretion as to the point which you may select for your Head Quarters.[11]

A sudden explosion of events at Amelia Island had drawn the full attention of authorities in Washington, D.C. The enigmatic Scottish-born soldier of fortune Gregor MacGregor appeared off Fernandina in June 1817 and took the town and island from the Spanish. Supposedly commissioned by the South American revolutionary Simon Bolivar, MacGregor raised the Green Cross of Florida flag and declared that he had revolutionized Spain's Florida colonies. The adventurer's dream of taking all of East and West Florida fizzled, however, and he sailed away for new adventures in September. The pirate/privateer Louis-Michel Aury (usually called Luis Aury) then took control of the island in the name of the Republic of Mexico. With his raising of the flag of Mexico, the number of national flags that had flown over Florida all or in part in a twenty-year time period increased to seven: Spanish, Muscogee, British, United States, Patriot, Green Cross and Mexican.

The United States was not thrilled with this turmoil on an island immediately across the St. Marys River from Georgia and the town of St. Marys. The Monroe Administration ordered U.S. troops to seize Amelia Island and Gen. Gaines was diverted from the Flint River to the Atlantic Coast to take command of the invasion. Before he could depart for his new command, however, the situation at Fort Scott exploded.

Gaines took command at Fort Scott in person in mid-November and on the 18th he dispatched a message down the Apalachicola to Maj. Muhlenberg telling him that the water level in the river "had risen sufficiently high" to allow the supply vessels to come up to Fort Scott. Lt. Scott's command was still on the river and Muhlenberg was authorized to use his detachment if needed. One of the schooners that Muhlenberg would try to bring up to the fort was a familiar site on the lower river. She was the *General Pike*, which had been part of the flotilla involved in the attack on the fort at Prospect Bluff. Along with a second schooner, the *Pike* was carrying the baggage and supplies of the First Brigade.[12]

The main bodies of the 4th and 7th Regiments marched into Fort Scott on the 19th and 20th of November. Gaines did not waste time in ordering his long-contemplated mission against Neamathla. Orders were given to Maj. David E. Twiggs to go to Fowltown and bring the chief back to the fort:

The hostile character & Conduct of the Indians of the Fowl Town, settled within our limits, rendering it absolutely necessary that they should be removed, you will proceed to the town with the detachment assigned you, and remove them. You will arrest and bring the chiefs and warriors to this place, but should they oppose you, or attempt to escape, you will in that event treat them as enemies. Your men are to be strictly prohibited, in any event, from firing upon, or otherwise injuring, women and children.

You will return to this place with your command as soon as practicable.

Should you receive satisfactory information that any considerable number of the neighboring Indians have joined those of Fowl Town, you will immediately return to this place without making any further attempt to execute first the above written orders.[13]

Twiggs marched out from Fort Scott on the evening of November 20, 1817, with 250 men from the 4th and 7th Infantry Regiments. Some additional volunteers from Donoho's Company of the 4th Artillery Battalion also joined the expedition. The soldiers followed the road up the west side of the Flint to the crossing at Burges's Bluff (today's Bainbridge, Georgia). There they crossed the river under cover of darkness and then started down the parallel road on the east side during the predawn hours of the 21st:

…Having marched all the night of the 20th I reached the town before day light on the morning of the 21st & posted the troops in order of Battle intending silently to surround it & without blood shed bring to you the chief & warriors, but the fled from the companies of Majr. Montgomery & Cpt. Birch on my right & fired upon my left under Capts. Allison & Bee when they were fired on in return.[14]

This first incident at Fowltown did not rise to the level of a battle, but was more of a one-sided skirmish. The troops fired only a single volley while the warriors opened only a brief scattering fire. None of the soldiers

97

were injured but Twiggs reported that 4 warriors and one woman were killed. They had been directly in front of the companies under Allison and Bee when the troops unleashed their single volley of fire.[15]

General Gaines had prohibited Maj. Twiggs to allow his men under any circumstance to fire upon or otherwise injure women and children. He now expressed great regret that his orders to this effect had failed:

> It is with some deep regret I have to add that a woman was accidentally shot with some warriors in the act of forcing their way through our line formed for the purpose of arresting their flight. The unfortunate woman had a blanket fastened round her (as many of the warriors had) which amidst the smoke in which they were enveloped, rendered it impossible as I am assured by the officers present, to distinguish her from the warriors.[16]

Warriors told Alexander Arbuthnot and his clerk Peter B. Cook that the soldiers came to their town in the dark and opened fire. They reported their casualties as 1 killed and 2 wounded in the blast of gunfire. If the report of Major Twiggs that one woman was killed in the battle and if the story as repeated by Cook and Arbuthnot are both correct, then the first American Indian casualty of the Seminole Wars was a woman of Fowltown.

The single volley fired in the night at Fowltown was the first of the Seminole Wars, a series of conflicts that would continue in Georgia, Florida and Alabama for the next 40 years. A prominent town had been attacked and blood had been shed. The spark had been ignited and there would be no turning back for either side.

The warriors did not try to mount much of a defense. They fired a few scattered shots at the soldiers but evaporated into the nearby swamp following the volley from Allison's and Bee's companies. Twiggs waited until full daylight and then moved his men into the village. They noted corncribs full of newly harvested corn and explored the houses and cabins of the still new town. Neamathla's home attracted particular attention:

> Among the articles found in the house of the chief, was a British uniform coat (scarlet) with a pair of gold epaulettes, and a certificate signed by a British captain of

marines, "Robert White in the absence of col. Nichols," stating that the chief "had always been a true and faithful friend to the British."[17]

Maj. Twiggs maintained tight control over his men while in the village and despite the discovery of such intriguing items, no looting was allowed. As soon as the sun rose, the major started his command back for Fort Scott. Twiggs informed Gaines that he left Fowltown "without destroying it or their provisions." He marched his man back to the fort, "bringing with me only a few head of horses & cattle."[18]

The fight for Fowltown was far from over, but two more days would pass before gunfire again erupted.

Despite its significance as the place where the first shots and first bloodshed of the Seminole Wars took place, the actual location of Fowltown has remained an enigmatic mystery for many years. Early land surveys of the area, which clearly show other key points from the Fort Scott era, do not show the site of the village, only the swamp that bore its name. There is a modern town of Fowlstown in Decatur County, Georgia, buts its distance from the old crossing over the Flint River at Bainbridge is too great for it to be on the site of the Creek village.

The answer to the mystery finally came into focus in the fall of 2014. A new look at the original copies of the military reports on the raids against Fowltown revealed that the American approaches to the town on November 21 and 23, 1817, had come from different directions. Twiggs and his force had crossed the Flint River at present-day Bainbridge and marched back south for 3-4 miles to reach the village. The soldiers sent out on the 23rd, however, crossed the river at Fort Scott and marched north to the village, which Lt. Col. Matthew Arbuckle described as being locating on the southwest rim of a large swamp.[19]

The only large swamp four miles below the old crossing point at Bainbridge is still known as Fowltown Swamp today. By superimposing the old road or trail down the east side of the Flint over modern topographic maps, it was possible to identify a small area on the southwest edge of the swamp that appeared to be a likely site for the village. A site visit resulted in the surface collection of brushed and plain Creek pottery and a flattened lead rifle ball. The material was indicative of a Creek Indian site and the only village historically reported in the vicinity was Fowltown.[20]

Gen. Gaines listened to the report of Maj. Twiggs on the evening of the 21st and immediately decided to send a larger expedition against Neamathla's town. The stated purpose of this movement was to reconnoiter the countryside east of the Flint and to learn more about any enemy groups in the area, but the force also carried along wagons to be filled from the corncribs at Fowltown. Provision stocks were dwindling at Fort Scott and raiding the village for corn and beef clearly was on the mind of the general.

The force this time included 300 men and command of the movement was entrusted to the second highest ranking officer at Fort Scott, Lt. Col. Matthew Arbuckle of the 7th Infantry. He crossed his men at Fort Scott and followed a trail that led up the west (or south) bank of the Flint River. This would allow him to approach Fowltown from the opposite direction of Maj. Twiggs' approach two days earlier. Neamathla's warriors were better prepared this time:

> ...On our approach several signal guns were fired by the Indians who we no doubt discovered one of our flanking parties but at the time that all the troops had reached the town no Indians were seen and a few yells only were heard from a swamp which skirts its north east side. I took a position near the town so as to secure the troops from any fire which might issue from the swamp, and after posting such sentinels as would prevent us from being surprised I ordered the men to refresh themselves while the waggons were loading with corn. This was done and the troops were about to march when the Indians, fifty or sixty in number (as I judge) were perceived advancing by the sentinels posted in the swamp and fired on.[21]

The encounter was the first real battle of the Seminole Wars and took place on the late morning of November 23, 1817. Lt. Col. Arbuckle reported that his men had reached the town at around 10 a.m. Allowing for an hour or so for the troops to load the wagons, the time of the engagement was probably somewhere between 11 a.m. and noon.

100

Arbuckle quickly realized that the warriors were trying to get to some houses on the edge of the town. From these, with the troops in the open ground of ahead of them and the swamp offering an avenue of retreat behind them, they would be able to direct fire on the American lines from protected positions. He immediately ordered part of his force to advance and seize the cabins. The soldiers reached them first, but the warriors would not withdraw:

> A spirited fire was then kept up for twenty or twenty five minutes when the Indians retreated into the Swamp. During the affair the Indians frequently appeared in the open ground and from the number which were seen to fall, there can be no doubt but six or eight were killed and many severely wounded yet as the swamp was large and uncommonly thick I deemed it not prudent to pursue them into it or search for those who fell on its edges.[22]

The warriors themselves told Alexander Arbuthnot and his clerk Peter B. Cook that they suffered the loss of two men killed in this battle. Since Arbuckle did not actually count the bodies of the warriors "which were seen to fall," it is certainly probable that he overestimated the number killed. The United States also suffered casualties in the battle:

> ...The skill and valor displayed by the officers and men engaged in the little affair affords a pleasing prospect should their services be required on another important occasion. The Indians must have been deceived as to our numbers otherwise they should not have had the temerity to attack us. On our side one Musician was killed and two privates were wounded.[23]

The musician killed in the battle was Aaron Hughes of Marlborough, South Carolina. The young fifer had joined the army at the age of 15 in 1814, when the War of 1812 was shifting to its southern front. The farm boy was 5'1" tall with blue eyes, dark hair and a fair complexion. He was 18 years old when he was killed at the Battle of Fowltown where one later account claimed he was standing on the roof of an Indian cabin so his fife could be

101

heard above the noise of the battle. The former farm boy from South Carolina was the first U.S. soldier killed in the Seminole Wars.[24]

Allegations surfaced after the battle that not all of the soldiers had been as valiant as Hughes. Lt. Milo Johnson of Capt. Donoho's artillery company wrote to Gen. Gaines one week later requesting in inquiry into his own behavior:

> Having understood that a report is calculating through the camp, that I behaved unlike a soldier in being separated from my company. and while separated in the affair at Fowl Town, on the 23d of Nov. 1817.
> I am compelled in justice to myself to demand a court of enquiry, to investigate the truth of sd. report.[25]

The specific nature of Johnson's alleged offenses is not clear but the implication of the rumors was that he had shown cowardice on the battlefield. If the court of inquiry ever took place, no record of it could be found. It is likely that subsequent events quickly erased concerns about conduct in the Battle of Fowltown.

Another account of the battle, included in a letter from an unknown officer to his father in Baltimore, Maryland, provided a small amount of additional detail:

> I have just been informed that an express will start for Fort Hawkins in 23 minutes, I therefore send you this hasty note. I marched from Fort Hawkins on the 15th Nov. and arrived here on the 19th, at night. On the 23d, Col. Arbuckle crossed Flint river with 300 men, for the purpose of destroying an Indian town, about 20 miles off. We arrived in the town about 12 o'clock, next day – at 3, the Indians attacked us, and after an action of about 15 minutes, they retreated into a large swamp which nearly surrounded their town. – The loss cannot be ascertained – Ours, 1 killed, 1 severely and 3 slightly wounded.[26]

The withdrawal of the warriors into Fowltown Swamp gave Lt. Col. Arbuckle a chance to assemble his men and withdraw from the town. He headed north up the trail to Burges's Bluff where Twiggs men had crossed the river two days before. He halted his men there to bury Aaron Hughes and build a small fort that was named in the fifer's honor.

The First Seminole War of 1817-1818 was now firmly underway. The United States had struck the first blow at Fowltown, but its officers had severely underestimated the size and fury of the hornets' nest they were provoking. Warriors now flooded to the Apalachicola and Flint Rivers from as far away as the Suwannee. The Red Stick Creek/Seminole alliance would soon strike back, and the result would shock the nation.

---

[1] Maj. Gen. Edmund P. Gaines to the Commanding Officer, 8th Military Department, west of the Alabama river at Bay of St. Louis or New Orleans, May 11, 1817, Andrew Jackson Papers, Library of Congress.
[2] Maj. Gen. Edmund P. Gaines to Maj. P. Muhlenberg, October 11, 1817, Adjutant General, Letters Received, NARA.
[3] *Ibid.*
[4] George Graham, Acting Secretary of War, to Maj. Gen. Edmund P. Gaines, October 30, 1817, American State Papers, Indian Affairs, Volume II,
[5] *Ibid.*
[6] *Ibid.*
[7] Maj. David E. Twiggs to Maj. Gen. Edmund P. Gaines, November 1, 1817, appeared in the New York Evening Post, p. 2., December 2, 1817.
[8] Maj. Gen. Edmund P. Gaines to Chiefs and Warriors, November 1817, (Referred to as Enclosure No. 3 in Gaines to Secretary of War, December 2, 1817) ASPMA Vol 1, No. 164. p. 688.
[9] *Ibid.*
[10] Maj. Gen. Edmund P. Gaines to Maj. Gen. Andrew Jackson, November 9, 1817, *American State Papers*, Indian Affairs, Volume II, p. 160.
[11] Hon. George Graham to Maj. Gen. Edmund P. Gaines, November 12, 1817, Adutant General, Letters Received, NARA.
[12] Maj. Gen. Edmund P. Gaines to Maj. P. Muhlenburg, November 18, 1817, American State Papers, Foreign Affairs, Volume IV, p. 599.
[13] Maj. Gen. Edmund P. Gaines to Maj. David E. Twiggs, November 20, 1817, Adjutant General, Letters Received, NARA.
[14] Maj. D.E. Twiggs to Maj. Gen. Edmund P. Gaines, November 21, 1817, Adjutant General, Letters Received, NARA.

[15] Maj. Gen. Edmund P. Gaines to Maj. Gen. Andrew Jackson, November 21, 1817.

[16] *Ibid.*

[17] *Ibid.*

[18] Maj. David E. Twiggs to Maj. Gen. Edmund P. Gaines, November 21, 1817.

[19] Lt. Col. Matthew Arbuckle to Maj. Gen. Edmund P. Gaines, November 30, 1817, Andrew Jackson papers, Library of Congress.

[20] Personal visit to the site by the author on November 21, 2014. The small surface collection remains in the possession of the author pending its donation to the Decatur County Historical Society for permanent preservation.

[21] Lt. Col. Matthew Arbuckle to Maj. Gen. Edmund P. Gaines, November 30, 1817, Andrew Jackson papers, Library of Congress.

[22] *Ibid.*

[23] *Ibid.*

[24] Enlistment Records of the U.S. Army, NARA.

[25] Lt. Milo Johnson to Maj. Gen. Edmund P. Gaines, November 30, 1817, Adjutant General, Letters Received, NARA.

[26] Extract of a letter from an officer at Fort Scott to his father in Baltimore, December 2, 1817, New York Daily Advertiser, December 27, 1817, p. 2.

CHAPTER EIGHT

The Scott Massacre

The Battle of Fowltown sparked a series of conflicts that would become the most expensive Indian wars in U.S. history. Taxpayers spent $40,000,000 to support military operations during the Second Seminole War (1835-1842) alone. In modern terms, this figure exceeds $800,000,000. When the expenses of the First and Third Seminole Wars are added to the total, American taxpayers were charged more than $1,000,000,000 in 2010 values for the effort to defeat the Seminoles, a remarkable sum in an era when the country had no personal income tax. The Seminole and Miccosukee people of today regard the three conflicts as a single war. It lasted more than 40 years and by the time it ended they had been driven from their homes in North Florida, thousands had been shipped west on the Trail of Tears but the last survivors still clung to Florida soil deep in the Peninsula. Their descendants remain there to this day as members of the Seminole Tribe of Florida, the Miccosukee Tribe of Indians of Florida and some smaller non-federally recognized groups.

In the view of the American Indian people of Georgia, Florida and Alabama, the Seminole Wars were started by the United States. American troops under Maj. David E. Twiggs had come to Fowltown in the dark of night and fired on women and children. The soldiers had come back two days later under the command of Lt. Col. Matthew Arbuckle to raid the town of its corn and cattle. Outnumbered warriors had resisted in a fight for their homes, food and families. U.S. officers of the time, however, blamed the Indians themselves for starting the war, first by firing on the troops sent to kidnap Neamathla and take hostages at Fowltown and then by staging an attack that forever changed the course of American history.

The raids against Fowltown outraged the warriors of the alliance of American Indian bands arrayed against the United States along its southern border. They responded by flooding to the scene of the action. It was decided by them to attempt to starve out the garrison of Fort Scott by laying siege to the post and by attacking the supply ships then known to be slowly making their way up the Apalachicola River. Led by Chenubby, Yuchi Billy and Homathlemico, the first large force of warriors gathered around the site of the evacuated Nicolls' Outpost just below the confluence of the Chattahoochee and Flint Rivers. Present in this group were Tuttalossees, Red Sticks, Yuchis, Black Seminoles and others. As they moved into position, other reinforcements flooded to Neamathla while smaller parties of warriors were sent to hover around and harass the U.S. garrisons at Fort Scott and Fort Gaines. A much larger army would concentrate and follow for the purpose of thoroughly blocking river traffic on the Apalachicola.

Lt. Richard W. Scott of the 7th Infantry, who led the advance of the water movement of baggage and supplies, had reached Fort Scott in mid-November. Aware that his planned raids on Fowltown might increase danger for the primary supply vessels, escorted by troops under Maj. Peter Muhlenberg, Gen. Gaines ordered Scott to take 40 men and go back down to support Muhlenberg in his effort to bring the *General Pike* and another schooner up the river. The lieutenant left the fort shortly before – but without knowledge of – the first attack on Fowltown. Neither he nor Maj. Muhlenberg had any way of knowing that a war had started with the raids

106

of November 21st and 23rd. Consequently and even though they had been warned to be on their guard, the officers were not prepared for the onslaught that followed.[1]

Scott traveled down river until he came up with Muhlenberg's flotilla slowly warping its way upstream against high water. Instead of keeping the lieutenant and his men, however, the major decided to unburden himself of 20 men who were too sick for duty, along with seven women and four children. The latter were the wives and children of soldiers at Fort Scott. He then ordered the lieutenant and his remaining 20 men to take these individuals back up to the fort. When the boat reached the plantations of William Hambly and Edmund Doyle at present-day Bristol and Blountstown, Florida, however, the lieutenant was firmly warned that danger awaited at the head of the river:

> Enclosed you will receive Major Muhlenberg's communication, which he directs me to forward to you by express from this place. Mr. Hambly informs me that Indians are assembling at the junction of the river, where they intend to make a stand against those vessels coming up the river. Should this be the case, I am not able to make a stand against them. My command does not exceed forty men, and one-half sick and without arms. I leave this immediately.[2]

Why Lt. Scott and his men continued on after he acknowledged that he was "not able to make a stand" against an attack is one of the great mysteries of the Seminole Wars. The prudent thing would have been to wait for a reply from Gen. Gaines and for additional troops to come down from Fort Scott to help him. Instead he continued onward.

Scott's last message reached the fort on November 30, 1817. The general immediately ordered Capt. J.J. Clinch of the 7th Infantry to lead a rescue party:

> You will embark with the party assigned you on board the two covered boats; descend the river until you meet with Lieutenant Scott; deliver to him a cover for his boat, and

give him such assistance as, in your judgment, shall be necessary to secure his party, and expedite his movement to this place. You will then proceed, with the residue of your command, down the river, until you meet with Major Muhlenberg; report to him, and act under his orders. You will, in no case, put your command in the power of the Indians near the shore. Be constantly on the alert. Remember that United States troops can never be surprised by Indians without a loss of honor, to say nothing of the loss of strength that might cause.[3]

It was already too late. By the time Capt. Clinch and his boats could reach the forks, the first U.S. defeat of the Seminole Wars had already taken place. Darkness had fallen and he passed by without seeing any sign of the disaster that struck Lt. Scott and his party. As the lieutenant and his men were navigating their boat around a bend at what is now Chattahoochee, Florida, they were suddenly fired upon by hundreds of Red Stick, Seminole, Yuchi and Black Seminole warriors concealed along the east bank of the river. By the time the battle was over, Scott, 34 of his men, 6 women and 4 children had all been killed. The news reached Fort Scott two nights later as Lt. Col. Matthew Arbuckle was completing the monthly returns for the 7th Infantry:

> Since making out the enclosed report I have received the unpleasant news of Lieut. Scott and thirty three or four men, being killed by the Indians on the 30th Ultimo. This took place on the Appalachicola River (as the party was ascending in a boat) a short distance below the junction of the Flint and Chattahoochie Rivers.[4]

The magnitude of the news settled over the stunned fort when some of Yellow Hair's warriors brought five survivors through the Red Stick lines to the safety of the military post. An unidentified officer described the situation at the fort when the wounded men came in:

> ...Lieut. Scott, of the Seventh, had been ordered down the Appalachicola with about 40 men, to assist the vessels

which were coming up with supplies. Maj. Muhlenburg, who commanded the troops on board the vessel ordered Lieut. Scott back, and put on board the clothing of our regiment, and several women and children. Yesterday, 5 of his men came in, all wounded. They state, that Lieut. Scott was attacked by the Indians just below the forks of the rivers, and the whole party killed except themselves. – This is truly lamentable. I expect we shall have some very warm work before many days. The whole Indian force is supposed to be 2800.[5]

As the officer finished his letter he noted that warriors had just opened fire from the opposite bank of the Flint on some women who had been washing clothes at the foot of the bluff. An additional man came in on the morning of December 2nd and Gen. Gaines placed the total number of known survivors at six when he penned his report to Acting-Secretary of War George Graham later that day:

...It is now my painful duty to report an affair of a more serious and decisive nature than has heretofore occurred, and which leaves no doubt of the necessity of an immediate application of force and active measures on our part. A large party of Seminole Indians, on the 30th ultimo, formed an ambuscade, upon the Appalachicola river, a mile below the junction of the Flint and Chatahouchee, attacked one of our boats, ascending the river near the shore, and killed, wounded, and took, the greater part of the detachment, consisting of forty men, commanded by Lieut. R.W. Scott of the 7th infantry. There were also on board, killed or taken, seven women, the wives of soldiers. Six men of the detachment only escaped, four of whom were wounded. They report that the strength of the current, at the point of attack, had obliged the lieutenant to keep his boat near the shore; that the Indians had formed along the bank of the river, and were not discovered until their fire commenced; in the first volley of which Lieutenant Scott and his most valuable men fell.[6]

Gaines promised the secretary that he would immediately strengthen the detachment under Maj. Muhlenberg that was lower down the river. He reported that the survivors told of having seen upwards of five hundred enemy warriors watching them at various points along the Apalachicola River. They could not say the size of the force that had attacked, but reported that the fire had burst from a stretch of woods some 150 yards long suggesting that hundreds of warriors had taken part.[7]

A brief account of the attack as described by the warriors was included in a letter from Arbuthnot's clerk, Peter B. Cook, to his fiancé Elizabeth Carney in the Bahamas:

> …There was a boat that was taken by the Indians, that had in it thirty men, seven women, and four small children; there were six of the men got clear, and one woman saved, and all the rest of them got killed; the children were taken by the heels, and their brains dashed out against the boat.[8]

Despite Lt. Col. Clinch's observation in 1816 that the area immediately around the confluence was not suitable for the building of a military post, Gen. Gaines now proposed moving from Fort Scott with his main force to that point:

> …I shall, moreover, take a position, with my principal force, at the junction of the rivers, near the line; and shall attack any force that may attempt to intercept our vessels and supplies below; as I feel persuaded the order of the President, prohibiting an attack upon the Indians, below the line, has reference only to the past, and not to the present or future outrages, such as the one just now perpetrated, and such as shall place our troops strictly within the pale of natural law, which self defence is sanctioned by the privilege of self preservation.[9]

In a separate letter written the same evening to Gov. William Rabun of Georgia, the general reported that a settler had been killed near Fort Gaines and that many warriors from the towns in the vicinity had headed south into

Florida to join the alliance fighting against the United States. Others, meanwhile, were offering their assistance to the soldiers and he had promised to notify them as soon as he was ready to march.[10]

From the time of the attack on Scott's party until the arrival of the army of Maj. Gen. Andrew Jackson in March 1818, Fort Scott was under siege. Warriors hovered around the stockade, firing at any soldier who dared show his face above or outside the walls of the post. They often fired into the fort from the opposite side of the Flint. Troops often responded with cannon fire but, so far as is known, no one was hurt on either side.

News, meanwhile, continued to come in about the attack on Lt. Scott's party. Maj. Clinton Wright, the Assistant Adjutant General to Maj. Gen. Gaines, informed Maj. Muhlenberg that the number of known survivors had increased to eight:

> ...I am instructed by Maj. Genl. Gaines to acknowledge the receipt of your letter forwarded by Jno. Blunt, who reached this Post this morning and to apprise you of the disastrous fate of Lieut. Scott, and his party who were fired on by a party of Indians about two miles from the mouth of the river, and without being able to make any defence fell into their hands, except seven, six of whom came in the succeeding day (five of them wounded) the seventh I understand is at this time with some friendly Indian. The women and children were all killed at that time or since murdered except one who not being wounded is at this time a prisoner with them.[11]

Wright told Muhlenberg to keep his boats near the center of the river and "in no case suffer your men to approach the bank of the river." Instead of warping as the vessels had been doing, he instructed them to "take advantage of every wind that will enable you to progress." As soon as the Georgia militia reached Fort Scott, he promised, a movement would be made by regular forces to Spanish Bluff or a point below to help Muhlenberg make it up to the fort. The men on the boats were urged to use the planking sent down on the 30th by Capt. Cummings to construct bulwarks to protect themselves in the event of attack.[12]

A careful analysis of regimental returns, enlistment records, military reports and other sources shows that the final tally of casualties from the attack on Scott's command should include 34 men, 6 women and 4 children killed. Six men escaped, although five of them had been wounded. The only civilian survivor was Elizabeth Stewart, the wife of a soldier. She was captured by the Red Sticks and taken away with them. Of the total force with Lt. Scott, only one person escaped without injury of some type.

Post returns dated December 4, 1817 reveal that just four days after the destruction of Scott's party, the total number of men present at Fort Scott was 496. Of this number, 32 officers and soldiers were too sick for duty. Gen. Gaines, who had brought on the war by sending soldiers to Fowltown, now waxed philosophical about the unwillingness of the "savage man" to seek peace and join the advancement of civilization:

> I would much more willingly devote my time and humble faculties in the delightful occupation of bringing over savage man to the walks of civil life, where this is practicable without force, than to contribute to the destruction of any one of the human race; but every effort in the work of civilization, to be effectual, must accord with the immutable principals of justice. The savage must be taught and compelled to do that which is right, and to abstain from doing that which is wrong. The poisonous cup of barbarism cannot be taken from the lips of the savage by the mild voice of reason alone; the strong mandate of justice must be resorted to and enforced.[13]

"It is a melancholy truth," he continued, "that in no Indian nation within my knowledge (the Chickasaws excepted,) has the scalping knife been laid aside for any considerable length of time until after every hope of using it with impunity had been defeated.[14]

It was at this moment, with Red Sticks and Seminole warrior flooding to the Apalachicola River intent on blocking the supply boats, Fort Scott and Fort Gaines under siege, supplies running low and the frontier in flames that Gaines received his orders to leave Fort Scott for Amelia Island. Realizing that the situation there was equally critical, he made immediate plans to comply. General Orders were read to the troops to notify them of the general's pending departure and Lt. Col. Arbuckle was placed in command of the post:

> The whole will be put in readiness for a vigorous attack on the enemy, whose long continued hostility and recent massacre of sick men and helpless women and children, demand and shall receive a full measure of retaliation. The Genl. calculates upon returning in time to participate in the service. In the mean time he tenders to the officers and men of his command his best wishes for their health, military distinction and personal prosperity.[15]

General Gaines had departed Fort Scott by December 10, 1817, and was making his way across Georgia when an earthquake rumbled across the state. Although the tremor was not mentioned by military officers at the fort, it likely was felt there. The *Georgia Journal* reported that it was "distinctly felt" in Milledgeville at about 11 p.m.[16]

Earthquakes had been interpreted by the Creeks to be signs of divine intervention on their behalf before the outbreak of the Creek War of 1813-1814. The 1817 Georgia earthquake, perhaps, signaled the arrival of news in Washington, D.C., of the destruction of Scott's command. On the same day that the *Journal* reported the shaking of the ground in Georgia, Secretary of War John C. Calhoun reacted harshly to the loss of so many men, women and children at the hands of the Red Sticks and Seminoles:

> On the receipt of this letter, should the Seminole Indians still refuse to make reparation for their outrages and depredations on the citizens of the United States, it is the wish of the President that you should consider yourself at liberty to march across the Florida line and to attack them within its limits, should it be found necessary, unless they should shelter themselves under a Spanish post. In the last event, you will immediately notify this Department.[17]

It would take time for the United States to take the fight to the towns of the Seminoles and Red Sticks. The reassignment of Gen. Gaines from Fort Scott ended any plan to move a large force down the Apalachicola River to assist Maj. Muhlenberg. Lt. Col. Arbuckle was ordered to act on the defensive and with great caution. The war was entering a new phase and the warriors, elated by their success over Scott's boat, were preparing for additional attacks.

---

[1] For a detailed history of the destruction of Scott's party, please see *The Scott Massacre of 1817* by this author.
[2] Lt. R.W. Scott to Maj. Gen. Edmund P. Gaines, November 28, 1817, *American State Papers,* Foreign Affairs, Volume IV, Page 599.
[3] Maj. Gen. Edmund P. Gaines to Capt. J.J. Clinch, November 30, 1817, *American State Papers*, Foreign Affairs, Volume IV, Page 599.
[4] Lt. Col. Matthew Arbuckle to Brig. Gen. Daniel Parker, December 2, 1817, Adjutant General, Letters Received, NARA.
[5] Extract of a letter from an officer at Fort Scott to his father in Baltimore, December 2, 1817, *New York Daily Advertiser*, December 27, 1817, p. 2.
[6] Maj. Gen. Edmund P. Gaines to Capt. J.J. Clinch, December 2, 1817, *American State Papers*, Military Affairs, Volume I, pp. 687-688.
[7] *Ibid.*
[8] Peter B. Cook to Miss Elizabeth A. Carney, January 19, 1818, *American State Papers*, Foreign Relations, Volume IV, p. 605.
[9] *Ibid.*
[10] Maj. Gen. Edmund P. Gaines to Gov. Rabun, December 2, 1817, appeared in the *Independent American*, p. 2., January 14, 1818.
[11] Maj. Clinton Wright to Maj. Philip Muhlenburg, December 2, 1817, Adjutant General, Letters Received, NARA.
[12] *Ibid.*
[13] Maj. Gen. Edmund P. Gaines to Hon. George Graham, Secretary of War American State Papers, Military Affairs, Volume I, p. 688.
[14] *Ibid.*
[15] Maj. Gen. Edmund P. Gaines, per Maj. Clinton Wright, General Orders, December 4, 1817, Adjutant General, Letters Received, NARA.
[16] Georgia Journal, December 16, 1817, p. 3.
[17] Hon. John C. Calhoun, Secretary of War, to Maj. Gen. Edmund P. Gaines, December 16, 1817, *American State Papers,* Military Affairs, Volume I, p. 690.

CHAPTER NINE

Fort Hughes

The establishment of Fort Hughes marked the first attempt by the U.S. Army to plant a foothold on the disputed lands east of the Flint River. The first encounter at Fowltown had likely convinced Gen. Gaines that future difficulties would develop in that direction. Neamathla's village was closely allied with the towns of Attapulgus and Miccosukee, both of which lay to the southeast along the old Pensacola-St. Augustine Road. The new outpost would block the road where it crossed the Flint at Burges's Bluff.

The bluff took its name from James Burges, am 18th century trader who settled there when it was the site of the Lower Creek town of Pucknauhitla (or Pucknawhitla). Exactly when Burges arrived on the Flint is not clear. in Pucknawhitla (Pucknawhitla), a Lower Creek town led by the Mad Warrior. Exactly when Burges arrived on the Flint is not known. A person of that name was born in Darien, Georgia, in 1737 and at the age of 19 joined a 1756 trading expedition into Florida. He likely settled on the Flint soon after as by 1765 he was described as an established trader well-versed in the Creek languages.[1]

Fort Hughes, 1817

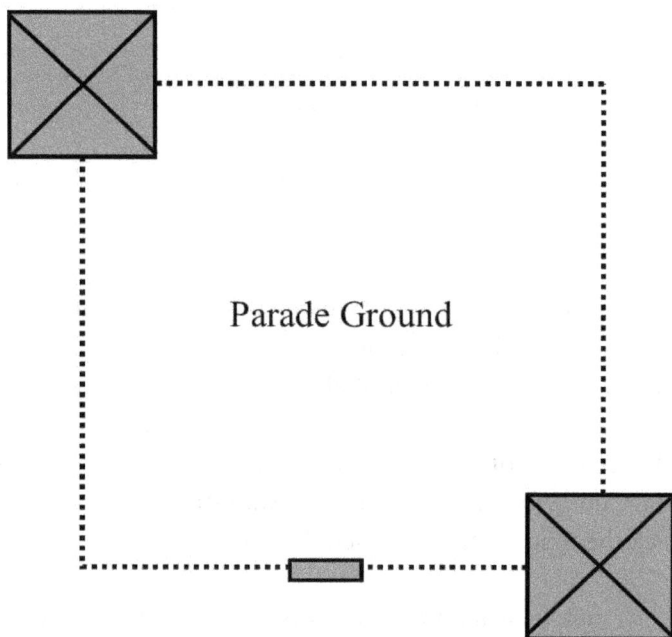

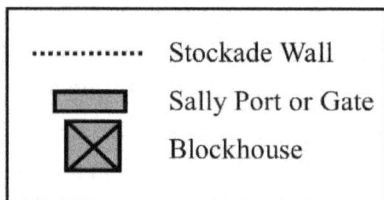

Parade Ground

·············· Stockade Wall	Exterior Walls 90' by 90'
Sally Port or Gate	
Blockhouse	Blockhouses 20' by 20' on lower floor 24' by 24' on upper floor

Burges remained at Pucknauhitla for the next 40 years, marrying a Creek woman and raising children there. His trading post was a major landmark in the borderlands and was prominently noted on the 1778 map of the Pensacola-St. Augustine Road. He allied himself with the British during the American Revolution and warriors from the town took part in the fighting along the Georgia-Florida border north of St. Augustine. He later served variously as an interpreter and assistant to United States Indian agents while also becoming a partisan of the adventurer and pirate William Augustus Bowles.

Mr. Burges had died by the time Fort Scott was established and his trading post site was abandoned when troops under Maj. Twiggs passed through on their way to Fowltown. Ruins of the old houses and other structures were evident as they could still be seen in 1820 when State of Georgia surveyors worked in the area.

The open fields of the old settlement along with the commanding view of the river crossing made Burges's Bluff the ideal site for a fort and Lt. Col. Arbuckle was instructed to build one there on his return from Fowltown. The decision was timely as the colonel's 300 men had been hard-pressed by a much smaller force of warriors during the battle of November 23, 1817. They likely would have faced attack again as they tried to cross the Flint had they not halted to build fortifications at the bluff. Arbuckle placed the strategic location of the new fort in his report to Gen. Gaines:

> The scite of the Fort is on a Bluff sixty or seventy feet above the River and distant about one hundred yards from its edge, the space between the fort and the River and for a considerable distance above and below is very open from this position both on and off the River. There is a considerable portion of good land. The surface of the country is very pleasant and from every appearance must be healthy. This I consider a very advantageous position for a post, it being eight or ten miles nearer to Fort Gaines than

[Fort Scott] is and more than that distance nearer to that
portion of the Creeks who have commenced the war.[2]

The point selected by Arbuckle for the construction of the new fort
overlooked a sharp bend of the Flint from the top of the bluff. The site was
in the west end of today's J.D. Chason Memorial Park in the city of
Bainbridge, Georgia. The view is as impressive today as when it was
described by the lieutenant colonel in 1817.

Although sometimes described as a "small house" in early documents,
the fort was actually similar to the work thrown up at Fort Gaines in 1817
by the 4th Infantry. Like that post it was designed to be defended by around
one company of men:

> ...[W]e marched to Burgess' Bluff on the River where in
> compliance with your instructions I erected a strong
> stockade work ninety feet square with two Blockhouses at
> opposite angles; the lower stories of which were sixteen and
> the upper twenty feet square. I left Captain McIntosh in
> command of the work with a subaltern and forty men, a
> garrison sufficient to maintain it against any Indian fire.[3]

It took around three days for Arbuckle's 300-man force to complete the
fort. The positions of the two blockhouses diagonally opposite from each
other allowed the men assigned to each the ability to completely sweep the
approaches to the stockade with musket fire. The overhanging design of the
second-floors also allowed soldiers to fire directly down on any warriors
who might successfully reach the log walls of the lower floors. Forts of this
design were easy and quick to build but impressively strong against attack
from lightly armed forces.

The young American soldier killed at the Battle of Fowltown was buried
at the new post, which was named Fort Hughes in his honor. It is believed
that fifer Aaron Hughes still rests somewhere at the site. A monument was
placed there by order of the U.S. Congress during the 1880s, but the exact
location of his grave could not be determined by that time. Consisting of a

massive 32-pounder cannon mounted breech down in a block of Stone Mountain granite, the monument still stands adjacent to the fort site.

A portion of the orders given to Arbuckle by Gen. Gaines required him to reconnoiter the lands on the east side of the Flint:

> During the time I was detained at the Bluff I had small parties reconnoitering every day and from the number of fresh trails reported to lead in a direction for Fort Gaines there can be no doubt that an understanding exists between the hostile Indians and those residing on the Chattahoochie and that a considerable number of the latter will join the hostile party. On our tour we took from the hostile Indians four horses, fifteen head of cattle, and about Eighty bushels of corn.[4]

The main body of the expeditionary force remained at Fort Hughes for 4-5 days before crossing the Flint River and returning to Fort Scott. Captain John N. McIntosh of the 4th Infantry was left in command of the new fort. He reported in 1819 that the real object of the second expedition to Fowltown had been to secure provisions. The amount of corn and beef taken, however, was "just sufficient for the support of the troops during their absence from Fort Scott."[5]

By the time Arbuckle left Capt. McIntosh and his 40 men at Fort Hughes on November 27th or 28th, a Creek/Seminole expedition against the new fort was already underway. Peter B. Cook, the clerk at Alexander Arbuthnot's store on the Suwannee, was sent by the Scottish trader and another new arrival, former Colonial Marines lieutenant Robert Ambrister, to locate and fight the Americans responsible for the attack on Fowltown. He led out 32 warriors from the Suwannee towns on December 1, 1817. The weather had turned extremely cold and rainy.[6]

Cook's party advanced for six days and nights, exposed to cold weather and rain the entire time. "For six days and six nights we had to encamp in the wild woods and it was constantly raining night and day," he told his fiancé, "and as for the cold, I suffered very much by it; in the morning the water would be frozen about an inch thick." The United States and Europe were then experiencing unusual climactic cooling due to the 1815 explosion of the volcano Tambora in Indonesia. So much ash was thrown into the atmosphere that the entire planet cooled as a result and severe winter weather was reported for a three-year time period remembered today as the "Year without a Summer."[7]

Cook and his warriors finally reached Fort Hughes after nearly one week of battling ice, freezing rain and below-freezing temperatures. Although he does not mention it in his brief account, his party was apparently reinforced along the way. News of the attack on Scott's party was the talk of Miccosukee and other villages along his route and Cook heard first-hand accounts of the bloody victory as he passed. Exactly when the clerk's little army reached the fort is somewhat in dispute. Cook's account appears to establish the date as December 7th, but correspondence from Fort Scott places it as the 15th.[8]

Peter Cook's previous experience in battle is not clear. Regardless, he led the warriors at his command into battle:

> …After seven days' march we arrived at the fort; and after our men got rested, I went against it. We had an engagement for four hours, and seeing that we could do no good with them, we retreated and came off. The balls flew like hail-stones; there was a ball that had like to have done my job; it just cleared my breast.[9]

Other warriors, likely from Fowltown, Attapulgus and Miccosukee, continued the siege for several days. The compact little fort, however, was too secure and McIntosh's men had plenty of ammunition. The Battle of Fort Hughes ended with American victory. Reports of the affair by U.S. reports were minimal, other than to note that McIntosh and his command had held out "without losing a single man."[10]

The destruction of Scott's command on November 30th followed by attacks on Blunt's Town and Muhlenberg's flotilla two weeks later convinced Lt. Col. Arbuckle that he had erred in leaving Capt. McIntosh at Fort Hughes with such a small force. Supplying the fort was proving impossible and the attack – although beaten back by the little garrison – would likely be followed with a strong effort. Consequently, he decided to evacuate the fort.[11]

The threat of an attack during the withdrawal was a serious one so Arbuckle sent a detail of 60 men with 2 corporals and 2 sergeants under Capt. Sanders Donoho to provide additional firepower to McIntosh's men as they crossed the Flint River and marched back to Fort Scott. Donoho left for Fort Hughes on December 18, 1817, and the fort was evacuated and McIntosh and his command escorted back to Fort Scott by the following day. No attack materialized and the withdrawal took place without incident.[12]

The military history of Fort Hughes was now all but over. U.S. troops would pass by from time to time and Maj. Gen. Andrew Jackson's army marched down the road on the opposite side of the river on its way to Fort Scott, but no garrison would ever again occupy the little fort on Burges's Bluff. The city of Bainbridge would be established on the site within a few years and its residents remembered the fort for many years, often assigning it greater importance than it had held during its actual history.

---

[1] Mark F. Boyd, "Historic Sites in and around the Jim Woodruff Reservoir Area, Florida-Georgia," River Basin Survey Papers, No. 13, *Bulletin 169*, Smithsonian Institution, Bureau of American Ethnology, 1958: 301; "The Indian Frontier in British East Florida: Letters to Governor James Grant from British Soldiers and Indian Traders," Florida History Online, University of North Florida, Online resource at www.unf.edu/floridahistoryonline/Projects/Grant/letters.html (transcribed by James Hill).

[2] Lt. Col. Matthew Arbuckle to Maj. Gen. Edmund P. Gaines, November 30, 1817, Andrew Jackson papers, Library of Congress.

[3] *Ibid.*

[4] *Ibid.*

[5] Capt. John N. McIntosh to Hon. A. Lacock, February 5, 1819, *American State Papers*, Indian Affairs, Volume 1: 747.

[6] Peter B. Cook to Miss Elizabeth A. Carney, January 19, 1818, *American State Papers*, Foreign Relations, Volume IV, p. 605.

[7] *Ibid.*; See *The Scott Massacre of 1817* by this author, Old Kitchen Books, Bascom, FL.

[8] *Ibid*; "Indian War," *Niles Weekly Register*, Volume 13, January 14, 1818.

[9] Peter B. Cook to Miss Elizabeth A. Carney, January 19, 1818, American State Papers, Foreign Relations, Volume IV, p. 605.

[10] "Indian War," *Niles Weekly Register*, Volume 13, January 14, 1818.

[11] Lt. Col. Matthew Arbuckle to Major General Edmund P. Gaines (dated Fort Scott), December 20, 1817, ASPMA Vol 1, No. 164 p. 689-690.

[12] Register of Details for Command from Fort Scott, from the 18th of December, 1817, until the 19th of March, 1818, whilst under the command of Lt. Col. Arbuckle, Office of the Adjutant General, Letters Received, 1805-1821.

CHAPTER TEN

The Siege of Forts Scott & Gaines

The situation at Fort Scott continued to grow increasingly dire in December 1817. The list of disasters striking U.S. troops became longer with each passing day. Lt. Scott's command had been wiped out, war parties were firing into the fort on a daily basis, Arbuckle's raid on Fowltown failed to produce much in the way of food, provision stocks were declining and Fort Hughes had been surrounded and besieged. More bad news was coming, but first there would be one last attempt to make peace.

As war exploded along the frontier, the Lower Creek chief William Perryman appeared at Fort Scott along with one of his brothers and an allied chief named Johnson. They were horrified by the situation and were leading a desperate mission to stop the fighting and return peace to the borderlands around the confluence of the Chattahoochee and Flint Rivers. They had already talked with both Cappachimico (Kenhajo) and the Autossee Mico ("Otessee Micko") and both had authorized them to speak with the U.S. commander on their behalf. William Perryman did not know it at the time, but the end of his life was just days away.[1]

Command of the fort had now passed from General Gaines to Lt. Col. Matthew Arbuckle. He received them courteously and listened as Edmund Doyle, the trader from Prospect Bluff who had accompanied them, explained that he had also spoken with the Autossee Mico and was authorized to speak on his behalf. The talk delivered by the American officer to Perryman and his associates made clear that efforts by intermediaries to find common ground with the warring chiefs were not authorized by the military. Arbuckle also made clear that more than one year after the U.S. destruction of the fort at Prospect Bluff, capturing the African Americans living among the Indians was still a major objective:

> I have understood that Mr. Doyle has had a talk with Ottossee Micko about making peace. I did not ask Mr. Doyle to make this, or any other Talks with the hostile Indians, but I shall be glad if the talk has enduced them to wish for peace, as their Great Father the President of the United States, has always wished for peace with them.
>
> The army did not come here to make war on the Indians, but expected their assistance in getting the negroes belonging to the White People who are in their country, and to ask that some offenders should be given up.
>
> During the last summer, Genl. Gaines sent two talks to the Mickysoockee chief, who did not answer like a friend but still the General did not believe that he wished for war.[2]

The lieutenant colonel was referring to the exchange between Gaines and Cappachimico (Kenhajo) the previous summer. The general had demanded the surrender of the warriors responsible for the murders of Mrs. Garrett and her children on the St. Marys. The chief had responded by pointing out that Indians had been killed as well and that a kettle belonging to one of these victims had been found in the Garrett home. Arbuckle then went on to blame Neamathla's people for shooting at the American troops who were trying to surround and take them hostage. He also referenced the attack on Lt. Scott:

Some complaints has been made of the Indians of Neamatla's town, and when Genl. Gaines came here, he sent for Neamathla to talk with him, but he would not come. The General then sent some men after him, to bring him to the fort, and ordered that no one should be hurt, unless the Indians fired on our people. This party did not expect to get to the town before day light but they got there sooner than they expected, and went to the town for the purpose of taking Neamatla. As they went up the Indians fired on them. They then fired and some of the Indians were killed. Since that time a boat on the Apalachicola R., with an officer and many sick men and women & children was attacked by Indians not belonging to Neamatla's town, and the officer, all of the women except one, and all the sick men and children were killed & the property belonging to the United States, onboard of the boat, was taken or destroyed.[3]

Arbuckle then told the Perrymans and Johnson that if the chiefs now at war wished for peace, they should send their talks and be heard. He agreed to withhold any movements against the war faction for six days to give them time to send in peace emissaries. He warned, however, that any more gunfire would lead to talks not being heard until the Seminoles and Red Sticks had been "severely punished." The lieutenant colonel also promised that no lands would be taken from chiefs and warriors friendly to the United States:

> Should the hostile Indians still want war, nothing is asked of the friendly Indians but to remain Peacibly at their homes and to keep the hostile Indians from among them, and if the army should march by a friendly town, they have nothing to do but hoist a white flag.
> Chiefs Johnson & Perrymans, I am well pleased with your conduct as honest men, and with your good intentions in endeavoring to bring about a peace. If you should fail

you have only to remain quietly at your homes, where you will be unmolested.

Your Great Father the President of the United States will not take from the friendly chiefs and warriors their land or property but the Indians of the hostile towns will be expected to pay the expenses of the war they have made.[4]

Paying for the expenses of war was the same requirement that had led to the imposition of the Treaty of Fort Jackson on the Creeks following the Creek War of 1813-1814. Neamathla had not been a party to that treaty but it gave away his land just the same. His statement that the "land was his" and that he had been directed by the "Powers above" to defend it had led to the U.S. raids on Fowltown and the beginning of the war that was now underway. Whether U.S. officers understood this connection or not, the chiefs and warriors at war with the United States did and none came in to make peace.

The council at Fort Scott over, William Perryman and a party of his warriors escorted Edmund Doyle back down to his plantation at Spanish Bluff on the Apalachicola River. Doyle's business associate William Hambly was already there and Chief John Blunt had come across the river from Blunt's Town (now Blountstown) with a few of his warriors as well. Any hope that Doyle and Perryman might have had of negotiating a peace ended tragically when the plantation at present-day Bristol, Florida, was attacked by Red Sticks who were assembling on the river in vast numbers:

> ...On the 13th instant, Hambly and Doyle were made prisoners by this party, and, I presume, killed, and their property of every description taken possession of. The chief, William Perryman, who had gone down with a party to protect Hambly and Doyle, was killed, and his men forced to join the opposite party. All of the Indians on the Chattahoochee, below Fort Gaines, who are not disposed to

126

go to war, I fear will be compelled to remove above for security.[5]

While William Perryman was killed in the Battle of Spanish Bluff, Hambly and Doyle survived. They were carried first to Ocheesee Bluff where the main Red Stick and Seminole army was assembling under the Prophet Francis. From there they were taken to Tallahassee Talofa and Miccosukee before finally winding up at Boleck's town on the Suwanee. Alexander Arbuthnot ordered them killed, but a Black Seminole chief named Nero intervened and took them to the Spanish fort of San Marcos de Apalache. They remained there in safety until Maj. Gen. Andrew Jackson's army arrived at the post the following spring.

The death of William Perryman at Spanish Bluff marked the end of one of the most remarkable men of his time. The son of Thomas Perryman, the onetime principal chief of the bands on the Apalachicola and lower Chattahoochee Rivers, and the grandson of the English trader Theophilus Perryman, he was a noteworthy chief and leader of Lower Creek forces. Commissioned a captain by the British during the American Revolution, he had led Creek warriors on their behalf during numerous battles along the Georgia frontier. Surviving that war, William became an ally but still later an enemy of the adventurer and pirate William Augustus Bowles. The enigmatic Bowles had married his sister and used his connection with the Perryman family to build a following in the borderlands. He made the mistake of threatening William's father, however, and the younger Perryman turned on his brother-in-law and signed an agreement with the Spanish to help bring Bowles to justice.

William Perryman is believed to have been the "Indian Willy" who warned U.S. Commissioner of Limits Andrew Ellicott of a pending attack in 1799, allowing Ellicott and his party to prepare a defense and then escape without major harm. Perryman was a leader in the party of Lower Creek chiefs that went to Pensacola in 1813 to meet with an English sea captain and plead for help. The Creek War of 1813-1814 had just erupted and they feared that the United States would come down on them with no regard as to whether they had actually participated in the war. It was this overture that resulted in the dispatch of Lt. Col. Edward Nicolls and Maj. George Woodbine to Spanish Florida during the closing days of the War of 1812. He had allied himself with the British once again and was a signer of the Nicolls Outpost Treaty on March 10, 1815.

The failure of the British to return and the subsequent American destruction of the fort at Prospect Bluff convinced Perryman that it was time to make peace with the United States and he did so. He relayed word of the partial burning of Fort Scott after his brother, the caretaker of the abandoned fort, was forced to flee to William's town by the Red Sticks. He then relayed several messages upriver to Fort Gaines to keep U.S. troops apprised of the situation in Spanish Florida and otherwise did what he could to help American officers. It was at his request that Major David E. Twiggs convened a council of chiefs at Fort Scott during the summer of 1817. Perryman and others hoped to use the meeting as an opportunity to flog his former ally Neamathla for putting them at risk of war with the United States, but were disappointed when the Fowltown chief refused to appear.

William Perryman's final acts were efforts to preserve peace and protect friends. He led the delegation that met with Lt. Col. Arbuckle on December 10, 1817, and was successful in negotiating a temporary truce. The war factions of the Red Sticks and Seminoles were not interested, however, and the distinguished chief gave his life to protect Edmund Doyle and William Hambly in the battle at Spanish Bluff on December 13, 1817.

John Blunt escaped Perryman's fate and carried the news of the attack to Lt. Col. Arbuckle at Fort Scott. He also warned that major attacks against U.S. troops were coming. His warning was verified when simultaneous attacks were launched against both Fort Hughes on the Flint and the vessels under Maj. Peter Muhlenberg on the Apalachicola on December 15, 1817:

> On Monday morning the transports were attacked by Indians from both sides of the river with a heavy fire of small arms. We returned their fire, the firing has continued ever since. We have lost two men killed and thirteen wounded, most of them severely. Whether we have injured

them any I am not able to say. We are now compelled to remain here, as it is impossible for us to carry out a warp, as a man cannot shew himself above the bulwarks without being fired on. I can assure you that our present situation is not the most Pleasant not knowing how soon or whether we are to receive succor from above, the wounded are but in a bad situation owing to the vessels being much crowded, and it is impossible to make them any ways comfortable on board. Not having other means to communicate to you, I am compelled to dispatch the keel boat with instructions to make the best of his way to Fort Scott. I hope to hear from you soon with instructions [on] how I am to proceed in my present situation.[6]

The Battle of Ocheesee would continue for weeks and become the longest sustained engagement of the Seminole Wars. The point of the attack at Ocheesee Bluff was ideal for the Red Sticks and Seminoles. The Apalachicola River passes through a sharp "S"-shaped bend there, making it possible for Francis and his warriors to fire on the boats not just from east and west, but north and south as well. The high bluffs on the east side of the river at today's Torreya State Park, also gave the attackers excellent views down into the vessels. Confederate forces later picked this same section of river for the placement of a battery of heavy cannon for exactly the same reasons. The Prophet had clearly learned some valuable military lessons during the Creek War and War of 1812.

Muhlenberg's ships, one of which was the seasoned old *General Pike*, were pinned down midstream and forced to drop anchor. News of the battle was alarming to Lt. Col. Arbuckle at Fort Scott, perhaps even more so because of Maj. Muhlenberg's post script that "I have but a few days' provision on board. The men have been on half allowance for some time."[7]

Supplies were running low at Fort Scott and the chiefs and warriors were doing their best to make sure that no more made it through. Large parties were sent up the Chattahoochee and Flint Rivers to cut-off communications between Fort Scott and Fort Gaines with the upriver garrisons at Fort

Mitchell and Fort Hawkins. The movements of these warriors were brought home to U.S. officials in an alarming way:

> An express from Gen. Jackson to Gen. Gaines, who left here on Friday, returned to night. He took the route by fort Gaines, but was unable to proceed even that far. He penetrated within ten miles of the fort, where he observed fresh Indian signs; and a few miles further came to where white men had been killed, one of whom was Mr. John Chambers, of fort Gaines.[8]

The courier had gone out apparently not knowing that Gen. Gaines had been ordered from Fort Scott to the St. Marys. He tried to get his message to the general by way of Fort Gaines. He was trailing behind another party of whites and was only five miles away when the attack took place:

> The express had heard from them frequently, by persons whom he met, and was trying to overtake them; and at the time of the murder could not have been more than five miles behind. They were killed last Monday morning, within a few miles of the place where they had encamped the night before. The appearance indicated about twenty Indians, and the trail entered the road in the direction of fort Gaines, at which place there is merely a sergeant's guard of twelve men, and a few of the neighbouring inhabitants, who have taken refuge there. So safe, however, have the inhabitants considered themselves there, that some, it is save, are so credulous as to make their yard railing their only breast-work; and the alarm has come so sudden upon them, that retreat is impossible, or at least dangerous.[9]

The settlers around Fort Gaines once again fled into the stockade. News of the attack led Georgia authorities to order a detachment of militia to the fort with orders to assist in its defense. According to the reminiscences of one of the participants, famed frontiersman Thomas Woodward, the relief party made it through and reached the fort at night. The unidentified officer who relayed word of the situation near Fort Gaines to a Georgia newspaper editor also provided some detail of the military situation on the frontier:

> ,,,Fort Gaines is said to be of considerable strength; fort Scott is a mere camp, having very partial defences. Two expresses dispatched from fort Gaines to fort Scott, have not been heard of; nor has the one sent from this place since he left fort Mitchell. Jackson's express says that he was informed by a friendly chief, that Gen. Gaines had sent advices to fort Mitchell, requesting that as few passages should be made through the nation as possible. This is probably correct and necessary, as the hostile influence seems to be extensive and scattered, and one middle town on the rout to Fort Gaines, which is avowedly hostile, lies only thirty-seven miles below the Alabama road. Governor Mitchell is at Fort Mitchell, and will use his influence and authority with the nation in courting their neutrality, or directing their vengeance.[10]

General Thomas Glasscock of the Georgia Militia was at Fort Hawkins with some of his men when the courier arrived. He told the editors of the *Augusta Chronicle* that two men had been killed in the incident and also relayed news of the destruction of Lt. Scott's party. He expected to be ordered into combat soon:

> I feel a conscious pride that the small detachment under my command will participate in avenging the death of our slaughtered breathren, as I have no doubt but that gen. Gaines's feelings are sufficiently roused to pursue them to the last extremity, or at least so far as prudence may dictate. I am fearful ere this reaches you, Fort Gaines will fall, and

from the success the Indians have lately met with, they will be very bold and daring.[11]

It would take longer than Glasscock hoped to get into action, but he and his men would soon play an important role in American war preparations by advancing to the Flint River and building Fort Early. This post, near present-day Cordele, Georgia, would serve as a key supply depot for U.S. forces being ordered to assemble on the border.

Many historians have written that Fort Early was rebuilt on the site of a breastwork thrown up my General David Blackshear during the War of 1812. While it is true that Blackshear did build a small earthwork nearby in 1814, the new fort was built a short distance away from the old. Accounts of Georgia militia troops indicate they once used Blackshear's old fort as shelter when they were confronted by a party of warriors not far from the new Fort Early.

As the war parties hovered around Fort Scott and Fort Gaines, occasionally firing on each, former Georgia governor David B. Mitchell, now the U.S. Agent for Indian Affairs, attended a council at the Lower Creek town of Broken Arrow. This town was the seat of the Little Prince, the principal leader of the Lower Creeks:

> ...[A] meeting of the Principal Chiefs had been called by the Little Prince, at the Town of Thla-Cotch-Cau, on the Chatahoochie River, near Fort Mitchell, at which I attended; the object of which was, to take into consideration the state of the Nation, and particularly, the measures which it would be proper for them to take, in relation to those Indians residing between Fort Gaines and the Spanish Line; and also the conduct they should pursue with regard to the War with the Seminoles. They unanimously expressed much regret, that hostilities should have commenced between the Troops under General Gaines, and the Fowltown Indians, who reside within our Boundary;

because these Indians, although they did not unite with the friendly ones during the late War, neither did they join the Red Sticks, and had recently expressed a great desire to become decidedly friendly. They were, however, perfectly willing, that their Warriors should join General Gaines against the Seminoles.[12]

Mitchell told the assembled chiefs that the United States did not want a war with the Seminoles and that he could not approve of Creek warriors crossing the border into Spanish Florida to attack them. He urged them to send a trusted chief to the towns between Fort Gaines and the Spanish line with an urgent appeal that they relocate above the line into the newly defined Creek Nation. This emissary should then go on to Miccosukee to meet with the chiefs there. Once again, the subject of the African Americans living on the Suwannee came into the picture:

…[They agreed that] the same Chief should then proceed directly to the Mackasukie Town (the Head-quarters of the Seminoles and Red Sticks of the Late War,) and propose to them certain terms of peace, and a junction of their Force to go against the Negro Camp. The objects which this Chief was instructed to hold out to those Indians, as attainable, by adopting this course, were various, and of sufficient importance, in the view of those making the proposition, to induce a belief, that they would be favorably received; in which event I should proceed to Fort Scott to adjust their differences. This course of proceeding was immediately adopted, and the head man of the Osoochies, Hopoi Haijo, set out on the same day, charged with the Mission.[13]

The chiefs felt that it was best to allow this emissary time to meet with the Seminoles and Red Sticks before sending their warriors to assist U.S. forces. They agreed to reconvene on January 11, 1818. Maj. William McIntosh and the warriors would be told to attend with arms and supplies in hand and would march immediately if they were needed to reinforce the army.[14]

Mitchell's efforts to make peace were not received well by U.S. officers at Fort Scott and Fort Gaines. They were under siege and at risk of being either overrun by enemy warriors or forced to evacuate their posts due to provision shortages. They had hoped that McIntosh and his warriors would come down the Chattahoochee to break the siege and help drive back the Seminoles and Red Sticks. Lt. Robert Irvin, the commanding officer at Fort Gaines, expressed his astonishment that McIntosh was not coming in a report to Lt. Col. Arbuckle at Fort Scott:

> …[T]he agent had told the Indians that Genl. Gaines had no business to go to the Indian's Town and fire on them in the night, that he had acted like the Indians themselves in doing so – McIntosh had come as far as Fort Mitchell on his way, and the agent has sent him home and told him to meet him at the agency for a Talk in 30 days, 18 of which yet remains, and that he should not move till the general government should give the order. This I expect is the case for they have sent Onos Hadjoe a talk that he was doing wrong to be in service in this country till the agent should give him orders – He further states that the agent has sent a talk to Simanola, to the chiefs to meet him and he would make peace for them, and the white people should have no satisfaction for what was done.[15]

The peace council that Mitchell proposed convening at Fort Scott never took place. The arrival of the report on the massacre of Lt. Scott's party in Washington, D.C., ended any restraint on the part of the United States. Orders went down authorizing Gaines to cross the line into Spanish Florida to find and punish those responsible. A similar order went to Maj. Gen. Andrew Jackson, the hero of both New Orleans and Horseshoe Bend, instructing him to assemble an army on the frontier and put an end to the threat from below the Spanish border.

General Gaines wrote to Washington as he passed through Georgia en route for St. Marys. His letter offers a good understanding of the American view on why the Seminoles especially had gone to war:

>...The Seminole Indians, however strange and absurd it may appear to those who understand little of their real character and extreme ignorance, entertain a notion that they cannot be beaten by our troops. They confidently assert that we have never beaten them, or any of their people, except when we have been assisted by "red people." This will appear the less extraordinary when it is recollected that they have little or no means of knowing the strength and resources of our country; they have not travelled through it; they read neither books nor newspapers; nor have the opportunities of conversing with persons able to inform them. I feel warranted, from all I know of these savages, in saying that they do not believe we can beat them. This error of theirs has led them, from time to time, for many years past, to massacre our frontier citizens, often the unoffending and helpless mother and babes.[16]

Gaines went on to explain he had truly believed that his raids on Fowltown would "be adequate to stop these outrages." He had felt "pleased" with his ability to be "instrumental in effecting an object of so much importance to our exposed frontier settlements." Things had not, he admitted, gone as he expected and he requested permission from Secretary of War Graham to go back to Fort Scott:

>...You can more readily conceive than I can describe the mortification and disappointment I have experienced in being compelled to suspend or abandon my measures at a

moment when the loss of Lieutenant Scott and his party had given the enemy an occasion of triumph, and a certain prospect of increasing his strength, by enlisting against us all who had before wavered or hesitated. Permit me, then, to repeat my request that I may be permitted to return.[17]

The general concluded by telling the secretary there was then little to fear about troops crossing into Spanish Florida because so many warriors had come north of the line to lay siege to Fort Scott and Fort Gaines.

---

[1] Lt. Col. Matthew Arbuckle, Talk to three Indian chiefs, December 10, 1817, Adjutant General, Letters Received, NARA.

[2] *Ibid.*

[3] *Ibid.*

[4] *Ibid.*

[5] Lt. Col. Matthew Arbuckle to Major General Edmund P. Gaines (dated Fort Scott), December 20, 1817, ASPMA Vol 1, No. 164 p. 689-690.

[6] Maj. P. Muhlenburg to Lt. Col. Matthew Arbuckle, December 16, 1817, Adjutant General, Letters Received, NARA.

[7] *Ibid.*

[8] Staff officer to the editor of the Reflector in Milledgeville, December 10, 1817, printed in the Massachusetts Spy, p. 2., December 31, 1817.

[9] *Ibid.*

[10] Staff officer to the editor of the Reflector in Milledgeville, December 10, 1817, printed in the Massachusetts Spy, p. 2., December 31, 1817.

[11] Gen. Thomas Glasscock to the editors of the Augusta Chronicle, December 11, 1817, appeared in the Augusta Chronicle on December 17, 1817.

[12] Hon. David B. Mitchell to Hon. George Graham, Secretary of State, December 14, 1817, British Foreign and State Papers, pp. 1106-1107.

[13] *Ibid.*

[14] *Ibid.*

[15] Lt. Robert Irvin to Lt. Col. Matthew Arbuckle, December 23, 1817, Andrew Jackson papers, Library of Congress.

[16] Maj. Gen. Edmund P. Gaines to Hon. George Graham, Secretary of War, December 15, 1817, American State Papers, Military Affairs, Volume I, p. 689.

[17] *Ibid.*

CHAPTER ELEVEN

Winter on the Flint

The Seminole and Red Stick siege of Forts Scott and Gaines was remarkably effective and it was extremely fortunate for the U.S. troops at these installations that reinforcements were already mobilizing. The Georgia militia had been called out and was forming, Maj. William McIntosh was expected to march with his Creeks on January 11th, and orders were in route to Maj. Gen. Andrew Jackson for his movement to the frontier. It would be up to Lt. Col. Matthew Arbuckle to maintain his position near the border until help reached him. He could not have known that it would take three full months.

The beleaguered Arbuckle learned of the attack on Maj. Peter Muhlenberg's ships at Ocheesee Bluff when Capt. J.J. Clinch arrived at Fort Scott early on the morning of December 18, 1817, in a keel boat. The stocks of provisions at Fort Scott were also rapidly diminishing, but Arbuckle immediately dispatched Capt. Blackstone with fifteen days' rations of meat and bread for 160 men, along with some soap and liquor. The lieutenant colonel also advised Muhlenberg of a plan he had devised to help move the ships forward:

> I am making some alteration in the boat Captain Clinch came in which I think will render her safe and convenient in carrying forward a kedge by which means you will have it in your power to progress a little every day and should the wind be favorable I shall have hopes of your reaching this in eight or ten days, but should it take longer it cannot be avoided as I have not the means of doing more for you at present.[1]

A kedge is a small anchor that can be carried forward of a ship or boat and dropped. The crew can then pull on the rope or cable to slowly edge the vessel forward. Once the ship reaches the kedge, it is then carried forward again and the process is repeated. Kedging is a slow and laborious but effective process. From his letter to Maj. Muhlenberg, it sounds as if Arbuckle had devised a way for Capt. Clinch's boat to carry forward a kedge without exposing its crew to the fire of the Prophet Francis's forces.

Arbuckle expressed concern over the condition of the men who had been wounded in the battle. After reporting that he had a large boat under construction at Fort Scott that would carry up to 300 barrels in safety, he noted that he was worried about whether he had enough iron to finish it. If it did not come down within eight days, he urged the major to send Capt. Clinch back up in the keel boat with the wounded men and "five or six hundred weight [500-600 pounds] of iron."[2]

Muhlenberg was urged to protect his men as much as possible to keep Fort Scott apprised of his progress:

> In any event you will be compelled to progress slowly and I request that you will have no greater object in view than to prevent your men from exposure or injury from the fire of the enemy. I wish you to fire a morning gun at sun rise every morning (and one at sun set should it be

convenient). This will enable us to find you should information justify a movement of the troops from this place for your support.[3]

The attack on the supply flotilla forced Arbuckle to order the evacuation of Fort Hughes. By the time that garrison was brought back to Fort Scott, however, the total food stocks at the main post had declined to less than a 20-day supply. The lieutenant colonel pleaded with Col. David Brearley of the 7th Infantry to do what he could to get supplies to the fort:

> General Gaines has made a requisition on the contractor at Fort Hawkins for provisions to be delivered at this post. Do all you can to have them forwarded soon, as we have not a supply of more than twenty days rations of meat, and flour for about double that time. Beef cattle could be brought here from above on this river if escorted by a strong detachment of dragoons.[4]

Unless he could somehow get a new supply. Arbuckle had only enough food on hand to feed his men until the second week of January 1818. The men at both the fort and on the flotilla had been on half-rations for a long time and situation was growing dire. One of the symptoms or side effects of a dramatic reduction in caloric intake is depression or sadness. The mood of the men on both the ships and at Fort Scott likely was plunging by late December. This may explain the increasingly pessimistic tone that began to surface in Lt. Col. Arbuckle's pleadings with superior and supply officers as the day slipped past and hunger grew at Fort Scott. He would later face court martial for this despondency. Fatigue and increased stress are also side effects of a major drop in food intake and the garrison definitely showed signs of both during the winter of 1817-1818.

Arbuckle's stress was definitely increased when Lt. Gray arrived back at the fort in the keel boat during the third week of December. The lieutenant was carrying a letter from Maj. Muhlenberg that bordered on despondency. The battle was clearly not going well for his detachment:

> I was in hopes you would have been able to afford some relief to the command, as our situation demanded that something should have been done immediately, that we are not able to progress is evident, as we have the enemy on both sides of the river and therefore impracticable to carry out a warp, had we not heard from you by the keel boat this morning, it was decided that we should have attempted to return to the bay this morning. I shall now dispatch the keel boat under the command of Lieut. Gray and try to retain our present position until the night of the 21st. In case we should not hear from you or be reinforced by land we shall make the attempt to reach the Bay.[5]

At Fort Scott itself, troops continued to work feverishly to finish the fortifications. Unlike smaller posts such as Fort Gaines and Fort Hughes, the fort was a massive affair designed to house a full brigade of U.S. troops.

No ground plan of the fort has ever been found nor has any detailed description of its appearance by the winter of 1817-1818 surfaced. The surviving descriptions are vague and generally say little more than that the fort was formerly a cantonment that had been surrounded by an "irregular" quadrangular stockade. The only detailed maps showing the fort's outline are the survey plats of Lots 224 and 227 of District 21 in the original Early County, Georgia. Both of these lots were surveyed on February 18, 1820, when the post was still occupied by U.S. troops.[6]

The outline of the fort appears to have been drawn by hand and it is unclear whether it was to scale, although surveyors usually attempt to be as accurate as possible. If the fort outline is to scale, then the fort enclosed 11-12 acres of land making it one of the largest such facilities ever built in the Southeast. The shape was an irregular polygon with four sides counting the Flint River. Major John Davis inspected the original cantonment in 1816 and noted there were no plans to erect a stockade wall along the river side since it was impossible for an enemy to approach from that direction. This defect was likely corrected with a wall after warriors repeatedly fired into the fort from the opposite bank. Davis indicated that the permanent works consisted of a line of connected barracks built all in a row about 100 yards from the river and parallel to it. The rear wall of these log structures would also serve as one of the outer walls of the fort. Between the barracks and the Flint, he reported, an Officers' Quarters structure had been built.[7]

Red Stick warriors burned the barracks at Fort Scott following the departure of the troops there but U.S. soldiers undoubtedly rebuilt these during the summer of 1817 to provide themselves with comfortable quarters. If they were restored according to the original design, then the fort in 1818 probably consisted of a long line of barracks about 100 yards from the river. Between these and the river were the Officers' Quarters, "Hospital House," magazine and other structures. The main gate was likely about the mid-point of the eastern wall, while a second smaller gate was near the northwest corner of the fort. The sheer size of the complex explains why it took the garrison from June until December of 1817 to finish their construction work.

The heavy labor of finishing the fort combined with food shortages obviously affected the health of the soldiers. In addition to symptoms such as depression and chronic exhaustion, they also likely suffered from bone or joint pain, weak muscles, dry skin, brittle nails, hair loss and other symptoms of malnutrition. Their weakened condition also made them more susceptible to colds, influenza and fever. The severe cold weather of that winter did not help either the soldiers or the warriors trying to battle them.

The fear and depression being felt by the officers and soldiers in the isolated fort on the Flint was clear in a letter written by an officer to an unidentified correspondent on December 20, 1817:

> An attempt is to be made to-morrow to get an express to Fort Hawkins.
> Our situation is really an alarming one. An enemy around us of treble our force, and but 20 days provisions.

141

How we are to be relieved I know not. Major Muhlenburg has two schooners about 30 miles below – the Indians and Negroes all around him, keeping up a constant fire; some of his men have been killed and wounded, and the rest left entirely to the mercy of the winds, for they cannot move in any other way.[8]

Lt. Col. Arbuckle wrote to Maj. Muhlenberg one day later in a desperate effort to convince him not to drop back down the Apalachicola with the vessels under his charge. Arbuckle pointed out that the major's position would not be bettered even if he marched to his relief with every healthy soldier at Fort Scott. He reported that he was sending out four mounted men in a desperate attempt to slip through to call for help from the Georgia mounted militia or Maj. William McIntosh and his Creeks.[9]

Arbuckle expressed disappointment that Muhlenberg had not tried to use the keelboat to kedge his vessels upstream but urged him to at minimum maintain his position and at most to try other methods of moving the ships forward. The lieutenant colonel made no secret of his fear that the ships were going to withdraw back down the river. "Do not loose hope," he pleaded, "and be assured sir that every thing which can be done for your vessels without making the destruction of the whole force here certain, shall be done."[10]

Muhlenberg responded on Christmas Eve by reporting a lessening in the severity of gunfire being directed at his vessels:

…I had hoped that you would have been able to have marched to our relief, but as that is impossible for the Present we shall have to remain in our present situation. Every means has been tried to ascend the river but in vain, and I am fearful we never shall get up without we are relieved from above. The Indians still continue to annoy us, but I do not think they are in such force as they were the three first days that we were attacked. Our situation at

Present is a tolerable secure one, and we shall retain it as long as it is practicable.[11]

Arbuckle sent the keel boat back on the 26th with a cargo of planks, moss and other materials that could be used to further strengthen Muhlenberg's vessels against rifle fire. He also sent down "some sweets and fire wood" to improve the comfort of the men. He promised to shortly send down "the only small boat at this place" along with one of the new flat boats he had been building. The flotilla could make use of these to either assist in its movements or cargo could be transferred onto them for shipment up to Fort Scott. The lieutenant colonel hoped that the schooner, sloop and other vessels would begin to make some progress soon and he instructed the major to fire two cannon in quick succession should he reach the mouth of the Flint River sooner than expected.[12]

Secretary of War John C. Calhoun returned to his office after his Christmas holiday on the same date and found three letters waiting from Maj. Gen. Gaines. News of the outbreak on the frontier shocked him and he immediately regretted the previous orders instructing the general to relocate to the St. Marys:

> ...The fate of the detachment under Lieutenant Scott is much to be regretted; but, under all the circumstances, no blame can attach to yourself or the officers immediately concerned. When the order of the 12th November was given, directing you to repair to Amelia Island, it was hoped that the Seminoles would have been brought to their reason without an actual use of force, and that their hostility would not assume so serious an aspect. It is now a subject of much regret, that the service in that quarter has been deprived of your well known skill and vigilance.[13]

Calhoun told Gaines that Maj. Gen. Andrew Jackson was being ordered to the frontier. If U.S. troops were already in possession of Amelia Island by the time the letter reached St. Marys, however, Gaines was to immediately return to Fort Scott and resume the command there until Jackson could arrive on the scene. The general was to consider a movement to Fort Scott directly through the Seminole country of Spanish Florida if he thought that such a march could be made without great danger:

> ...I am not sufficiently acquainted with the topography of the country between Amelia and their towns, to say whether it is practicable, or what would be the best route; but it is not improbable that some advantage might be taken of the St. John's river, to effect the object. Should it be practicable, it is probable efficient aid might be given to the attack on them, as the attention of their warriors must be wholly directed towards Fort Scott. Should you think it practicable and advisable to co-operate, with the force under your command, you will leave a sufficient number at Amelia Island to retain the possession of that place.[14]

The sound of two cannon shots in quick successful could be heard by the garrison at Fort Scott on the morning of December 29, 1817, announcing the arrival of Maj. Muhlenberg's flotilla at the mouth of the Flint River. The attack on the ships had finally come to an end and the vessels were able to reach Fort Scott the next day. While they brought no desperately needed supplies for the garrison, the arrival of the boats ended great anxiety at the post about the fate of the men on board.[15]

The year 1817 came to an end with the men at Fort Scott on half-rations. Ten days had passed since Lt. Col. Arbuckle reported that he had only 20-days' rations left and no new supply had been received during that time. The Georgia Militia was finally on the march to build Fort Early on the Flint River. At Fort Hawkins, meanwhile, the sergeant and three privates sent on horseback arrived with the pleas for help from the lieutenant colonel. American authorities were growing more aware of the desperate situation at Fort Scott, but New Year's Eve was cold and bleak for the hungry men huddled by their fires low down on the Flint River.

[1] Lt. Col. Matthew Arbuckle to Maj. P. Muhlenburg, December 18, 1817, Adjutant General, Letters Received, NARA.

[2] *Ibid.*

[3] *Ibid.*

[4] Lt. Col. Matthew Arbuckle to Col. David Brearly, December 19, 1817, from the National Standard, January 28, 1818, p. 3.

[5] Maj. P. Muhlenburg to Lt. Col. Matthew Arbuckle, December 19, 1817, Adjutant General, Letters Received, NARA.

[6] Plats of Land Lots 224 and 227, District 21, Early County, Georgia, February 18, 1820, Survey Book EEE, Office of the County Clerk, Decatur County, Georgia.

[7] *Ibid.*; Inspection report of Major John M. Davis, April 30, 1817.

[8] Officer to unknown individual, December 20, 1817, Alexandria Gazette, February 12, 1818, p. 2.

[9] Lt. Col. Matthew Arbuckle to Maj. P. Muhlenburg, December 21, 1817, Adjutant General, Letters Received, NARA.

[10] *Ibid.*

[11] Maj. P. Muhlenburg to Lt. Col. Matthew Arbuckle, December 24, 1817, Adjutant General, Letters Received, NARA.

[12] Lt. Col. Matthew Arbuckle to Bvt. Maj. P. Muhlenburg, December 26, 1817, Adjutant General, Letters Received, NARA.

[13] Hon. John C. Calhoun to Maj. Gen. Edmund P. Gaines, December 26, 1817, American State Papers, Military Affairs, Volume I, pp. 689-690

[14] *Ibid.*

[15] Lt. Col. Matthew Arbuckle to Maj. P. Muhlenburg, December 29, 1817, Adjutant General, Letters Received, NARA; Lt. Col. Matthew Arbuckle to Maj. Gen. Edmund P. Gaines, January 6, 1818, Adjutant General, Letters Received, NARA.

CHAPTER TWELVE

Waiting for Jackson

January 1818 marked a temporary return to offensive action for the troops at Fort Scott. Lt. Col. Matthew Arbuckle left for a third raid on Fowltown this time adding the nearby village of Attapulgus to his itinerary as well. The objectives of the new raid were to find provisions and reconnoiter the area east of the Flint River for signs of enemy activity. The withdrawal of the little garrison from Fort Hughes two weeks earlier had left the army blind as to the activities of Neamathla and his supporters.

The total strength of the force selected for the raid was 23 sergeants, 73 corporals and 304 privates. A number of lieutenants, captains and other officers also took part and Lt. Col. Arbuckle led the movement in person. The size of the force was roughly the same size of one that had assembled three days earlier for a planned march to help Maj. Peter Muhlenberg reach Fort Scott, but the major's flotilla arrived before the troops could head out.[1]

The troops were assembled and equipped on New Year's Day but did not march until early on the 4th:

[I] crossed the Flint River about fourteen miles above this post and proceeded to Fowl Town, which had been deserted. I burnt it, and on the next day arrived at Attapulgis a small town about fourteen miles south east of this post, it had also been abandoned, and the cattle and stock of every kind removed, as had been the case at Foul Town. I am informed they have gone to or beyond the Oaklocny River, there to place their women and property in greater security, and better prepare themselves for war. They continue to have considerable intercourse with the Indians on the Chatahooche, many of whom were with them and assisted in the destruction of Lieut. Scott and his party, and in the attack on our vessels ascending the river under the command of Brevt. Major Muhlenberg.[2]

No opposition was encountered during the expedition and no supplies were found, but it still provided worthwhile intelligence on the situation in the wilderness across the Flint. The destruction of Fowltown finally accomplished the removal of that town from the Fort Jackson treaty lands that Gen. Gaines had envisioned six weeks earlier when he first sent U.S. troops to capture Neamathla. Attapulgus was targeted because its warriors had gone to support their friends at Fowltown following the first attack on that place.

The failure of the raid to locate beef and corn led Arbuckle to inform Maj. Gen. Jackson that his situation was becoming extremely serious:

No provisions has yet reached us. We are now on half rations & have but a few days supply at that rate without a prospect of receiving any more soon.

The contractor's agent left here some time since for Fort Gaines for the purpose of procuring cattle, I have not heard how he has succeeded & fearing that he may not be able to furnish a supply in time, I have ordered Captain Birch with a party of men to repair to Fort Gaines, with a view of collecting cattle or assisting the contractor's agent, in bringing in what he may have collected.[3]

Secretary Calhoun's orders for Jackson to proceed to the frontier reached Nashville not long after Arbuckle returned from Fowltown and Attapulgus. In a circular published to a number of state officers, he announced his plans to march without delay:

> The Seminole Indians have raised the war hatchet. They have stained our land with the blood of our Citizens; their war spirit must be put down; and they taught to know that their safety depends upon the friendship and protection of the U States. To accomplish this the aid of one Regiment of mounted Gun men, of one thousand strong, completely armed and equipped, and to serve during the Campaign is asked from West Tennessee: can you raise them and be ready for the Field in ten days?[4]

As the hero of New Orleans was preparing to take the field, conditions continued to worsen at Fort Scott. Warning that his force was "much too small to advance against the enemy," Lt. Col. Arbuckle told Jackson that he had not heard a word from the Georgia Militia or McIntosh's Creeks since Gen. Gaines left the fort in early December. He had only two days' rations of meat left, although his flour stocks were sufficient for 30-days:

> ...[S]hould Capt. Birch who is now at Fort Gaines, with a command of one hundred and twenty men, for the purpose of obtaining beef, not succeed, and the contractors agents persist in neglecting their duty much longer, the consequences must be greatly disastrous to the Troops and Inhabitants of the Chattehooche.[5]

Arbuckle informed Jackson that he had sent Capt. Alex Cummings to Apalachicola Bay to see if any ships had arrived there with provisions. He promised to do all he could to hold his position at Fort Scott, but expressed fear that "my best exertions will fail."[6]

Cummings reached Apalachicola Bay on January 14, 1818, but not without considerable resistance from warriors still positioned along the river:

> About one o'clock of the day we left you we passed the Ochesee town, a little below which we were fired on: a ball passed through our bulwarks, but fortunately did no other injury. We passed Hambly's a little after dark, where the Indians have collected in considerable force, & where we exchanged a number of shot with them without receiving any injury.
>
> At Stefanulga Bluff, about eight miles below Hambly's, we were again attacked and had (for a little time) a very sharp firing, a ball passed through the bulwarks of the keel boat and wounded the Srgt. (slightly) but did not other injury.
>
> On the morning of the 12th we were again attacked at a low Bluff, but we passed so rapidly that we recd. no injury the enemy not being able to load and fire a second time.[7]

Cummings found Lt. Christian waiting for him at Apalachicola Bay aboard a schooner from Mobile. Unfortunately, the vessel carried only 42 barrels, of which no more than six or seven were filled with salted pork. He did not believe the supply would be even sufficient for the crew of the ship if it tried to ascend the river. The river was running high and he questioned whether his men would be able to row the keelboat back upstream:

> I shall make the attempt to move up tomorrow and will be glad to hear from you at the Negro Fort. From the time we leave this place our difficulties will increase hourly, and I am really apprehensive that with all our exertions we shall not be able to ascend much higher.[8]

The captain asked Arbuckle to send down medical officers and soldiers experienced in the use of artillery. Although Lt. Christian's schooner did not bring much food, it was loaded with 200-300 axes, other tools and extra clothing for the men of the 4th and 7th Infantries. The lieutenant reported that two other ships loaded with provisions had sailed 10 days ahead of him, but no sign had been seen of them at Apalachicola Bay. Since they had no escort troops aboard, they would be forced to wait in the bay until men could come down river – assuming, of course, that they arrived at all.[9]

The message from the mouth of the Apalachicola reached Fort Scott, probably by Indian courier, on the 18th. Arbuckle received intelligence on the same day that the Red Sticks and Seminoles were preparing for a major campaign. He urged Brig. Gen. Thomas Glasscock of the Georgia Militia to undertake extraordinary measures to send supplies downriver to supply his garrison:

> I have received information this evening which I have no doubt may be relied on, that the whole or the greater portion of the hostile Indians are to have a meeting some where near the mouth of Flint River the 21st inst. for the purpose of concerting measures for the destruction of the inhabitants on the Chattahochie and the reduction of this post. In the latter object, they expect to succeed, owing to our want of supplies, and their calculations are not without a reasonable prospect of success, should not uncommon exertions be made to supply us from your quarter, as this command has been without meat at this time for five or six days, and have barely a hope of receiving a temporary supply by a command sent to Fort Gaines for the purpose of collecting a few beef cattle.[10]

It was at this point of desperation that Maj. Gen. Edmund P. Gaines suddenly reappeared on the scene. The U.S. occupation of Amelia Island having taken place with little difficulty, Gaines was back at Hartford, Georgia, by January 19th. He immediately sent orders for contractor Benjamin G. Orr to provide for the immediate issue of 2,000 rations per day at the "new Fort now building on Flint River near the Chehaw Village." The reference was to Fort Early. The contractor was further required to have 60,000 complete rations in store at that post within 30 days, the majority to consist of "good pickled pork or bacon."[11]

The general also notified Gen. Jackson that due to the failure of the contractor's agent to supply necessary provisions to that point, he had ordered the immediate purchase of 40,000 rations, the meat portion of which was to be delivered to Hartford within four days. One half of the meat would be driven out on foot immediately under escort for Fort Early, while the balance would be slaughtered and salted at Harford. All of the meat was pork and the purchase price was eleven cents per pound.[12]

In Nashville, meanwhile, Andrew Jackson announced plans to march for Georgia on January 22nd. He informed Gen. Gaines that two regiments of mounted Tennessee volunteers would assemble at Fayetteville, Tennessee, on the 31st and march immediately for Fort Scott by way of Fort Jackson. Maj. A.C.W. Fanning had been sent to Fort Hawkins with orders to purchase the necessary supplies of forage and provisions for the Tennesseans:

> ...I most particularly enjoin upon you not to hazard a general engagement with the Seminoles unless with such force as will ensure a decisive victory. The lives of our citizens are too precious to be wantonly exposed in an unequal conflict with Savages. You will therefore have your Forces prepared to march at a moments warning. As soon as reinforced by the Tennessee Volunteers, our strength will be sufficient to inflict, and speedily, merited chastisement on the deluded Savages – Let your supplies be abundant; I would not wish my movements retarded an hour on that account – If there is the least suspicion of the contractors failing, issue the necessary orders to the Qr Master to supply all deficiencies.[13]

General Jackson reached Huntsville in the newly established Alabama Territory on the night of January 26, 1818, and reported to Secretary of War Calhoun that the Tennessee Volunteers would follow. In Georgia, Maj. Gen. Gaines learned to his dismay that flour being stored at the Creek Agency on the Flint River for use by the troops had been issued to Creek volunteers. He informed Col. David Brearley that he was to make no further such issues until the regular soldiers of the army had been supplied. He further reported that the pork he had hoped to receive had been delayed:

The pork mentioned in my last will not be delivered in the time promised. I shall however order some beef cattle to the Militia Fort to be sent with your first boats to Fort Scott, where I fear the meat part of the ration is much wanted. Send them, I pray you, as much as possible from the Agency. [Lt.] Keiser is ordered to send out all that can be procured at Fort Hawkins.[14]

The movement of troops and supplies to Fort Scott was now accelerating and the presence of Gen. Gaines at Hartford allowed him to exert the pressure of his rank on the supply officers and contractors. In Florida, the warriors were also preparing for a resumption of the conflict. Alexander Arbuthnot wrote to Lt. Col. Edward Nicolls in England on the 30th from his store on the Suwannee:

When I last took the liberty of writing to you, by the desire of the chiefs of the Creek nation, I little expected that war would so soon have commenced between the Americans and them. It is, however, actually begun, by the wanton aggressions of the former, in an attack on Fowl Town, during the night. Though this wanton attack has been disavowed by General Mitchell, the American agent for Indian affairs, and he has made reparation for the injury and loss sustained by Inhimathlo and his people, yet the continued aggression of the Americans, and the numbers pouring into the nation, not from the land side alone, but from Mobile and elsewhere, by the Appalachicola river, have compelled the Indians to take arms as their only resource from oppression.[15]

"Your friend Hillis Hadjo has been called by his people to put himself at their head," Arbuthnot continued, "and he is now encamped at Spanish Bluff, the residence of Doyle and Hambly." The strength of the Prophet's force was estimated at 1,000-1,200 men, most of them Red Sticks. A few hundred Seminoles, he reported, had also joined the fight.[16]

General Jackson was at Fort Hawkins by February 10th, writing to Gov. William Rabun of Georgia to urge that he use what influence he could with the press to encourage respect for operational security:

> ...It has caused me much pain to discover the publicity which has been given by the Journalists of this State to all communications from the Army - & I have to request that you will make use of your influence to check for a time this general practice – You will readily perceive the propriety of my request – Whatever is to be effected against the Seminoles must be done secretely & expeditiously; They doubtless have their emissaries among us, & if all our movements and intentions are made public, we are ourselves defeating the very objects we wish to effect – Surely our citizens can restrain their curiosity, or are willing to remain ignorant for a time of facts, when necessary for the general good.[17]

Jackson did not order a muzzling of the Georgia press and the reaction of the state's newspaper editors to his request is not known. His movements would soon quickly outpace the printing presses anyway and from mid-February until the end of the war Jackson was well ahead of the publication of news about his campaign.

The general reached Hartford on February 12th and found Maj. Gen. Gaines waiting there for him. He reported to Secretary Calhoun that the contractors had utterly failed in their mission to deliver supplies for his army or the troops at Fort Scott. Never the less, he planned to make a "prompt & speedy march for the relief of Fort Scott." His only hope, he reported, was to continue to move forward in expectation of meeting provisions that had been ordered to the Apalachicola River by way of the Gulf of Mexico:

> ...The plan which has been adopted to procure the necessary supplies for the Army, to transport them to Fort Scott, & the quantity otherwise ordered to that point, will I hope relieve me from any embarrassment on that account, until a decisive blow has been struck upon the enemy. I have been so frequently embarrassed from the failures of

Contractors that I cannot but express a hope that some other
more efficient & certain mode of supplying our Army may
be adopted – Such a Plan as will render those charged with
the execution of so important a trust responsible to military
authorities, & exposed to severe & merited chastisement,
whenever defaulters, at the discretion of a Court Martial.[18]

The general also informed Calhoun of a litany of allegations that had
been made about the new Indian Agent, former Governor David B. Mitchell.
The Creeks were complaining that Mitchell had withheld $85,000
appropriated by Congress to indemnify them for losses experienced at the
hands of the Red Sticks. Of greater concern, though, were complaints that
the agent was involved in smuggling slaves from Spanish Florida into the
United States and for this reason had prevented McIntosh's warriors from
marching to the support of Fort Scott:

> …It is alledged in the first instance that he has used his
> influence in preventing the Creek Indians from joining
> General Gaines; That he was induced to this act to assist
> himself & others in smuggling into this country a large
> number of Affrican Negroes which they had purchased at
> Amelia Island; that upwards of one hundred have been
> carried to the Agency, part of which have been seized by
> the officer of the Customs, but that a large number have by
> the Agents written passport been carried to some point
> unknown. That thirty were transported from the Agency On
> the day the custom house officer arrived there & I am this
> day informed that upwards of one hundred Affrican
> Negroes, some time since, passed Mr. Barnets on the Flint
> river bound to the Agency.[19]

Col. Brearley informed Jackson that he had seen not only some of the
slaves in question, but a passport from Mitchell allowing for their movement
through the Creek Nation.
Col. A.P. Hayne led 1,100 mounted Tennessee Volunteers across the
Tennessee River on the same day (February 14, 1818) to begin their march
to Fort Mitchell. They had left Nashville with 220 days of provisions, more

than enough to make a planned rendezvous with Jackson at Fort Scott, but the food would give out faster than the men could move.[20]

Lt. Col. Arbuckle at Fort Scott was unaware of the speed with which Jackson was approaching his post. His food stocks were almost exhausted and on the 15th he penned a letter to Maj. Gen. Gaines that would earn for him the eternal enmity of Andrew Jackson's officers:

> Your express has brought me such information as to alarm me much for the safety of Fort Gaines. He states that about forty miles above this he discovered where at least two hundred Indians had passed in that direction, about three or four days since, and it is unfortunate that we have at this time but twelve or fourteen men at that Post.
>
> If supplies do not arrive here in eight days or there is a certainty by that time of their arriving within a few days after, I shall be compelled to abandon this post with perhaps the whole force, and if Fort Gaines has fallen, that will probably not be the only disaster in this quarter, as the reduction of that Post will much more increase the force of the enemy. Should I be compelled to leave this, I shall march on the west bank of the Flint and endeavor to make Fort Early.[21]

The dispatch reached Gen. Gaines near Hartford on February 20th and he immediately shared it with Gen. Jackson. The latter officer had held his possession on the Coosa River during the Creek War under even more difficult circumstances and the idea of an American officer abandoning his post in the fact of the enemy ignited an explosion of Jacksonian proportions. Subordinates of the general would heckle Arbuckle over his threat to flee the Flint River for years to come.

To prevent the catastrophe that likely would follow an evacuation of Fort Scott, Gen. Gaines headed for Fort Early. There, with Jackson's approval, he boarded a supply boat manned by only 12 men on the afternoon of the 22nd and started down the Flint River. His goal was to reach Fort Scott before Arbuckle could abandon the post and time was of the essence. The date given by the lieutenant colonel for leaving the fort was February 23rd so Gaines moved day and night down the rocky and twisting river.

The rapid voyage downstream under high water conditions was an invitation for disaster. The general's boat is thought to have been near today's Daugherty-Mitchell County line about 12 miles south of Albany when it slammed into a rock on the night of the 23rd. The boat sank in high water, taking eight barrels of meat and other supplies to the bottom. Gen. Gaines was saved by an interpreter and reached the west bank of the river. Four other soldiers made it to the same side but at different points than the general, who now found himself alone in the wilderness wearing nothing but his shirt and pantaloons. The weather had turned severely cold with ice in the creeks and ponds and even accumulations of snow reported. Major John Nicks reached the opposite side of the river with three soldiers and the general's private servant. Two other men – one of them Gaines' longtime aide-de-camp Maj. Clinton Wright – drowned. The presumed site of the disaster is known today as Deadman's Island.[22]

A freezing cold wilderness in the midst of a war with Creek and Seminole warriors was no place for any of the survivors to be, especially a major general. Maj. Nicks and the three men with him started down the east side of the river for Fort Scott on their own. The other three men on the west bank apparently did the same. Gen. Gaines sent the interpreter to Fort Scott for help after pointing out a place where he would wait for the arrival of rescuers. Not long after the departure of his courier, however, he decided to attempt a cross-country journey to Fort Gaines on his own.[23]

The courier reached Fort Scott in safety and soon led a company under Capt. Allison back to the point where Gaines had promised to wait. The men found no sign of the general other than a note written in pencil explaining that he had decided to make for Fort Gaines. Allison set out in that direction as well and soon found the spot where Gen. Gaines had crossed Chickasawhatchee Creek. He lost the trail after that point, however, and returned to Fort Scott after detaching a portion of his force under Capt. Bee with orders to proceed to Fort Gaines. He did succeed in rescuing three other victims of the wreck.[24]

Maj. Nicks and his small party reached Fort Scott on February 28th as the search continued for any trace of the missing general. Captain Bee reached Fort Gaines on March 1st without finding him. Gen. Gaines had changed his mind about reaching that post, however, and instead headed in the general direction of Jackson's army. Likely he stumbled across the trail that Jackson expected to follow on his way down to Fort Scott. He finally stumbled into the head of Jackson's command on March 4th, suffering severely from exposure and hunger but otherwise unharmed.[25]

Jackson began his final advance to Fort Scott during the time that Gaines was wandering lost in the wilderness and feared dead. The best known account of the march is from the diary of John Banks, a lieutenant in Captain John Mann's company of Georgia Militia. He described it as a miserable time of torrential rain, severe cold, snow, ice and roads so miserable that the army had to abandon its baggage wagons. It took his company eight days to march from Hartford to Fort Early, a distance of only 45 miles. The men ran completely out of flour and lived on nothing but pork and kernels of corn for two weeks.[26]

Banks reported that his company left Fort Early for Fort Scott on Saturday, February 28, 1818, and crossed the Flint River four miles below the former post. The men then advanced on to the Creek village of Chehaw from which they began their southbound movement to Fort Scott. Snow, ice, mud and severe cold continued to impede their movements, as did hunger. The people at Chehaw and the nearby town of Jack Kinnard supplied what food they could but the amounts they could provide was limited. Many of the warriors of these towns joined the army as it passed.[27]

As the troops marched south, Lt. R.M. Sands of the 4th Infantry reached Apalachicola Bay aboard the sloop *Phebe Ann*. He took aboard the cargo of the schooner *Perdido* and reported to Lt. Col. Arbuckle on February 28th that another large sloop had crossed the bar into the bay the previous day. The supplies on board his vessel included flour, pork, whiskey and vinegar.[28]

Good news also arrived from another direction. Maj. Enos Cutler wrote from Fort Gaines on March 1st that Capt. Burch would leave his post the next morning with additional provisions of beef. He had cleared all of the cattle on the east side of the Chattahoochee that still had the strength to travel to Fort Scott. The flight of settlers from their farms into Fort Gaines had left stock with no one to tend for it and in the severe winter the animals were suffering. Cutler also reported that the long expected Creek warriors under Maj. William McIntosh were finally on their way:

158

Colo. Brearley writes to me that five hundred Indians
are ordered here. They are expected this evening. He directs
me to enroll them and to give them orders. I am this day
driving up cattle on the other side of the river to give them
a little provisions, and shall send them immediately in
pursuit of the Red Ground Chief and Mico de coxe.[29]

There is some confusion over which Red Ground Chief is referred to in
Cutler's report. Most likely he meant Econchattimico ("Red Ground King")
who lived on the west bank of the Chattahoochee just below today's
Alabama line. The leader of the large Creek town of Ekanchatte or "Red
Ground," he had joined the forces at war against the United States and
withdrawn with his people into the swamps of the upper Chipola River in
what is now Jackson County, Florida. The other possibility was a lesser
known Red Stick chief named Holmes. This leader was believed to be
somewhere in the vicinity of the Choctawhatchee River.

The "Mico de coxe" was an old chief of long standing in the
borderlands. He had allied himself with William Augustus Bowles during
the adventurer's second sojourn in Florida.

It took a bit longer for the Creeks to reach Fort Gaines than expected.
Maj. McIntosh was now Brig. Gen. McIntosh. He reported from the "Uche
Old Fields" between today's cities of Eufaula and Phenix City that the
creeks were extremely high which was causing great difficulty for his men.
He had already captured three warriors involved in firing on the boats on
the Apalachicola, one of them wounded, and was carrying them to Fort
Gaines.[30]

Col. A.P. Hayne reached Fort Mitchell with the Tennessee Volunteers
on March 2nd. They found Col. David Brearley in command of the post and
in a state of great alarm about the lack of supplies at Fort Scott. He showed
the colonel letters from the post that contained reports of starvation and
hunger. Unsure of what to do, Hayne wrote to Lt. Col. Arbuckle on the same
day:

I have just arrived at this post with the Brigade of
Tennessee Volunteers & wish to know whether you will
have it your power to feed us, or in other words whether the

contemplated supplies of provisions have arrived from New Orleans.

I shall proceed from this place to Fort Gaines where I shall certainly expect to hear from you by express. Our men will draw from this place ten days rations which is all that can be had.

Our route will by way of Fort Perry along the east bank of the Chattahoochee.

I have seen your letter of the 24th of last month & most seriously lament the suffering of the brave troops under your command.

Pray as not fail to let me know whether you can be able to feed us.[31]

Jackson had previously instructed Hayne and his Tennesseans to proceed to Fort Scott as quickly as possible, but the rumors reaching Fort Mitchell halted them in their tracks. Col. Brearley, unaware that the supply ships expected by Jackson had arrived at Apalachicola, further told Col. Hayne that the expected ships had not been heard from and were feared lost in a storm. Finally deciding not to wait for word to come back up from Fort Scott, Hayne headed east for the settled areas of Georgia in hopes of finding provisions there. The move would infuriate Jackson, who could not understand why the colonel would march away from the direction in which supplies were expected to see provisions in an area that had already been stripped clean by the passing of the Georgia brigade. The Tennesseans would not reach Fort Scott until well after Jackson and Col. Brearley would face a court martial for his role in the confusion.

Lt. Col. Arbuckle, meanwhile, was making arrangements to help bring supplies up the Apalachicola River. Capt. George Vashon was ordered to leave for the bay on the large keel boat built over the winter at Fort Scott. The vessel, which was of sufficient size to carry 300-400 barrels, had been named the *Support* and would remain in use on the Apalachicola for several years to come. Vashon was to make contact with the supply boats and then return with meat, bread, salt, soap and candles. He was not to waste time loading whiskey, then an important part of an army's rations. Arbuckle made clear to Vashon that he was to return with as much food as possible as fast as possible. Thousands of men were converging on Fort Scott and without meat and bread to feed them, a disaster of unimaginable magnitude would take place.[32]

The movement of the supplies did not take place a moment too soon.

[1] Register of Details for Command from Fort Scott, from the 18th of December, 1817, until the 19th of March, 1818, whilst under the command of Lt. Col. Arbuckle, Office of the Adjutant General, Letters Received, 1805-1821.
[2] Lt. Col. Matthew Arbuckle to Maj. Gen. Edmund P. Gaines, January 6, 1818, Adjutant General, Letters Received, NARA.
[3] *Ibid.*
[4] Maj. Gen. Andrew Jackson to Col. R.H. Dyer et. al, January 11, 1818.
[5] Lt. Col. Matthew Arbuckle to Maj. Gen. Andrew Jackson, January 12, 1818, Andrew Jackson Papers, Library of Congress.
[6] *Ibid.*
[7] Capt. Alex Cummings to Lt. Col. Matthew Arbuckle, January 14, 1818, Adjutant General, Letters Received, NARA.
[8] *Ibid.*
[9] *Ibid.*
[10] Lt. Col. Matthew Arbuckle to Brig. Gen. Thomas Glasscock, January 18, 1818, Andrew Jackson Papers, Library of Congress.
[11] Maj. Gen. Edmund P. Gaines to Benjamin G. Orr, Esq., January 19, 1818.
[12] Maj. Gen. Edmund P. Gaines to Maj. Gen. Andrew Jackson, January 19, 1818.
[13] Maj. Gen. Andrew Jackson to Maj. Gen. Edmund P. Gaines, January 20, 1818.
[14] Maj. Gen. Edmund P. Gaines to Col. David Brearly, January 28, 1818.
[15] Alexander Arbuthnot to a person of rank in England (i.e. Edward Nicolls), January 30, 1818, from the London Times of August 7, 1818.
[16] *Ibid.*
[17] Maj. Gen. Andrew Jackson to Gov. William Rabun, February 10, 1818.
[18] Maj. Gen. Andrew Jackson to Hon. John C. Calhoun, February 14, 1818.
[19] *Ibid.*
[20] Annette McDonald Suarez, "The War Path Across Georgia Made By Tennessee Troops in the First Seminole War," *The Georgia Historical Quarterly*, Vol. 38, No. 1, (March 1954), pp. 32.
[21] Lt. Col. Matthew Arbuckle to Maj. Gen. Edmund P. Gaines, February 15, 1818, Adjutant General, Letters Received, NARA.
[22] Mark F. Boyd, "Historic Sites in and around the Jim Woodruff Reservoir Area, Florida-Georgia, River Basin Surveys Papers, No. 13, *Bulletin 169*, Smithsonian Institution, Bureau of American Ethnology, 1958, pp. 245-247.

[23] *Ibid.*

[24] *Ibid.*

[25] *Ibid.*

[26] John Banks, *Diary of John Banks*, 1936.

[27] *Ibid.*

[28] Lt. R.M. Sands to Lt. Col. Mathew Arbuckle, February 28, 1818, Andrew Jackson Papers, Library of Congress.

[29] Maj. E. Cutler to Lt. Col. Matthew Arbuckle, March 1, 1818, Adjutant General, Letters Received, NARA.

[30] Brig. Gen. William McIntosh to Maj. Daniel Hughes, March 2, 1818, Camden Gazette, April 11, 1818, p. 3.

[31] Col. Arthur P. Hayne to Lt. Col. Matthew Arbuckle, March 2, 1818, Andrew Jackson Papers, Library of Congress.

[32] Lt. Col. Matthew Arbuckle to Captain George Vashon, March 3, 1818, Andrew Jackson Papers, Library of Congress.

CHAPTER THIRTEEN

Jackson's Trail to Fort Scott

Andrew Jackson spent a total of three days at Fort Scott but his passage through Southwest Georgia remains the stuff of legends even to this day. Jackson Street, for example, is one of the two streets that intersect at the site of Fort Hughes in Bainbridge. There are other Jackson Streets in Fort Gaines, Columbus and Albany along with a Jackson Avenue in Blakely. The Three Notch Road, which has Jackson connections, runs through Seminole and Miller Counties, while old maps show today's Ten Mile Still Road in Decatur County as the "Jackson Trail." Terrell County has an Andrew Jackson Monument while in Bainbridge a massive stone commemorates the Andrew Jackson Trail. Other communities have trees, roads and campsites where the general supposedly once lingered or passed.

Reconstructing the story of Andrew Jackson's march to Fort Scott is largely made possible through the writings of his officers and men. While his image has suffered a bit in recent years and at this writing there was a serious move underway to remove his image from the $20 bill, there can be no doubt that Andrew Jackson was a tough and determined military commander. Much has been written about his iron-willed determination during the Creek War of 1813-1814 when he kept his army in the field despite provision shortages and threatened desertions. The general's march through Southwest Georgia was some ways even tougher than his Creek War success.

As was noted in the previous chapter, Maj. Gen. Jackson reached Fort Early at the head of a brigade of Georgia Militia on February 26, 1818. The situation there was dismal and Maj. Gen. Gaines had disappeared following his disastrous boat wreck on the Flint. Supplies were all but nonexistent and the weather was miserable. Major Hugh Young, Jackson's topographical engineer, gave an excellent description of the problems offered by building roads around Fort Early:

> …Fort Early is situated on the east side of Flint river, on a high hill. It is simply a picketed square with two block houses, the water is excellent and the country healthy. – The most singular features of the country between Hartford and Fort Early is the extreme rottenness of the soil during the winter months. This character extends even to the top of the hills, and frequently when the surface is perfectly dry and seemingly hard a wagon will sink to the body…When the rainy months commence the falling water easily penetrates the surface but is stopped at the depth of a few feet by a bed of clay on which it remains pervading and swelling the sandy soil above and giving it that spongy penetrable character so destructive of the roads.[1]

While Young's description borders on the scientific, the conditions made life nothing short of miserable for the soldiers in Jackson's column. Lt. John Banks of the Georgia Militia left a vivid account of the march from Hartford to Fort Early:

> …It rained nearly all the time, the waters were very high, we had to build some bridges and flats to cross the creeks

on. We carried our baggage wagons till we got in ten miles of the fort, found it impracticable to carry them any further. They were dismissed and we took our provisions on our backs, officers and all, and performed the balance of the expedition without a wagon.[2]

On Saturday, February 28th, the growing army marched down the east bank of the Flint River to a crossing point 4.5 miles below Fort Early. Major Young described the terrain as "sand and pine." The pathway followed by the general crossed a "creek with sandy banks" roughly two miles south of the fort and then a "small thicket branch" one-quarter of a mile further along. The first of these was Swift Creek, now much larger than in 1818 due to the construction of the Warwick Dam and creation of Lake Blackshear in 1925-1930, and the second was Flournoy Branch. The route of the march was along a now vanished trail just west of Georgia Highway 300.

From Flournoy Branch the route of march continued on for another 2.25 miles to the crossing point on the Flint River. Young described the river at the ferry site as 180 yards wide, with a low pine bluff on the east bank and a thicket on the west. From the crossing, he wrote, "the path goes up the river one quarter mile to a place where the open pine woods are near the bank – but separated from it by a bayou with a deep rapid current and a width of twenty yards." It was necessary to cross a bridge across this bayou.[3]

Once across the Flint and this bayou, which may have been running much higher than normal due to the heavy rains reported that winter, the troops followed the old trail down to the Chehaw town on Muckalee Creek. This large village was about eight miles up the creek from its mouth:

> …It consisted of fifteen or twenty cabins with a large council house in the center which on our arrival was decorated with the white flag. The creek at the town is eighty-five feet wide with a swamp on the west side one-quarter of a mile wide and a high open bank on the east. The banks and bottom are firm and sandy. The swamp is not miry except near the highland where for one hundred

165

yards there is a mixture of stiff white clay. It has the usual varieties of bottom growth of Palmetto.[4]

The site of Chehaw is marked by a large stone monument on New York Road just east of U.S. 19 in Lee County, Georgia. Lt. Banks wrote that his company had lost contact with the main army after crossing the Flint River:

> ...On Sunday night, the first of March, we marched till 9 o'clock P.M. We had a rough time of it that night, the rain fell in torrents while it was so dark we could not see to follow the rail. We were endeavoring to overtake the main army which had left us crossing the river. In this, however, we were disappointed, for we could no longer follow their track.[5]

Whether the two forces followed the same trail from the crossing place to Chehaw is not known. The heavy rain obscured everything. The Georgia company caught up with the main body of the army on the next morning:

> On the 2d we overtook the army in Chehaw town. This was an old Indian town in the Creek nation, which tribe refused to join the Seminoles in the war, and as we passed through, most of their warriors joined us. The town is about ten miles from Fort Early. They had a white flag hoisted in a prominent place in the town. We purchased some provisions of them, such as corn, potatoes, ground peas, etc.[6]

"Ground Peas" are known today as peanuts. The army was delayed in Chehaw for a full day as the men built a bridge across Muckalee Creek and Jackson conferred with the town's chief, Major Howard. Banks wrote that he "went about 4 miles to Kenard (an Indian chief) and bought some provisions." Like the Perryman family on the lower Chattahoochee, the Kinnards were an extensive and well-known family in the Creek Nation.

Jack Kinnard was reputedly the wealthiest man in the Nation. There is a bit of disagreement between Young and Banks as to the distance from Chehaw to Kinnard's town. Banks gave the distance as four miles while Young said it was more like 5 ¼ miles.

The army continued its march on the 4th, crossing the new bridge at Chehaw and then fording Kinchafoonee Creek about 3.5 miles downstream from Kinnard's town. The trail being followed by the soldiers took them generally southward between Albany and Dawson, Georgia. Lt. Banks wrote that it snowed on the night of the 3rd and that the march on the 4th was exceedingly miserable. "We were constantly wet from wading ponds and creeks," he noted, "and we had ice to encounter in the ponds." The year without a summer was definitely being felt in Southwest Georgia.

The next natural barrier to be crossed was Fowltown Creek, which flows into Muckalee Creek just northwest of Albany. The crossing place was 20 miles up this stream at a point where it flowed within about three miles of the Muckalee:

> Fowl [i.e. Fowltown] Creek is three miles from Canards [sic.] Creek – shallow but wide with a thick undergrowth of evergreens. On the south side are the remains of an ancient and very large town, large trees are growing on innumerable little mounds disposed with some regularity and on which the houses were probably built.[7]

Fowltown Creek is so named because Neamathla's band of Tuttollossees had lived there before relocating down to modern Decatur and Seminole Counties. Although the ancient town described by Maj. Young has sometimes been confused with Neamathla's earlier village, the two were not the same. They were, however, in reasonably close proximity.

It was somewhere during this phase of the march that the hungry and cold Maj. Gen. Edmund P. Gaines stumbled into the vanguard of the army after more than one week alone in the wilderness.

After crossing Fowltown Creek the army angled more to the south-southeast even as the Flint River began its slow curve to the southwest. The solders came down the north (or east) bank of Ichawaynochaway Creek, likely following the present route of Jericho Road to a point around 5 miles upstream from the point where the creek meets the Flint River. Young states that the creek was forded at this point and that the soldiers continued on to Big Cypress Creek. The latter was crossed at a point 4.5 miles from the Ichawaynochaway and less than two miles from the Flint River. It should be noted, however, that Young was not saying that the two creeks were this distance apart, only that the march of the army covered about that many miles.[8]

The 1819 plat of survey for District 12 of the original Early County, Georgia, shows a trail cross today's Big Cypress in the southeast corner of Land Lot 100. The creek was then called "Dry Creek," although Young described it as being about 30-feet wide at the time of the crossing. It is considered an intermittent stream by the U.S. Geological Survey, however, so the old plat identification makes sense. The trail shown on the 1819 plat is almost certainly the one that was followed by the army and a road following the approximate route is still in use today. County Road 47 (Hoggard Mill Road) leads from a crossing on Ichawaynochaway Creek down to a crossing of Big Cypress Creek in the position shown by the 1819 survey. The site is in Baker County today.[9]

The trail used by Jackson's army to reach Fort Scott now becomes much easier to follow. After crossing the Ichawaynochaway and Big Cypress Creeks, the army followed the old Creek Indian trail down the west bank of the Flint through today's Baker and Decatur Counties to the fort:

> ...Struck the river in one and a half mile further the road going down the last creek [i.e. Big Cypress Creek]. From this point the route continues down the river – generally in sight of it to Fort Scott. The country gets more uneven and altho' the soil and timber differ but little from the flatter districts, the ground is much firmer and better adapted to roads. Flint rock is here very abundant – the path intersects

the road from Fort Hughes, nine and a half miles from Fort
Scott.[10]

The District Plat of Survey for District 15 of the original Early County,
Georgia, was completed in 1821 and confirms that the old road down the
west side of the Flint was the path used by the American army. Clem
Powers, who conducted the survey, labeled the path as "Jackson's Trail" on
his plat. Careful comparison with modern roads shows that much of this
section of the route of march is still in use today. Georgia Road 253 follows
the approximate – and in some cases actual – Jackson Trail from just south
of the mouth of Ichawaynochaway Creek to West Bainbridge.[11]

A good example of how the modern highway follows the original trail
can be found by comparing its route as shown on the 1821 plat with today's
Georgia Road 253 in the vicinity of its intersection with Pinehill Road north
of Bainbridge. The two follow virtually the same exact line as they brush
against the west side of the river at the sharp bend just south of Pinehill
Road.

"Jackson's Trail" as shown on the 1821 plat intersected with the "road
from Fort Hughes" in today's West Bainbridge. From this point on, the trail
is labeled "Road to Fort Scott." The same trail used by Maj. David E.
Twiggs during his raid on Fowltown and later by Lt. Col. Matthew Arbuckle
on his way back from the village, this road was well established by the time
Jackson arrived and continues on down the west side of the Flint to the fort.[12]

Maj. Young did not provide great detail on the route from Fort Hughes
to the fort, but it is clear that the army followed the "Road to Fort Scott" in
order to reach the post. This section of the trail can also be followed with
relative ease today. Leaving West Bainbridge it continued along State Road
253, which south of Bainbridge is called "Spring Creek Road." At a point
just west of Little and Big Horseshoe Bends of the Flint River it departed
from Spring Creek Road and continued southwest on today's 10 Mile Still
Road. The route is still in use all the way down to the end of the road where
it meets a canal or "cut" that separates the mainland from Fort Scott Island.[13]

Young described the area of today's Fort Scott Island as "a high flat of
sandy second rate soil." Of the fort itself, he simply noted that it was

"formerly only a cantonment and was afterwards irregularly enclosed by a quadrangular picketing." The nature of the terrain has changed dramatically due to the 1958 completion of the Jim Woodruff Dam and Lake Seminole. Instead of being a high sandy flat or plateau today, the site of the fort is much lower and wetter. A portion of the site has been inundated by Lake Seminole but a significant portion of perhaps 8-9 acres remains above the level of the reservoir. A short section of the old road can be seen at the site, a surviving trace of Jackson's original trail to Fort Scott.[14]

Lt. John Banks of the Georgia militia indicated in his account that the army was joined on March 6, 1818, by around 600 Creek auxiliaries under Majors Billy Lovett and Noble Kinnard. This was part of the Creek Brigade raised under Brig. Gen. William McIntosh to operate in support of Jackson's primary movement. Lovett and Kinnard had been ordered to scour the east side of the Chattahoochee River from Fort Gaines south to root out any Red Stick or Seminole warriors in the area. No enemy contact was reported by tem.[15]

The combined force reached Fort Scott three days later:

> ...On the 9th we reached Fort Scott after dark. We found provisions scarce at the fort, and the army entirely destitute. One the tenth we drew three days' rations of corn and pork, and crossed back on the eastern side of Flint River. We crossed about midnight in a little boat; the river was very high. Here the regular army joined us, being nearly one thousand of them.[16]

Lt. Col. Arbuckle had disappointed Gen. Jackson in other areas, but he was able to provide the important news that supply boats had reached the Apalachicola River and that Capt. George Vashon had been sent down to collect as many provisions as possible and bring them back up the river.

Jackson's own description of his time at Fort Scott is brief. Unfortunately, it is the most detailed account of the future President's visit to the post on the Flint:

At seven o'clock P.M. on the 9th instant, I reached Fort Scott, with the brigade of Georgia militia nine hundred bayonets strong and some of the friendly Creeks who had joined me on my march a few days before, where finding but one quart of corn per man, and a few poor cattle which added to the live pork I brought along, would give us three days' rations of meat, determined me at once to use the small supply to the best advantage. Accordingly, having been advised by Col. Gibson, quartermaster general, that he would sail from New Orleans on the 12th of February with supplies, and being also advised that two sloops with provisions were in the bay, and an officer had been despatched from Fort Scott in a large keel-boat to bring up a part of their loading, and deeming that the preservation of these supplies would be to preserve the army, and enable me to prosecute the campaign, I assumed the command on the morning of the 10th; ordered the live stock slaughtered, and issued to the troops with one quart of corn to each man, and the line of march to be taken up at twelve meridian.[17]

The general added in a letter to his wife that he had not "lost one man by sickness or any other casualty" on the march from Fort Early to Fort Scott and that his troops were all in good health. It took until the morning of the 11th for the army to continue its crossing of the Flint at Fort Scott but the men finally took up their line of march at 9 a.m. and headed south for Florida. Maj. Young noted that the ferry landing was one-quarter mile below the fort and that the current was rapid at the time of the crossing.[18]

From Fort Scott the army marched to the southwest along the high hills that overlook today's Lake Seminole from the community of Recovery, Georgia, down to the city of Chattahoochee, Florida.

Maj. Gen. Andrew Jackson never returned to Fort Scott or Southwest Georgia and his two night stay at the fort was the longest sojourn of his march through the region. The route described above is the only "real" Jackson Trail in Southwest Georgia, although other roads associated today with the general were used by troops of the U.S. Army during the First Seminole War. A good example is the "Three Notch Road" that leads from Fort Gaines down to Fort Scott. This path, originally called was opened by soldiers of the 4th and 7th Infantry regiments in 1817 to connect the two forts. It remained in use by the military until both posts were evacuated in 1821.

---

[1] Maj.. Hugh Young, "A Topographical Memoir of East and West Florida with Itineraries," 1819, Records of Reports, July 3, 1812-October 4, 1823, pp. 292-336, Records of the Chief of Engineers.

[2] John Banks, *Diary of John Banks*, 1936.

[3] Maj. Hugh Young, "A Topographical Memoir."

[4] *Ibid.*

[5] John Banks, *Diary of John Banks*, 1936.

[6] *Ibid.*

[7] Maj. Hugh Young "A Topographical Memoir."

[8] *Ibid.*

[9] *Ibid.*; District Plat of Survey for District 12, Early County (now Baker County), Georgia, 1819, State Archives of Georgia; Topographic Map for Hopeful, Georgia, U.S. Geological Survey, Washington, D.C., 1971.

[10] Maj. Hugh Young, "A Topographical Memoir."

[11] *Ibid.*; District Plat of Survey for District 14, Early County (now Decatur County), Georgia, 1821, State Archives of Georgia.

[12] *Ibid.*

[13] *Ibid.*

[14] Maj. Hugh Young, "A Topographical Memoir."

[15] John Banks, *Diary of John Banks*, 1936.

[16] *Ibid.*

[17] Maj. Gen. Andrew Jackson to Hon. John C. Calhoun, Secretary of War, March 25, 1818, American State Papers, Military Affairs, Volume I, pp. 698-699.

[18] *Ibid.*; Maj. Gen. Andrew Jackson to Rachel Jackson, March 26, 1818, Jackson Papers, Library of Congress; Maj. Hugh Young, "A Topographical Memoir."

CHAPTER FOURTEEN

Fort Scott and the Florida Invasion

Andrew Jackson's departure from Fort Scott marked a dramatic change in the role of the post. In one single day the fort was transformed from its previous significance as the southernmost U.S. defensive post on the Florida frontier to its new role as the supply and logistics base for operations during the First Seminole War.

Fort Scott was left with few men and few supplies after Jackson swept through on March 9-11, 1818. The main bodies of the 4th and 7th Infantry regiments joined the march into Florida, as did the men of the 4th Artillery with their field guns. Captain John N. McIntosh, the former commander of Fort Hughes, was left behind with a small detachment to hold the fort. The captain quickly assumed a communications role, assuring that dispatches arriving at Fort Scott made their way forward to Jackson in Florida. On March 14th, for example, he reported that two expresses had reached the fort with dispatches for the general. These had been sent forward with an escort of Creek warriors. McIntosh also reported that a boat with sale and 180 barrels of corn was expected that day at the confluence of the Chattahoochee and Flint Rivers. A large herd of swine was also on the way down from Fort Gaines under the protection of another large detachment of Creeks. There were also still signs of enemy activity in the vicinity:

> ...The second day after your departure large fires were discovered some distance up the river but on the opposite shore. Yesterday a number of guns, say 20 & some whooping were heard by the detachment of Indians who arrived from Fort early, one hundred & forty strong, in addition to that force I have added forty Indians from the detachment left at this post & intend crossing them where the troops crossed the river with orders to reconnoiter as far up the river as Fort Hughes which I hope will meet your approbation.[1]

After leaving Fort Scott, Jackson had pushed down the Apalachicola River. His line of march took him through the modern city of Chattahoochee and across Mosquito Creek near present-day River Junction. From there he followed the high hills of Gadsden and Liberty Counties south to Alum Bluff. This remarkable bluff is now part of the Nature Conservancy's Apalachicola Bluffs and Ravines Preserve and is the tallest exposed section of the earth's crust in Florida. The view from the top is phenomenal and the army's advance scouts could see the supply boat coming upstream. The army halted and the men ate their first full meal in weeks. The general then pushed on down the river to Prospect Bluff where he instructed his engineer, Capt. James Gadsden, to build a new fort. Jackson was pleased with the project and named the post Fort Gadsden.

A second large force, meanwhile, was moving down the west side of the Chattahoochee River under the brigadier general and Coweta chief William McIntosh. His command included some 900 warriors and his immediate objective was the Red Ground chief. McIntosh learned from spies that Econchattimico had moved his people from their town on the Chattahoochee to the swamps on the upper Chipola River in what is now Jackson County, Florida. He was trying to protect the women and children of his town, as well as his vast herds of cattle and horses:

...I went down the creek Chaubellee [i.e. Chipola] the 12th day of March, about ten miles above the camp of Chunchattee Micco or Red Ground Chief, and the creek swamp was so bad we could not pass it for the high waters; my men had to leave their clothes and provisions, and swim better than one half of the swamp, about six miles wide; we marched within about two miles of his station, and the next morning we surrounded his place, but he was gone and we could not follow him till we could get some provisions we had left behind us; and Maj. [Samuel] Hawkins followed him and overtook his party, and he got away from us with about 30 men. We have taken 53 men, and about 180 women and children prisoners, without the fire of a gun; and we killed ten men that broke to try to make their escape. I have not lost one man since I left Fort Mitchell.[2]

The encounter between McIntosh and Econchattimico took place in the vicinity of today's Bellamy Bridge Heritage Trail north of Marianna. The detachment under Maj. Hawkins caught up with the chief again in the area of Florida Caverns State Park, an indication that the escaping warriors were heading for the Natural Bridge of the Chipola River so they could drive their remaining cattle to safety. A second skirmish took place there. Hawkins and his men captured most of Econchattimico's cattle, but the chief and his retinue of warriors once again escaped.[3]

His raid down the upper Chipola complete, McIntosh turned his command for Fort Scott.

The movement of supplies down the Flint River from Fort Lawrence at the Creek Agency to Fort Scott remained a difficult enterprise, even after Jackson's army had pushed into Florida:

The communication with Fort Scott has become so dangerous, that the boats which descend the river from fort Lawrence, are compelled to construct bulwarks of plank higher than the heads of the men, to protect them from the fire of the enemy. Even this precaution has been nearly rendered useless by the ingenuity of the savages – for finding they can make no impression upon the bulwark, they direct their fire against the oars of the boat, with such certainty, that they soon destroy them, and if sufficient changes of oars have not been provided, the boat is in danger of being wrecked by a sawyer, or of falling into the hands of the enemy.[4]

That supply boats could make it from as far upriver as Fort Lawrence is quite remarkable. The paddlewheel steamboats of rarely ventured farther upriver than Albany and even then only during high water.

Col. A.P. Hayne and his mounted Tennessee Volunteers showed up on the frontiers of Georgia even as Jackson was driving his main army south down the Apalachicola River. Still searching for supplies, Hayne divided his force on March 13th, two days after Jackson left Fort Scott, sending the main body to Fort Hawkins while he took a smaller group of 350 men to Hartford. He expected to move from there to Fort Early and down to Fort Scott.[5]

At Fort Scott on the 15th, meanwhile, Capt. McIntosh found himself in the embarrassing situation of having to report that three captured African Americans had escaped from the post:

> I...regret extreamly the necessity I am under of informing you of the Escape of the negroes Joe, Charles & John last night, from a competent guard to have kept them in perfect security, they were all in front & I had used every precaution that was in my power to keep them secure. We were however left destitute of a Guard House or place to confine the prisoners in. I had therefore commenced & nearly completed one when they made their escape.
>
> In consequence of nearly every man of the Regulars capable of performing duty having marched from this Post & having not others but sick Militia I had further found it difficult to mount a sufficient guard; at least such a one as I should have mounted for the security & protection of the Garrison to which cause I must measureably attribute the escape of the negroes.[6]

Little is known about the capture of these prisoners or their fates following the escape. McIntosh also informed Jackson that he would forward a letter to Col. Hayne by express, but feared that the Tennessee troops "contrary to your expectations" was either at Fort Hawkins or Hartford.[7]

The captain wrote to the general again on the following day, reporting the arrival of Col. Homer V. Milton from Fort Early with 40 Georgia Militia, 40 barrels of flour, 50 bushels of corn, 700-800 pounds of salt pork and four bushels of salt. Milton and Jackson had known each other well during the Creek War of 1813-1814 when the former was still in the U.S. Army. He had returned to civil life after that conflict but was now serving with the Georgia Militia to help support the regular army in its campaign against the Red Sticks and Seminoles.[8]

McIntosh also noted that a detachment of Creek warriors sent from Fort Scott to reconnoiter around Fort Hughes had returned without detecting any signs of the enemy. Another force of Creeks, led by the Yuchi warrior Timpoochee Barnard, had passed through Fort Scott on its way to join forces with Jackson's army in Florida.[9]

A rather interesting report of the voyage necessary to supply Fort Scott by water was written at the post on March 17th by an officer with the Georgia Miltiia, possibly Col. Milton himself or one of his staff. He reported the distance from Fort Early down seemed to be 250 miles by water:

> ...The first two days run from Fort Early we had a very narrow river, rapid current, numerous small islands, abrupt windings, and on the whole rather dangerous navigation – The third day the river became wider, the current more gentle, the lowlands, which before had been very narrow and poor, more extensive and fertile, and the country began to appear desirable. For about thirty miles by land above this, the navigation will be tolerably good for small keel boats, but above that, it can never be made good – It may possibly be as good as the Oconee, to Milledgeville, as high up as the Agency; but the land on it will never afford anything like a respectable settlement. Between the agency and Thirty Mile Creek, (30 miles above this place) from

there to the mouth the low grounds are good: and below here, between this and the mouth of the Appalachicola, is some of the finest country in the United States, but the advantages of navigation are not equal to those of Tombigby and Alabama.[10]

The unidentified officer also gave a brief description of Fort Scott itself. Unfortunately, it reveals little about the appearance of the fort after the completion of the 1817 rebuilding project:

This Fort is situated upon a Bluff, on the western side of Flint River, 12 miles above its confluence with Chatahoochie, & has complete command of the river, with strong defences; but from the hostility of the Indians, and the Spaniards having in possession the mouth of the river it will be many years before the lands can be rendered valuable.[11]

The officer had no way of knowing, of course, but Florida would become a U.S. Territory in only three years. The settlement of Southwest Georgia then took place at a pace he could not have imagined.

Col. Arthur P. Hayne reached Hartford, Georgia, where on the 19th he received a letter from Maj. Gadsden, who was functioning as Jackson's Aid-de-Camp. Gadsden told him that the expected supply ships had arrived in Apalachicola Bay and that Gen. Jackson had met them on his way down the river. Realizing now that he had disappointed the general, Hayne ordered both wings of his command to march for Fort Scott, but fell ill with the measles before he could march. Col. Thomas Williams and Lt. Col. George Elliott took command of the 350 men at Hartford and marched with them to Fort Early. The men at Fort Hawkins, meanwhile, turned back west on the Federal Road to Fort Perry from which moved south and cut a new road through the Creek Nation to Fort Gaines. This wing of the Tennessee force was led by Col. Robert H. Dyer and Lt. Col. John H. Gibson.[12]

At Fort Scott, Capt. McIntosh reported to Gen. Jackson on the 19th of March that he was making arrangements to move heavy cannon from Fort Scott downstream to Fort Gadsden. The flatboats, he warned, were not designed for carrying such weight and likely would not move at night. Colonels King, Brearley and Brock would go on the boats with one company of Georgia Militia to escort the cannon and other supplies.[13]

The captain also noted the arrival at Fort Scott on March 17th of Maj. Minton with 180 men and 40 head of "poor beef cattle" and 57 head of hogs. He promised to send forward 40 head of cattle and 50 head of hogs under a guard of 60 men. He also promised to ship out 20 barrels of flower and half of the corn at the fort by water the next morning.[14]

Andrew Jackson was still at Fort Gadsden on the Apalachicola on March 25 when President James Monroe addressed the U.S. House of Representatives on the subject of the war:

> ...[T]he Hostilities of this Tribe were unprovoked, the offspring of a spirit long cherished, and often manifested towards The United States, and that in the present instance, it was extending itself to other Tribes, and daily assuming a more serious aspect. As soon as the nature and object of this combination were perceived, the Major-General commanding the Southern Division of the Troops of The United States, was ordered to the theatre of action, charged with the management of the War, and vested with the powers necessary to give it effect. The season of the year being unfavorable to active operations, and the recesses of the country affording shelter to these Savages, in case of retreat, may prevent a prompt termination of the War; but it may be fairly presumed that it will not be long before this Tribe, and its associates, receive the punishment which they have provoked and justly merit.
>
> As almost the whole of this Tribe inhabits the Country within the limits of Florida, Spain was bound, by the Treaty of 1795, to restrain them from committing hostilities against The United States. We have seen with regret, that her Government has altogether failed to fulfill this obligation, nor are we aware that it made any effort to that effect. When we consider her utter inability to check, even in the slightest degree, the movements of this Tribe, by her

very small and incompetent Force in Florida, we are not disposed to ascribe the failure to any other cause. The inability, however, of Spain, to maintain her authority over the Territory, and the Indians within her Limits, and in consequence to fulfill the Treaty, ought not to expose The United States to other and greater injuries. When the authority of Spain ceases to exist there, The United States have a right to pursue their Enemy, on a principal of self-defence.[15]

Monroe's message provides a good summary of the position of the United States government on the outbreak of the First Seminole War. Although he grouped the Seminoles and Red Sticks into a single entity, the President otherwise made very clear why he had approved an invasion of Spanish Florida. Many modern writers and commentators place the blame for this invasion on Jackson's shoulders alone, but Monroe makes clear that the general was following orders when he marched for the frontier.

Capt. McIntosh wrote to Gen. Jackson on the same date, reporting that prisoners of war were beginning to arrive at Fort Scott. Brig. Gen. William McIntosh had arrived there with his Creek Brigade and Capt. McIntosh accepted custody of 20 prisoners of war taken during the Chipola River operation from him. He also reported that the chief John Yellow Hair was on his way with six others. Gen. McIntosh had been furnished with one barrel of powder, 35 pounds of lead, 500 gunflints and 50 muskets along with 12 hogs and one sack of corn. The large Creek force left the fort that morning to meet Jackson in Florida, accompanied by Col. Milton and probably some of his Georgia militiamen.[16]

Jackson, meanwhile, was preparing to leave Fort Gadsden on his final march against the primary Red Stick and Seminole towns. He sent orders for Brig. Gen. McIntosh and his Creeks to join forces with him near Tallahassee Talofa. In a letter to his wife, Rachel, the general showed his frustration that Col. Hayne and the Tennessee Volunteers were not ready to support him as well:

At Ft Scott I expected to meet the Volunteers from Tennessee, in this I was disappointed, I had caused supplies to be laid in for them at Ft Mitchell and advised them of a supply of corn at Ft Gains. Colo. Hayne recd. my dispatch & the supplies at Ft Mitchel, with my instructions to pass by Ft Gains to Ft Scott, the idea of starvation had spread far & wide, and a panic was every where, he was told by officers of high grade that no supplies could be had at Ft Gains, if he advanced to Ft Scott he would starve, he changed his rout by Georgia, where the frontier has been drained of supplies, and where they will experience great scarcity. I hear the Tennesseens are in the wilderness and I hope will join me to day or tomorrow, But how grating to their feelings – how grating to mine, that those brave men, who have marched so far, should be thrown in the rear by false statements, by men of high grade in the army, whose duty it was to have urged them on to have saved the supplies coming by water & on which the safety of the army & the future progress of the campaign rested, but an enquiry has been entered into, which will bring to light those who have been & are to blame for our scarcity and the change of rout by Colo. Hayne – was the Tennesseens up, I, under present circumstances, would be contented.[17]

Much of the general's anger over Hayne's failure to arrive at Fort Scott when expected was directed at Col. David Brearley who had been in command at Fort Mitchell when the Tennesseans arrived there. Brearly was charged with unmilitary conduct at Jackson's instance, but the military court declined to try him on the grounds that the colonel had been asked for his advice by Hayne and that giving advice was not a military crime.

Capt. McIntosh reported from Fort Scott on March 26 that he then had 66 hogs, 130 bushels of corn, 300 pounds of salt pork, two barrels of salt and four barrels of flour in stock. He was daily issuing 400 rations, plus occasional additional issues for detachments, express riders and Creek warriors who were "daily passing and repassing this post." Brig. Gen. McIntosh, he indicated, was still camped on the opposite side of the Flint from Fort Scott and likely would be requisitioning more supplies soon. "I have however informed him of the scarcity," Capt. McIntosh continued, "& advised him to be frugal of that which he has in hand."[18]

The captain was able to report by the next day that the Tennessee Volunteers had finally started to arrive at Fort Scott. Lt. Col. George Elliott passed through the post on the 26th with the lead elements of the mounted force and a second force arrived a short time later. The men with Elliott moved on to meet Jackson in Florida, while the second command joined forces with Brig. Gen. William McIntosh's Creeks on the morning of the 27th. Two companies of Georgia militia under Capt. Pierce also joined the Creek force. Instructions were received from Gen. Jackson on the morning of the 27th for Brig. Gen. McIntosh to march for Ochlocknee Bluff on the river of the same name. Jackson was on the march from Fort Gadsden and would join forces with the Creeks, Georgians and Tennesseans there. Capt. McIntosh gave up as many provisions as possible to help the Creeks and other forces march that the garrison at Fort Scott was reduced to half-rations once again.[19]

Jackson's plan of campaign called for a joint land-sea movement against the warriors in the "Big Bend" region of Florida. Capt. Isaac McKeever of the Navy had sailed on the USS *Thomas Shields* with other vessels to prevent the escape of any enemy warriors by boat and to blockade the mouth of the St. Marks River. The general in turn had marched with his main army for Ochlocknee Bluff where he expected to meet Gen. McIntosh. His route took him in a large curve around the northern fringe of the vast wilderness preserved in today's Apalachicola National Forest. He crossed the Ochlocknee River and on March 31st arrived at Tallahassee Talofa, the first of the major Seminole towns. The people of the town evacuated ahead of the arrival of the troops. The primary town of Miccosukee would become the target on the following day.

At Fort Scott, the total garrison had fallen to only 50 effective men. Maj. Enos Cutler, then at Fort Gadsden, notified Maj. Gen. Gaines on the 31st that this number was wholly insufficient for the defense of the fort on the Flint. He also reported the presence of nearly 30 prisoners of war at Fort Scott and urged the general to have that post reinforced.[20]

Brig. Gen. McIntosh and Lt. Col. Elliott did not join Jackson's army at Ochlocknee Bluff as ordered but did finally make contact with the advancing force on the morning of April 1, 1818. The total force at

Jackson's disposal now numbered more than 4,000 men and he directed them immediately against the Miccosukee.

The Miccosukee town or towns stretched along the west side of Lake Miccosukee on the border between today's Leon and Jefferson Counties in Florida. Led by Cappachimico (Kenhajo), the town was the largest in Florida at the time and the whites credited them with as many as 500 warriors. As Jackson approached, he found a body of warriors waiting for him:

> ...[O]n the same day a mile and a half in advance of the Mekasukian villages, a small party of hostile Indians were discovered, judiciously located on a point of land projecting into an extensive marshy pond; the positio, designated, as since understood, for the concentrating of the negro, and Indian forces to give us battle – They maintained for a short period a spirited attack from my advanced spy companies, but fled and dispersed in every direction upon comming in contact with my flank columns, and discovering a movement to encircle them – The pursuit was continued through the Mekasukian Towns until night compelled me to encamp my army - The next day detachments were sent out in every direction to reconnoitre the country; secure all supplies found; and reduce to ashes the villages. This duty was executed to my satisfaction: nearly Three hundred houses were consumed; and the greatest abundance of corn cattle & c. brought in.[21]

The U.S. destruction of the Miccosukee towns was thorough, but Cappachimico (Kenhajo) and most of his people succeeded in escaping the grasp of the army. The chiefs and warriors in Florida had learned from the devastating losses inflicted on the Red Sticks by Jackson's army during the Creek War of 1813-1814. They did not try to wage full scale battles against the troops as the Red Sticks had done, but instead fought delaying and guerilla actions against Jackson as he advanced. The Battle of Miccosukee was a delaying action that kept the troops at bay long enough for the inhabitants of the towns to evacuate. Gen. Gaines was sent with a force the next day across Lake Miccosukee in pursuit of Cappachimico's people, but failed to come up with them. He did encounter a firefight with Neamathla's Tuttalossees and a party of Black Seminoles.

In Miccosukee itself the soldiers found a red pole (or "red stick") raised in the square ground with more than 50 fresh scalps attached. Many were recognized as having belonged to the soldiers, women and children of Lt. Scott's command. Another pole with 300 old scalps from previous wars was also found in the town.[22]

After completing the destruction of Miccosukee and rounding up as many head of livestock as possible, Jackson turned his army south for the Spanish fort of San Marcos de Apalache at St. Marks, Florida. He had been told that the warriors involved in the war had not only been receiving arms and ammunition from that fort, but also had threatened to take it over if necessary. The Spanish denied the former claim but confirmed that the security of their outpost had indeed been threatened.[23]

As the general continued his operations in Florida, Fort Scott continued to fill its role as a base for supplies. Capt. McIntosh reported on April 6th that a boat had arrived from the Creek Agency via the Flint River with 350-400 bushels of corn and 800-900 pounds of bacon. The vessel was commanded by a Mr. Ellis, one of the Tennessee Volunteers. McIntosh promised to dispatch he vessel to Fort Gadsden the next morning after taking out the bacon and 80-90 bushels of corn for the support of his own garrison.[24]

A second boat commanded by a Tennessee Volunteer named Mr. Cox was supposed to arrive at the same time as Ellis's vessel but had become stuck on a "ledge of rocks" upriver from the site of the earlier disaster involving the boat carrying Gen. Gaines. McIntosh sent a light flatboat upstream in an attempt to salvage the boat and its cargo of corn, salt and hospital stores.[25]

The captain concluded by reporting that he had received no intelligence of enemy warriors in the vicinity of Fort Scott. Some Black Seminoles had been raiding near Jack Kinnard's on Kinchafoonee Creek but no trouble had been reported nearer to the fort than that.[26]

Maj. Gen. Jackson arrived at San Marcos de Apalache on April 7th and demanded the surrender of the fort to his troops by its commander, Francisco Caso y Luengo. The Spanish commandant refused but U.S. troops stormed through his gates and occupied the post before the garrison could man the walls to fire in their own defense. To Jackson's surprise, Alexander Arbuthnot was found inside the fort. He was immediately arrested and placed in confinement. The magnitude of the victory achieved by seizing the fort became even more clear when Capt. McKeever brought his vessels up the river to the fort. He had succeeded in decoying the Prophet Francis and the Red Stick chief Homathlemico aboard and they were now his prisoners. The latter chief was blamed by the Americans for leading the massacre of Scott's command. Jackson ordered both to be summarily executed and his sentence was carried out.

The general was again on the march by April 9th, this time headed for the Suwannee. The fiercest battle of the campaign took place three days later when McIntosh's Creek Brigade located Peter McQueen's Red Sticks in a thick swamp along the Econfina River. Not to be confused with Econfina Creek in western Florida, this stream is a 44-mile long river that flows through Taylor County to Apalachee Bay and the Gulf of Mexico. The site of the engagement was near the natural bridge west of today's city of Perry.

McIntosh and his warriors delivered a hard defeat to McQueen's outnumbered men. The Red Stick chief suffered losses of 37 killed and 44 captured. Thirty-eight of the prisoners were women and children. He also lost 700 head of cattle, a large number of hogs, some horses and most of his supply of corn. McIntosh reported a loss to his own force of 3 killed and 5 wounded.[27]

Neither McIntosh nor Jackson had any reason to have known it, but they briefly held in their hands an individual who would help lead the Seminoles in their next war against the United States. Among the women and children taken at the Battle of Econfina was the young Billy Powell, a nephew of Peter McQueen. He would later rise to prominence as the Black Drink Crier among the Alachua Seminole and it was from this role that he received his title of Asi Yahola. Whites corrupted this to Osceola and it is by this name that he is remembered today.[28]

Another individual of note was also found on the battlefield. Elizabeth Stewart, the female survivor of the Scott Massacre, was heard calling for help during the heat of the battle and was rescued by McIntosh's officers. U.S. troops had heard rumors of her presence just ahead of them from the time they took Tallahassee Talofa. Her husband and father were traveling with Jackson and McIntosh was able to return her to them.[29]

The army pushed on from the Battle of Econfina for Boleck's town on the Suwannee River. They captured that place and the adjacent Black Seminole town on April 16, 1818. Another delaying action had taken place while Boleck evacuated the women and children across the Suwannee. Once again Jackson's troops destroyed the villages while failing to capture the inhabitants. They did succeed in taking Robert Ambrister, the former lieutenant from Lt. Col. Edward Nicolls' Colonial Marines. He along with Alexander Arbuthnot were tried and executed at San Marcos de Apalache (now called Fort St. Marks) for their role in leading and encouraging the Red Sticks and Seminoles in their war against the United States.

Jackson returned to Fort Gadsden after instructing the Georgia Militia and Creek Brigade to return home. From there he returned up the river, crossed over at Ocheesee Bluff and marched on to Pensacola. The Spanish capital was occupied by U.S. troops and the First Seminole War for the most part came to an end, although mopping up operations continued for some time.

Fort Scott continued to serve as a logistics base for the remainder of the war. Troops came and went and Capt. McIntosh did what he could to feed his own garrison as well as the prisoners and various parties of both refugee Creeks and soldiers that passed through. When Jackson decided to cross the Apalachicola River at Ocheesee, orders were sent for the rest of the 4th Infantry to come down to the Ocheesee village along with flats to be used by the army in crossing. Only the sick of the regiment were left behind at the fort.[30]

On April 22 the men at Fort Scott and on the march in Florida shivered through one of the worst spring cold snaps ever recorded in Southwest Georgia and Northwest Florida:

> …The Spring of 1818 was the coldest that has been known in Florida for many years. On the 22d of April a frost of most destructive kind blighted all the young vegetation along the southern frontier from Mobile to Sahwanne and probably to the Atlantic. It was followed by several days of excessively cold weather in which a large fire, even in the middle of the day, was far from uncomfortable. The effects

of this frost...were singularly various in situations and appearance. On some of the high grounds, the vegetation was scarcely effected, whilst in places much lower, and apparently sheltered, the frost had the same appearance as the blasting of a fire among the low bushes and shrubs. Even large trees had their small leaves partly withered and the foliage of some young oaks presented a singular motley show of russet and green.[31]

The severe cold probably contributed to the outbreak of sickness that followed at the fort. Major Enos Cutler took command when Capt. McIntosh marched with his men to join Jackson at Ocheesee Bluff. He reported to Gen. Gaines on May 16th that the situation was becoming critical:

The great number of sick which have been left at this post at different periods since the Brigade move, has nearly exhausted the medicines, and entirely so the hospital stores, some articles of which are absolutely necessary for the comfort of the sick. I have been compelled to take from the medicines belonging to the 7th Regiment a very small quantity until a supply can be received.[32]

Cutler enclosed a report of the provisions the on hand at the fort. It listed 25,000 rations of flour, 14,500 of salted pork, 35,000 of whiskey, 24,000 of soap and candles and 5,000 of vinegar. The major also reported there were about 20 bushels of salt in storage.[33]

Another individual who would figure prominently in the story of the next war between the Seminoles and the United States entered the story of Fort Scott in May 1818. Capt. Francis L. Dade reported from Savannah on the 26th that he had arrived in that city with 130 men. The soldiers were all recruits from Richmond, Virginia, and Baltimore, Maryland, and Dade was under orders to march with them to Fort Scott. Dade, in an odd twist of fate, had been on recruiting duty the previous year when Lt. Richard W. Scott was killed. Dade himself would suffer a similar fate in December 1835 when his command was wiped out by Seminole and Black Seminole warriors at the start of the Second Seminole War.[34]

Maj. Cutler at Fort Scott seems not to have known that Capt. Dade was on his way with the recruits. In a May 29th letter to Gen. Gaines, Cutler sought detail on what was being done to send additional troops to the post:

> Unofficial
>
> Will not this post be strengthened? We report but 27 privates for duty, and the total present of both companies is but 61, which number is almost daily diminishing by discharge. By a paragraph which I see in the newspaper, it appears troops have been marched from Virginia and North Carolina to Savannah. This must be Clinch's recruits and his route must have been changed by the Majr. Genl. The Floridas it is said are ceded to Alexander the Emperor. If this is true we shall have Cossacks as well as Indians to contend with.[35]

Russians, of course, were not on their way to the Gulf Coast but the rumor repeated by Maj. Cutler reveals how isolated Fort Scott had become since the passage of Jackson's army. The number of reports that mention or date from the fort diminished greatly in May and June 1818.

The body of Maj. Wright, who had drowned during the disaster that struck the boat carrying Gen. Gaines in February, was found in June 1818. Troops also recovered some of his personal effects. The remains of the unfortunate major were carried down to Fort Scott where they were interred with military ceremonies.[36]

The summer of 1818 saw an inquiry convene at Fort Scott with regard to the conduct of Lt. Col. Matthew Arbuckle while in command of the post. The voluminous interrogatories and documentation that he submitted saved his commission while also providing great detail on the situation at the fort during the First Seminole War. Gen. Jackson read the documents on his return to Nashville and wrote to Arbuckle in September expressing support for the measures the colonel had taken in keeping his post supplied under exasperating circumstances but restating his position that Fort Scott should not have been evacuated under any circumstances.[37]

Arbuckle was back at Fort Scott by mid-September 1818 from where he reported that many of the Red Stick Creeks and their families had given up the fight and were on their way up to Fort Gaines on their return to the Creek

Nation. He remained at his former post only briefly before continuing upriver to Fort Gaines as well and eventually on to the settled areas of Georgia. The last significant mention of Fort Scott in military records for 1818 was an order from Gen. Gaines that two companies be held in readiness there to escort a surveying party assigned to complete the work that had been interrupted by the outbreak of hostilities the previous year.

Fort Scott remained occupied but it would be some time before it regained significance as a strategic point.

---

[1] Capt. John N. McIntosh to Maj. Gen. Andrew Jackson, March 14, 1818, Andrew Jackson Papers, Library of Congress.

[2] Brig. Gen. William McIntosh to Maj. Daniel Hughes, March 16, 1818, Camden Gazette, April 11, 1818, p. 3.

[3] *Ibid.*

[4] *Augusta Chronicle*, March 15, 1818.

[5] Annette McDonald Suarez, "The War Path Across Georgia Made By Tennessee Troops in the First Seminole War," The Georgia Historical Quarterly, Vol. 38, No. 1, (March 1954), pp. 34-35.

[6] Capt. John N. McIntosh to Maj. Gen. Andrew Jackson, March 15, 1818, Andrew Jackson Papers, Library of Congress.

[7] Capt. John N. McIntosh to Maj. Gen. Andrew Jackson, March 15, 1818, Andrew Jackson Papers, Library of Congress.

[8] Capt. John N. McIntosh to Maj. Gen. Andrew Jackson, March 16, 1818, Andrew Jackson Papers, Library of Congress.

[9] Capt. John N. McIntosh to Maj. Gen. Andrew Jackson, March 16, 1818, Andrew Jackson Papers, Library of Congress.

[10] Officer of the Georgia Detachment to the editor of the August Chronicle, March 17, 1818, from the Newburyport Herald (Mass.), May 1, 1818, p. 1.

[11] Officer of the Georgia Detachment to the editor of the August Chronicle, March 17, 1818, from the *Newburyport Herald* (Mass.), May 1, 1818, p. 1.

[12] Annette McDonald Suarez, "The War Path Across Georgia Made By Tennessee Troops in the First Seminole War," The Georgia Historical Quarterly, Vol. 38, No. 1, (March 1954), pp. 35.

[13] Capt. John N. McIntosh to Maj. Gen. Andrew Jackson, March 19, 1818, Andrew Jackson Papers, Library of Congress.

[14] *Ibid.*

[15] James Monroe, Message from the President of the United States to the House of Representatives, relative to the War with the Seminoles, March 25th, 1818, British Foreign & State Papers, p. 1090.

[16] Capt. John McIntosh to Maj. Gen. Andrew Jackson, March 25, 1818, Andrew Jackson Papers, Library of Congress.

[17] Maj. Gen. Andrew Jackson to Rachel Jackson, March 26, 1818, Jackson Papers, Library of Congress.

[18] Capt. John N. McIntosh to Maj. Gen. Andrew Jackson, March 26, 1818, Andrew Jackson Papers, Library of Congress.

[19] Capt. John N. McIntosh to Maj. Gen. Andrew Jackson, March 27, 1818, Andrew Jackson Papers, Library of Congress.

[20] Maj. E. Cutler to Maj. Gen. Edmund P. Gaines, March 31, 1818, Adjutant General, Letters Received, NARA.

[21] Maj. Gen. Andrew Jackson to Hon. John C. Calhoun, Secretary of War, April 8-9, 1818, American State Papers, Military Affairs, Volume I, pp. 699-700.

[22] Maj. Gen. Andrew Jackson to Francisco Caso y Luengo, April 6, 1818, Jackson Papers, Library of Congress.

[23] *Ibid.*

[24] Capt. John N. McIntosh to Maj. Gen. Andrew Jackson, April 6, 1818, Andrew Jackson Papers, Library of Congress.

[25] *Ibid.*

[26] *Ibid.*

[27] Brig. Gen. William McIntosh to David B. Mitchell, April 13, 1818, from the Milledgeville Journal of April 27, 1818.

[28] Thomas Woodward, "Reminisces…"

[29] Brig. Gen. William McIntosh to Hon. David B. Mitchell, Agent for Indian Affairs, April 13, 1818.

[30] Capt. Alex Cummings to Maj. E. Cutler, May 5, 1818, Adjutant General, Letters Received, NARA.

[31] Captain Hugh Young, "A Topographical Memoir of East and West Florida with Itineraries," 1819, Records of Reports, July 3, 1812-October 4, 1823, pp. 292-336, Records of the Chief of Engineers.

[32] Maj. E. Cutler to Maj. Gen. Edmund P. Gaines, May 16, 1818, Adjutant General, Letters Received, NARA.

[33] Major E. Cutler, "Report of Provisions on hand at Fort Scott this 16th May 1818," enclosed in Cutler to Maj. Gen. Edmund P. Gaines, May 16, 1818, Adjutant General, Letters Received, NARA.

[34] Report of ca. May 26, 1818, from the American Beacon, June 8, 1818, p. 3.

[35] Maj. E. Cutler to Maj. Gen. Edmund P. Gaines (unofficial letter), May 29, 1818.

[36] *Hallowell Gazette* (Maine), June 24, 1818, p. 3.

[37] Maj. Gen. Andrew Jackson to Lt. Col. Matthew Arbuckle, September 2, 1818, Adjutant General, Letters Received, NARA.

CHAPTER FIFTEEN

The Fever Outbreak of 1820

The year 1819 found the United States engaged in critical negotiations with Spain over the future of Florida. U.S. troops had never given up Amelia Island, Fort St. Marks (San Marcos de Apalache) or Fort Gadsden after the First Seminole War. Pensacola had only recently been returned to Spain, but American authorities engaged in a diplomatic push to make sure the reoccupation was temporary. Garrisons were maintained at Fort Crawford, Fort Scott, Trader's Hill and Camp Pinckney on the St. Marys to add teeth to the diplomatic initiative.

Leading the charge was U.S. Secretary of State John Quincy Adams. He used accounts originally written at Fort Scott as a sledgehammer to batter the Spanish. The Scott Massacre, Adams charged, had been the result of Spain's weakness and inability to abide by its treaty obligations to prevent attacks from its territory. One example of how Adams used the attack against Spain can be found in a letter he sent to the U.S. Minister Plenipotentiary in Madrid:

After the repeated expostulations, warnings and offers of peace, through the summer and autumn of 1817, on the part of the U. States, had been answered only by renewed outrages, and after a detachment of forty men, under Lieutenant Scott, accompanied by seven women, had been waylaid and murdered by the Indians, orders were given to General Jackson, and an adequate force was placed at his disposal, to terminate the war.[1]

The diplomatic crisis had begun with Spain accusing the United States of violating its territorial rights and seizing its posts. Adams and his assistants, however, quickly used the deadly attack against Lt. Scott's party to turn the debate in their favor and the Spanish were now on the defensive. Either put a sufficient force in Florida to prevent a repeat of such attacks, the U.S. demanded, or turn over possession of the colony. The cost of meeting this demand was prohibitive and the King finally agreed to surrender Florida so long as the United States agreed to respect his claim to Texas. Secretary Adams of the United States and Don Luis de Onis of Spain drew up the Adams-Onis Treaty and the final terms were signed in Washington on February 22, 1819, but was not ratified by Spain until October 24, 1820.[2]

The Adams-Onis Treaty was in many ways similar to the Treaty of Fort Jackson that had ended the Creek War of 1813-1814. The First Seminole War had begun with the U.S. attack at Fowltown on November 21, 1817, but did not really end until Spain ceded its colonies of East and West Florida. The Fort Jackson treaty had exacted a 20,000,000-acre land cession on the Creek Nation but there had been no need for negotiations with a foreign power since the United States already claimed to be the exclusive power in the ceded lands. The situation was different at the end of the Seminole War, however, because the Red Sticks and Seminoles were living on lands claimed by Spain. Instead of forcing the chiefs and warriors to sign a treaty giving away their lands, then, the United States instead forced such a cession from Spain.

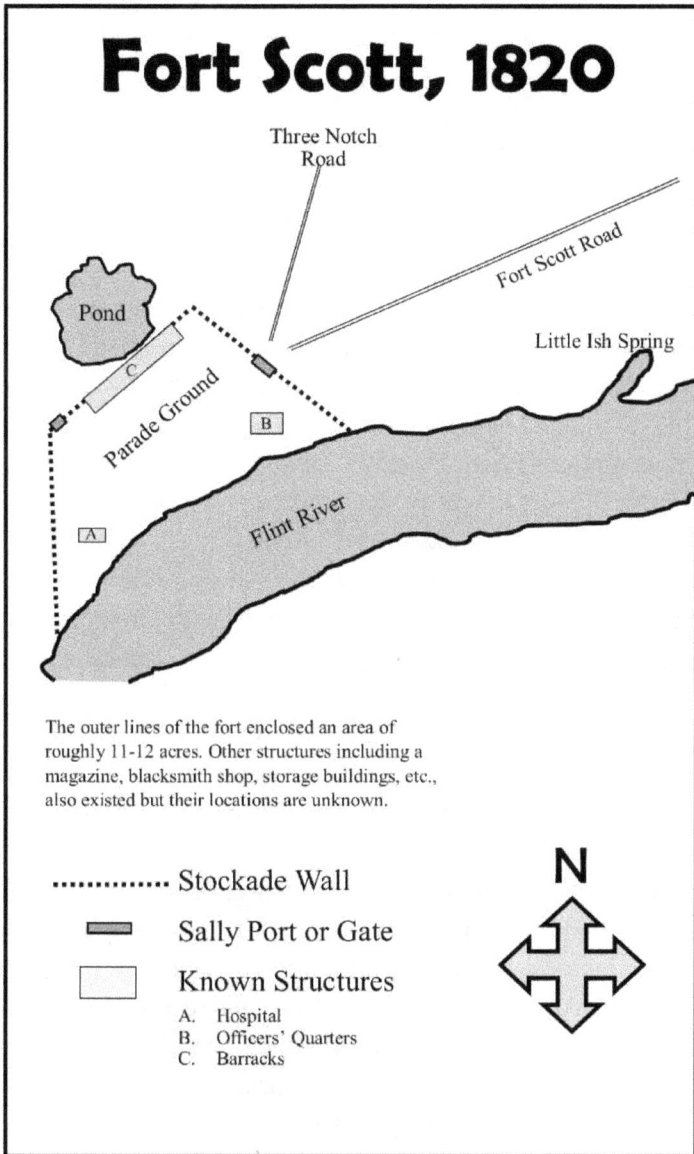

Fort Scott, 1820

Three Notch
Road

Fort Scott Road

Pond

Little Ish Spring

C

Parade Ground

B

A

Flint River

The outer lines of the fort enclosed an area of
roughly 11-12 acres. Other structures including a
magazine, blacksmith shop, storage buildings, etc.,
also existed but their locations are unknown.

············· Stockade Wall

Sally Port or Gate

Known Structures

A. Hospital
B. Officers' Quarters
C. Barracks

N

In terms of land ceded, the treaty that ended the First Seminole War was even more beneficial to the United States than the agreement imposed by Andrew Jackson at the end of the Creek War. The Florida cession included an estimated 34,721,280 acres – more than 14,000,000 than the Fort Jackson document. The deaths of 34 men, 6 women and 4 children on their way to Fort Scott had allowed the United States to complete its long dreamed of expansion to the Gulf of Mexico and Florida Straits. The nation could now look to the west for the realization of its Manifest Destiny.

The slowness with which Spain ratified the treaty caused the United States to maintain military pressure along the frontier. The size of the frontier garrisons, including Fort Scott, quickly grew back to and exceeded their pre-war sizes. Among the officers who returned to command the post during this time was Major David E. Twiggs, who had led the first U.S. raid on Fowltown. Twiggs was a tough officer and a severe disciplinarian. Charles Martin Gray, a soldier in Company A of the 7th Infantry, often watched as the major personally flogged soldiers for breaches of discipline. Gray described several of these incidents in his autobiography, among them the flogging of a soldier for leaving post without permission:

> [Twiggs] then pulled off his own coat, rolled up his sleeves, and inflicted upon his bare back, with a horse whip, twenty-five lashes, which made the blood spout and trickle down his manly form, and that scarred the skin at every stroke. At another time, for some small offense, he sentenced one of his command to pitch straws against the wind, for four or five hours without intermission. The wind was blowing a gale, and the penalty was that he should receive one lash for every straw he failed to produce. At the end of this delightful exercise…he found himself minus many a straw, and crowned with many a stripe, for he was compelled to pitch the straws as high in the air, as his strength, and the boisterous elements would allow, and an unrelenting

Orderly was present to report minutely every failure either of his strength or his skill.[3]

Nor was Major Twiggs the only officer at Fort Scott with a sadistic sense of discipline. Granville Leftwich was a lieutenant in Company I, 7th Infantry, who was promoted to captain during his years of service at Fort Scott and on the frontier. According to Gray, he used his prerogative as an officer to keep a "female friend" with him on post. On one occasion the woman approached a soldier named Stevens who was then serving as company cook to ask for a serving of food. Stevens gave her a "courteous, but decided refusal" pointing out that the food belonged to the military and he could not serve a civilian. Leftwich responded with fury:

> …[Leftwich had Stevens] stripped, tied up, and lashed by the drummer boy whilst he deliberately smoked out three Havanna Cigars. This surpassed in severity all the acts of petty tyranny I was ever called upon to witness. Stevens…suffered more death from the infliction, for if he was about to faint, and nature was giving away under the terrible scourging, he was stimulated with brandy to enable him to endure a little more, and I hesitate not to say that his Captain deserved, not a soldier's death, but to be hanged like a felon.[4]

Charles Martin Gray's account of life at Fort Scott also reveals some of the humor that goes with service on a military post. He told in particular of one trip down to Fort Gadsden in which he secreted an empty whiskey bottle in one pocket of an oversized coat and an identical bottle filled with river water in a second pocket. When his detachment of 24 men arrived at Fort Gadsden aboard the *Support*, he went immediately to the sutler, presented his empty bottle and requested to buy liquor to fill it. The sutler did so but then demanded payment. Gray had no cash so the seller demanded that his liquor be returned. The soldier then produced the bottle filled with river water which was poured back into the cask. After receiving his empty bottle back, he made off with the full botte of liquor without having paid for it.[5]

Other soldiers were amazed that Gray's scam had succeeded and it was not long before they decided to try it as well:

>...But the trick was too good not to be improved, and the same good bottles were passed again and again to different members of the detail, who all rejoiced in their own success as often as they tried the experiment, until we had obtained excellent whiskey enough to sustain my mess and colleagues in a royal spree.[6]

Gray and his buddies were almost caught red-handed by Major Twiggs, "who was then opposed to drinking in his command." Seeing the private return from the sutler's with his bottle, the major called out to him to display its contents. "With an air of innocence I handed him the empty bottle," Gray wrote, "when he immediately excused me, uttering at the same time the direst imprecations of what he had done, had it contained whiskey."[7]

Not long after the detachment returned to Fort Scott, Private Gray went to Major Twiggs to request permission to buy a bottle of whiskey "without stating the size." Twiggs approved and signed the necessary order. Ever the prankster, Gray then took a huge medicine bottle he had obtained from the surgeon and had it filled with more than one gallon of liquor. Since he had a signed order from the major, he felt confident that no trouble would follow:

>...When I had procured the liquor, therefore, I made no secret of it, but slinging the huge vessel on my shoulder, passed directly by the quarters of major Twiggs. When the latter beheld me as he walked to and fro along his little piazza he called me to him and demanded of me the authority I had for purchasing so much whisky, and received the answer that it was directly from him, as could be attested by the written order itself. He then turned to

Lieutenant Pierce M. Butler, who was promenading with him and inquired if Edgefield was composed of such men as Charles Martin Gray. Receiving an affirmative reply, he good humoredly said that he knew the devil must have his headquarters there, and beckoned me to go on.[8]

Gray, obviously, had been a resident of the Edgefield District of South Carolina before he joined the army. Like all of the privates at Fort Scott he suffered through many hardships and often found himself on the wrong end of attention from officers at the post. He and Lt. Richard Wash, also a South Carolinian, each developed a dislike for the other. This led to an event on the road between Fort Scott and Fort Gaines that is hilarious with the benefit of nearly 200 years of hindsight.

It was then the custom in the army for enlisted men to "piggyback" officers across creeks and streams so the latter would not get their feet wet. When the detachment approached Kolomoki Creek in today's Early County, Georgia, Wash demanded that Private Gray carry him across:

I began to reel and stagger under the weight that oppressed me, but recovering proceeded mildly forward until, when making the very middle of the swollen current, I stumbled...and fell in the waters and...disengaged myself entirely from any superincumbent load. The gallant Lieutenant to his great discomfiture, and to the inordinate merriment of all the men and officers present, was thus compelled to struggle alone...while his rich and gaudy uniform was soiled and begrimed with the mud, and rent in shreds by the rocks.[9]

Gray's account is filled with such stories. Combined they offer a fascinating view of life at Fort Scott in 1819-1820. Some are quite funny and others are horrifying, but such were the lives of the soldiers at the post.

Gray himself was a remarkable individual. Born at Edgefield, South Carolina, in 1800, he enlisted in the militia during the War of 1812 at the age of 13 but was forced back into indentured servitude by a chair maker in Augusta, Georgia. He enlisted again, this time in the regular service, after the furniture business failed and he was set free from his enslavement. His father brought a writ of *habeas corpus* and Gray once again was forced to leave the service. He then studied at the Edgefield Male Academy until he enlisted under Major Twiggs at Augusta on April 24, 1819. Assigned to Company A, 7th Infantry, he served ten years of frontier duty. A heavy drinker in his youth, he gave up liquor when he married Ann Green on September 3, 1841. He served as a deputy sheriff and constable in Edgefield and held the post of door-keeper to the South Carolina House of Representatives when that state seceded from the Union in December 1860. Despite being 60 years old and having four sons and three daughters, he enlisted in the 7th South Carolina and served as its color bearer in battles from First Manassas through Second Manassas. Finally given an honorable discharge due to age and infirmity, he returned home and lived out his life in Edgefield. He died there in 1870 at the age of 70 years old. During his lifetime, Charles Martin Gray served in the War of 1812, Seminole Wars and War Between the States.[10]

It proved expensive for the United States to maintain garrisons on the frontiers of Spanish Florida. A statement of the number of rations issued and the cost of providing them for June-August 1819 shows that 21,688 rations were issued at Fort Scott at a cost of $3,737.90. The list shows that the more remote the post, the higher the expense. Places like Fort Scott, Fort Gadsden and Trader's Hill were very expensive to supply, while posts at Mobile, Amelia Island and elsewhere along the cost were able to feed their soldiers at a lower cost per man.[11]

Expense and the lessening need for troops at so many points along the frontier led to some changes in early 1820. The *Savannah Republican* reported on February 23rd of that year, for example, that the troops from Trader's Hill had been ordered to abandon their post and take up the line of march to Fort Scott. Lt. Col. Arbuckle, meanwhile, was in Philadelphia enlisting new recruits for the 7th Infantry and sending them south to fill the ranks of the regiment that had become depleted when the last of the War of

1812 five-year recruits left the service. Arbuckle himself returned to the fort on July 25, 1820, and reported soon after that large numbers of new recruits had also arrived from the North.[12]

Things with the northern recruits did not go as well as expected. Surgeon Thomas Lawson reported that six had died almost immediately after they arrived at Fort Scott, five or six more had died on the voyage up the Apalachicola from Fort Gadsden and an additional seven had died at the later post where they first landed after their trip from Philadelphia. Lawson, who later became U.S. Surgeon General, blamed the deaths on the fact that the men had been cooped up in a small ship for more than 20 days.[13]

In view of the death statistics for April – June 1820, however, something much more serious was happening to the soldiers on the frontier. The "intermittent, remittent" fever was reported as was the bilious remittent fever. The former is recognized today as malaria, while the latter was the dreaded yellow fever. Thirty-seven men died at Fort Gadsden and Apalachicola Bay and many others were sick. Both of the deadly diseases were spread by mosquitoes and the infection rates soared.[14]

Doctors of the time, of course, did not recognize the role that mosquitoes played in the spread of malaria and yellow fever. Instead they blamed a variety of causes, including swamp air:

> The unhealthiness of the summer season in the south may be traced to the following causes: 1st. Excessively high and long continued atmospheric temperature, the mean temperature at 2 P.M. for the quarter being, at Fort Scott a fraction less than 86, at Montpelier and New Orleans 85, and at Baton Rouge 83. 2d. The insalubrious locality of some posts, especially Forts Scott and Gadsden. 3d The impracticability of preventing decomposition in some portions of the ration. 4th. The destructive effects of a southern climate, in an unhealthy season, upon northern constitutions already debilitated by indulgence in vicious habits. To these causes may be added others comparatively of minor importance; such as errors in diet and police, and a want of due attention in selecting the time and limiting the

duration of fatigue duty, during the prevalence of summer heats.[15]

Fort Scott proved to be an extremely unhealthy place to be during the summer of 1820. The diseases spread as sick soldiers moved up and down the Apalachicola River between hospitals at Fort Gadsden and Fort Scott, the surgeons not realizing that they were doing more harm than good by moving seriously ill men from the former fort to the latter. Dr. Thomas Lawson was the primary surgeon at Fort Scott and his accounts provide shocking detail on the situation there:

> The current summer has proven unusually sickly. An insalubrious atmosphere has pervaded the country, and disease and death have been everywhere present. That the troops have suffered in the utmost severity, the record of mortality affords melancholy evidence.
>
> About the 15th July, the simple inflammatory fevers began to yield to remittents; dysentery and diarrhea also gave ground; but intermittents maintained their position in the foremost rank. On the 1st August, remittents became more rife, and exhibited in a short time terrible phenomena. In September, they still gained ground, and eventually became so formidable as to prostrate every thing against which their force was directed.[16]

Yellow fever, he reported, was not the most prevalent disease at Fort Scott but was by far the most malignant. "The patient, in some instances, sinks directly under the weight of the primary disease," Lawson explained. In other cases, though, they often survived the first assault of the sickness but soon became so worn down by suffering and relapses that they willingly gave up their fights for life. "Whilst some expire in convulsions," he continued, "others pass away without a groan or a struggle."[17]

The first symptoms of yellow fever, Lawson continued in an October 1st report to the Surgeon General, included "mental anxiety, listlessness, languor, and lassitude on the least muscular exertion." From that stage it took on additional symptoms including nausea, back pain, severe headaches, vertigo, chills and fevers:

...During the stage of reaction, the pulse is frequent, full, and tense; an intolerable heat is diffused over the superficies of the body, with a similar sensation in the internal organs; the skin is dry and parched; the tongue is slightly moist, and covered with a white or greenish furl, great determination to the head and high delirium usually exist.[18]

The fever also appeared in several other forms. Dr. Lawson's description is lengthy and graphic, but is key to understanding the severity to which the sickness was devastating the unfortunate soldiers of Fort Scott:

In the second grade of the regular form, the disease is manifested by vertigo, imperfect vision, obtuse pain in the head, pain and anxiety in the region of the chest, difficulty of respiration, a tendency to coma, vomiting sometimes attended with purging, great prostration of strength, and the loss of the power of locomotion. In this modification, the reaction is less frequently preceded by a chill; the pulse is small and frequent; the skin is dry and contracted; the tongue is parched and constricted, with a glossy appearance; the thirst is intolerable; a horrible sensation of burning heat is felt throughout the intestines; and stupor prevails in every stage of the disease.

In the third variety, or first irregular form, the patient is suddenly affected with syncope, he falls down and remains in a state of insensibility for fifteen or thirty minutes, and on being resuscitated, a cold sweat appears; his respiration is laborious, with great anxiety about the proecordia; the stomach rejects its contents, and the bowls are often violently evacuated; and lastly, he is seized with general paralysis. In this condition, the pulse is small, quick, and frequently intermitting; the skin is very cold and shriveled; the tongue maintains its natural appearance; little or no delirium prevails but the tendency to syncope is so great, that the patient faints upon the least change of position, more expecially with placed in an erect posture.

In the fourth modification, or second irregular form, the victim seems affected with vertigo and total loss of vision; he totters, reels, and sinks exanimate to the ground.[19]

Lawson desperately tried to determine the cause of the devastating epidemic that continued to worsen as summer turned to fall. He blamed air from the swamps and marshes that surrounded Fort Scott. Drunkenness, fatigue, isolation, exposure to cold and damp night air were also on his list of causes:

> Our police, although far from commendable, is perhaps as well maintained as is practicable among recruits. Despite the efforts of officers, drunkenness will prevail. Whisky is smuggled into camp; moreover, as a few of the men dispose of their whisky ration, others are enabled to get daily a pint or a quart of ardent spirits. The fatigue endured by our men in transporting provisions, &c., from Fort Gadsden to this point, and in building and repairing barracks, &c., cannot be regarded as excessive to men of ordinary physical strength and accustomed to labor; but to the refuse of mankind, gathered from the purlieus of our cities, the burdens imposed may have been beyond the measure of their abilities. Our provisions have been in a state of such impurity, that were other supplies within reach, it is very probable that the greater part would be condemned. As the men have lately changed their mode of life, have come to an unfriendly clime, and are ignorant of their new provision, they have experienced just enough of military life to hate the service.[20]

Treatments attempted by the surgeons and their assistants ranged from the use of rudimentary medicines to the application of hot bricks to the feet of patients.[21]

By the end of October 1820, Lt. Col. Arbuckle knew that something terrible and deadly was taking place at Fort Scott. He submitted the monthly returns of the post to the Adjutant General on November 4th, nothing that "the number of deaths were unusually great during the month, and the sick list has but little if any diminished." From the weakened state of many of the men, he continued, "I greatly fear a number more must yet die." It was the worst outbreak of sickness ever witnessed by the lieutenant colonel:

> The present season I am confident is the most sickly I have ever known to the south, and in addition to this a great portion of my regiment arrived here (from the North) about the commencement of the warm season, and were compeled to build barracks to protect them from the heat of the sun and from the rains which were very heavy and almost daily from the 1st of June untill the 8th or 10th of the last month. During this time a considerable portion of the country, which is level and low for many miles around this post, was covered with water.[22]

The full magnitude of the outbreak at Fort Scott during the fourth quarter of 1820 is difficult to conceive. Of the 780 men at the post, 769 were on the sick list. The number of deaths totaled 32, more than doubling the size of the post cemetery.[23]

---

[1] Secretary of State John Quincy Adams to Minister Plenipotentiary of the U.S. to Spain at Madrid, n.d., from New York National Advocate, January 7, 1819, p. 2.

[2] Adams-Onis Treaty of 1819.

[3] Charles Martin Gray, "The old soldier's story: autobiography of Charles Martin Gray, Co. A, 7th Regiment, U.S.I., embracing interesting and exciting incidents of army life on the frontier, in the early part of the present century," Edgefield Advertiser Print, 1868 – 63 pages.

[4] *Ibid.*

[5] *Ibid.*

[6] *Ibid.*

[7] *Ibid.*

[8] *Ibid.*

[9] *Ibid.*

[10] John Abney Chapman, "History of Edgefield County: from the earliest settlements to 1897: biographical and anecdotical, with sketches of the Seminole

war, nullification, secession, reconstruction, churches and literature, with rolls of all the companies from Edgefield in the War of Secession, War with Mexico and with the Seminole Indians," E.H. Aull, 1897, 521 pages, pp. 191-196.

[11] Peter Hagner, Auditor, Statement showing the number of rations issued, and the cost, including sundry contingent expenses, and independent of the expenses of the Commissary Department, from 1st June to 31st August, 1819, ASP, Part 5, Volume 2, p. 74.

[12] Lt. Col. Matthew Arbuckle to Gen. Daniel Parker, Adjutant General, July 29, 1820, Adjutant General, Letters Received, NARA.

[13] Samuel Forrey, M.D., late of the United States Army, Thomas Lawson, M.D., Surgeon General, Statistical Report on the Sickness and Mortality in the Army of the United States: Compiled from the Records of the Surgeon General's and Adjutant General's Offices – Embracing a Period of Twenty Years, from January, 1819, to January, 1839, Washington, printed by Jacob Gideon, Jr., 1840, pp. 19-20.

[14] Samuel Forrey, M.D., late of the United States Army, Thomas Lawson, M.D., Surgeon General, Statistical Report on the Sickness and Mortality in the Army of the United States: Compiled from the Records of the Surgeon General's and Adjutant General's Offices – Embracing a Period of Twenty Years, from January, 1819, to January, 1839, Washington, printed by Jacob Gideon, Jr., 1840, pp. 19-20.

[15] Samuel Forrey, M.D., late of the United States Army, Thomas Lawson, M.D., Surgeon General, Statistical Report on the Sickness and Mortality in the Army of the United States: Compiled from the Records of the Surgeon General's and Adjutant General's Offices – Embracing a Period of Twenty Years, from January, 1819, to January, 1839, Washington, printed by Jacob Gideon, Jr., 1840, pp. 19-20.

[16] Samuel Forrey, M.D., late of the United States Army, Thomas Lawson, M.D., Surgeon General, Statistical Report on the Sickness and Mortality in the Army of the United States: Compiled from the Records of the Surgeon General's and Adjutant General's Offices – Embracing a Period of Twenty Years, from January, 1819, to January, 1839, Washington, printed by Jacob Gideon, Jr., 1840, pp. 21-26.

[17] Thomas Lawson, M.D., to the Surgeon General, October 1, 1820, in Forrey and Lawson, "Statistical Report on the Sickness and Mortality in the Army of the United States."

[18] *Ibid.*

[19] *Ibid.*

[20] *Ibid.*

[21] Samuel Forrey, M.D., late of the United States Army, Thomas Lawson, M.D., Surgeon General, Statistical Report on the Sickness and Mortality in the Army of

the United States: Compiled from the Records of the Surgeon General's and Adjutant General's Offices – Embracing a Period of Twenty Years, from January, 1819, to January, 1839, Washington, printed by Jacob Gideon, Jr., 1840, pp. 21-26.

[22] Lt. Col. Matthew Arbuckle to Gen. Daniel Parker, November 4, 1820, Adjutant General, Letters Received, NARA.

[23] Samuel Forrey, M.D., late of the United States Army, Thomas Lawson, M.D., Surgeon General, Statistical Report on the Sickness and Mortality in the Army of the United States: Compiled from the Records of the Surgeon General's and Adjutant General's Offices – Embracing a Period of Twenty Years, from January, 1819, to January, 1839, Washington, printed by Jacob Gideon, Jr., 1840, p. 26.

CHAPTER SIXTEEN

Camp Recovery

A monument made by standing a massive 32-pounder cannon breech down in a block of Stone Mountain granite still stands on a high hill across the Flint River from the site of Fort Scott. The weathered inscription notes that the gun was placed to mark the graves of men from the 4th and 7th Infantry Regiments who died at Camp Recovery "during the Indian Wars in the Flint and Chattahoochee river country, 1817 to 1821."

The actual name "Camp Recovery" never appears in the surviving documentation of Fort Scott, the 4th and 7th Infantry Regiments or the First Seminole War. The names "Camp Recruit," "Camp Curry," and "Fort Recovery" have also been used locally to describe the site, but neither do these names appear in the known documentation. Legend holds that the site was a hospital camp of Fort Scott and that the men buried there died from sickness.

From this clue it is possible to locate a single surviving document that makes reference to such an encampment. In a report completed on January 1, 1821, Dr. Thomas Lawson described how he had tried to save lives the previous September by carrying some of the desperately ill men from Fort Scott to a high hill about three miles south of that post. The severity of the malaria and yellow fever outbreak taking place at Fort Scott, the surgeon wrote, could only be ascribed to a "dispensation of Providence." The simplest illnesses suddenly became complex, more difficult cases turned malignant, and every case of sickness became so aggravated as to be "scarcely definable."[1]

Believing that the decomposing plant and animal matter in the swamps that surrounded Fort Scott might be responsible for the outbreak, which growing by the day, Dr. Lawson decided on about the 15th of September that "a portion of our invalids should be removed beyond the influence of the cantonment's atmosphere." Three days were spent making preparations:

> Accordingly on the 18th, such as were capable of enduring the unavoidable fatigue, and whose complaints were likely to be benefitted by a change of air, in number about 70, were removed under the charge of one of the Assistant Surgeons to a high pine ridge to the southeast of, and three miles distant from this place and the river. But scarcely were the tents pitched before a heavy rain came on, which, continuing five or six days, occasioned the immediate dissolution of several, and produced irreparable injury to all the sick. Many of those affected with intermitting fever, were also attacked with dysentery or diarrhea, and vice versa. Nay, the diseases generally became blended the one with the other.[2]

The description of heavy rains that lasted for five or six days may indicate that a tropical system of some type had moved into Southwest Georgia from the Gulf of Mexico. Lawson does not mention the high winds and other conditions associated with hurricanes, so it appears likely that a tropical depression or the remnants of a tropical storm settled over the area. Such events are relatively common in the area around the forks of the Chattahoochee and Flint Rivers during Hurricane Season and often bring remarkable amounts of rain.

Once the system finally moved out and things began to dry out, the sick men slowly began to show signs of improvement. Unfortunately, it was not to last:

> …As the weather soon grew mild, this little colony began to revive, one or two dropping off occasionally, until the 22d of October, when the sudden fall of the thermometer laid all prostrate, some of them never more to rise. This was the most fatal period. Every convalescent relapsed into his old, or contracted some new disease; and this state of things continued, with but little melioration, until the 23d November, when the establishment was broken up, and the surviving sick brought back to the cantonment. Thus did, in consequence of adventitious circumstances, the most disastrous results follow our best directed efforts.[3]

There is no indication that permanent structures were ever erected at the camp or that it was even given an official name. The only reference to housing is the brief mention by Dr. Lawson that tents were pitched at the site. Neither is the number of soldiers buried at the site known. Lawson mentioned that "several" died following the heavy rains and then that the cold snap on October 22nd laid all of the patients low, "some of them never more to rise."[4]

The late owner of the site, Mr. N.L. Sellers, believed that 30 or more men were buried in the traditional cemetery. The post returns for Fort Scott unfortunately do not distinguish men who died at the main fort from those who died at the hospital camp across the river. There could be 30 or more graves at Camp Recovery, but if so it is unlikely that all are soldiers. A total of 32 deaths were reported at Fort Scott in October-December 1820, the majority undoubtedly at the primary fort. It is certainly possible, however, that early settlers of the region also made use of the little cemetery and that it contains additional graves from the years following the military occupation.[5]

Any original grave markers at Camp Recovery had disappeared by the time its neglected condition was brought to the attention of Secretary of War Robert Todd Lincoln on February 20, 1882. Rep. H.G. Turner (Democrat,

Georgia) had received a letter from Hon. Maston O'Neal, a judge in Decatur County, Georgia, requesting that Congress do something to better mark the graves of soldiers at Camp Recovery, Fort Scott and Fort Hughes. He forwarded this letter to Lincoln, the son of President Abraham Lincoln, and the secretary instructed the Quartermaster General to look into the matter.[6]

Lt. J.D.C. Hoskins of the U.S. Army was sent from St. Augustine, Florida, to investigate the burial sites. Arriving in Bainbridge by train, he proceeded by land over the rough roads of the day to inspect the sites of Fort Scott and Camp Recovery. He visited the latter place and found it to be located in open pine woods on a hillside not far from a small spring. Depressions indicative of graves were evident but it was impossible to determine the number of burials or size of the cemetery.

The Quartermaster General, after reading the lieutenant's report, recommended against acquisition of the site by the U.S. Government, but suggested to Secretary Lincoln the placement of a gun monument. The area was prone to forest fires, he noted, but such a monument would easily withstand them. Lincoln agreed and approved the expenditure of $932.52 to cover the transfer of three 32-pounder cannons from Fort Clinch, Florida, and the purchase of three stone bases from Stone Mountain, Georgia.[7]

Orders to move the guns were issued on October 22, 1882. They were carried to Bainbridge by rail and from there moved to the sites where they would be installed by steamboat, animal and manpower. This took some time to accomplish but the *Bainbridge Democrat* reported that the monument at the Fort Hughes site was in the process of being erected on May 24, 1883. It is inferred that the Camp Recovery Monument was placed at about this same time.[8]

The monument was inscribed on two sides with identical descriptions:

> Erected on the site of Camp Recovery near which are
> buried officers and soldiers of the United States Army who
> died during the Indian Wars in the Flint and Chattahoochee
> river country, 1817 to 1821.

Owners of the property have been diligent in maintaining the monument and traditional site of the cemetery through the years. Both remain on private property today and are located in a grove of old trees and surrounded by a wire fence that encloses perhaps one-half acre of land. The Historic

Chattahoochee Commission has placed a permanent historical marker nearby on the shoulder of Booster Club Road a short distance east of Recovery Road in the unincorporated community of Recovery, Georgia.

The monument and cemetery are located on the gentle slope of a high hill or ridge. A spring flows from the base of this elevation and likely provided a source of water for the men. The actual camp probably lay on the gentle crest of the hill between Booster Club Road and the monument. Military cemeteries of the time were always located a slight distance away from actual camp or fort limits.

---

[1] Thomas Lawson, M.D., to the Surgeon General, January 1, 1821, in Samuel Forrey, M.D., late of the United States Army, Thomas Lawson, M.D., Surgeon General, Statistical Report on the Sickness and Mortality in the Army of the United States: Compiled from the Records of the Surgeon General's and Adjutant General's Offices – Embracing a Period of Twenty Years, from January, 1819, to January, 1839, Washington, printed by Jacob Gideon, Jr., 1840, pp. 26-27.
[2] *Ibid.*
[3] *Ibid.*
[4] *Ibid.*
[5] Personal Communication, Mr. N.L. Sellers of Recovery, Georgia, August 1980.
[6] Mark N. Schatz, Reference Service Report: Monuments on the sites of Fort Scott, Fort Hughes, and Camp Recovery, near Bainbridge, Georgia, NARA.
[7] *Ibid.*
[8] *Bainbridge Democrat*, May 24, 1883.

CHAPTER SEVENTEEN

The Final Year

The malaria and yellow fever outbreak began to diminish at Fort Scott when the "mosquito season" ended in mid-November 1820. The sickness, however, was far from over and many more men would sicken and die before the troops were withdrawn from the post. Spain had finally confirmed the Adams-Onis Treaty, but Florida would not become part of the United States until September 1821. The fort would remain garrisoned by a large force until the change of flags was final, regardless of the cost in lost and broken lives.

The first quarter of 1821 saw 541 cases of sickness and 7 deaths at Fort Scott, from an average garrison of 750 men. Most of the deaths then and the previous fall had been "confined to northern recruits, who are represented by the medical officers to have been unfit for military service in any clime or season." Few of the recruits brought south from Philadelphia by Lt. Col. Arbuckle in the summer of 1820 escaped without effect.[1]

Dr. Lawson and other surgeons of the time tried to explain why the diseases struck recruits from the north with much greater severity than those from the south. They blamed much of the problem on the living conditions of poor recruits from the north, many of whom had recently arrived from Europe and lived in the poverty-stricken slums of larger cities. Southern recruits, even those from poor homes, were more acclimated and lived in the outdoors more than many of those from the north. They also had more of a tradition of military service and many had performed duty in the militia during the War of 1812 before joining the regulars. Dr. Lawson felt this last fact contributed greatly to their higher survival rates:

> Many of the fatal diseases usually imputed to climate and locality arise, in a great measure, from defects in police and in the eternal economy of the camp. Cleanliness is the life of an army. The Jewish code, enjoining ablutions and purifications as religious rites, has been quoted as a system adapted to a camp. The general police of the camp, no less than the observance of personal cleanliness, should, at all times, be rigidly enforced. Attention in the selection of recruits is likewise all-important, and equally so is the mode of employing them during the first year of service. The mere labor performed by the recruit is generally but a minor part of the inconvenience arising from his new mode of life; for the fatigue and exposure that may be very well borne by a soldier after twelve months' service, will often prove destructive to him who has not yet learned to take care of himself when relieved from duty.[2]

The surgeons at Fort Scott, Fort Gadsden and Fort St. Marks also noted with interest a report from the medical staff at Fernandina that they had seen a dramatic reduction of sickness after the troops voluntarily gave up whiskey for the duration of the crisis. Whether it was the temporary elimination of liquor itself or whether the reduction in drunkenness and drunken habits that helped, the improvement in the health of the garrison was quick and lasting. The surgeons had substituted tea, sugar and other items for alcohol.[3]

The debate over how Lt. Col. Arbuckle and his officers had conducted themselves during the First Seminole War still continued in the first quarter of 1821. An interesting note from an officer who called himself only "Veritas" (Latin for "Truth") appeared in the *Arkansas Gazette* on February 10, 1821:

> ...During all these operations, no measures were taken to apprize Maj. Muhlenburg or Lieut. Scott, that hostilities had actually commenced. The latter, (after taking on board the sick and convalescent soldiers, women and children, who had been sent round in the transports, which, from the nature of the current, were not compelled to warp up, and being short of provisions it was the more desirable they should ascend with Lieut. Scott,) was ordered to return to Fort Scott; and having reached within a few miles of the mouth of the Flint river, (6 miles by land from Fort Scott,) himself and party, with the exception of six men and one woman, (some of whom were severely wounded), fell victims to an infuriated band of savages, who, but a few days before, had been attacked in their own town, in the dead of night, their superannuated men and women killed, their provisions plundered, and town destroyed.[4]

The identity of "Veritas" has not been established, but he likely was an officer who had served in the war but was now doing duty on the western frontier. He correctly pointed out that the Scott Massacre had been in retaliation for the attacks on Fowltown and also correctly noted that neither Maj. Muhlenburg nor Lt. Scott had been informed of the outbreak of hostilities.

That the issue was still being hotly debated three years after the war may seem surprising, but the Florida negotiations and the diplomatic flap with Great Britain over Jackson's executions of Arbuthnot and Ambrister had kept the conflict in the forefront of the American mind. When the American army encountered little resistance during its march through Florida in 1818, many of Jackson's officers concluded that the Red Sticks and Seminoles had never amounted to much of a threat. This led to much ridicule of Lt. Col. Arbuckle, but he had faced a full scale offensive instead of the delaying actions of the 1818 campaign. Andrew Jackson had nearly 10 times as many men in his army as Arbuckle had been able to muster during the standoff in 1817 and the warriors simply chose to withdraw ahead of the former army where they had engaged in fierce combat against the latter force.

A classic example of the ridicule that Arbuckle faced in later years is found in the papers of Richard Keith Call at the State Archives of Florida. Call was a young army officer in 1818 but later became Governor of Florida. The scrap of paper once in his possession is a tongue in cheek note written to appear as if it had come from Neamathla himself and addressed "from my bark cabin" at Tampa Bay. While it is not completely legible, the note jokingly refers to Arbuckle as "Old Mathew Shoebuckle" and refers to his "rapid retrograde from 'Fowl Town' on the 23d November" before noting that he was "still lurking about Flint River" and that it was "said there, that he lately told a lye or Two."[5]

It is not clear whether call was the author or the recipient of the letter, but he would one day find himself in a situation not unlike Arbuckle's after his army was bloodied at the Battle of Wahoo Swamp during the Second Seminole War.

Conditions at Fort Scott continued to make slow improvement during the second quarter of 1821. Reports indicate that seven men died at Fort Gadsden in April through June, but "at Fort Scott, the other most sickly position then occupied by troops, there was fortunately no death."[6]

Long-awaited news reached the fort, or so its commander thought, when a May 10th letter was received from the departing Adjutant & Inspector General announcing that the fort would be evacuated and the soldiers sent to a new station:

> …This information convinced me that the movement
> would take place very soon. Not having received further
> advice on this subject, I am now compelled to require a

further supply of provisions, which can barely arrive before the supply on hand is exhausted, and the surgeon informs me that the supply of the medicines and hospital stores on hand are by no means sufficient for the summer, and that many articles of the first importance are now wanting; add to these deficiencies I have not heard a word of the summer clothing required for my Regiment; the want of which is severely felt.[7]

Arbuckle reported on June 29th that he was unsure of what to do but needed these additional supplies to provide for his troops in their current position at Fort Scott. He would write to New Orleans to request resupply. The news that the solders would soon be moved to a new and hopefully healthier post must have buoyed the spirts of officers at the fort. The transfer of Florida from Spain to the United States was nearing completion and the long sojourn of the 7th and part of the 4th Infantry in the fever-infested swamps of the Flint River was nearing an end. Unfortunately, more men would have to die before the hopes of relocation were realized.

The massive surge of yellow fever and malaria during the previous year had come with the arrival of summer and 1821 would prove no different. Post returns for July-September reported 18 deaths at "Fort Scott and neighboring encampments" and another 14 at Fort Gadsden. The meaning of the term "neighboring encampments" is unclear. It is possible that men had again been moved across to Camp Recovery, but the "neighboring" camps could also have been those immediately surrounding the stockade itself.[8]

Samuel Forrey, a former Surgeon General of the United States, later teamed with Dr. Lawson to explain how the outbreak had devastated every aspect of life at the fort:

At Fort Scott, there were still in operation, the same causes of disease, - intemperance and irregularity of every description. The police was exceedingly defective; and the recruits, brought from the north, resembled the paupers which, in more recent years, have been transported to our shores from Europe. During this quarter, there were twelve cases of scurvy; and nearly every fatal case of disease might be traced to the abuse of spirituous liquors. 'For the last two years,' says Surgeon Lawson, 'our cantonment has never been encircled by a chain of sentinels; nay, the resemblance scarcely of guard duty has been maintained within our command.'[9]

As the fevers and deaths surged yet again, Lt. Col. Arbuckle was promoted to colonel of the 7th U.S. Infantry. The news must have come as a pleasant surprise to him and a shock to his enemies. Maj. Gen. Andrew Jackson was taking on a new role in his own life by accepting the governorship of Florida when that colony became a U.S. territory. Maj. Gen. Edmund P. Gaines was assuming higher command with the departure from the military of Jackson and may had a higher opinion of Arbuckle than did the hero of New Orleans. Andrew Jackson, however, was a complicated man who often appreciated those with the courage to approach him directly, as he demonstrated with his clemency of the Red Stick leader William Weatherford at the end of the Creek War of 1813-1814. Arbuckle had taken it upon himself to write to Jackson directly and at length during the controversy over his command decisions that had followed the First Seminole War. Jackson had responded with uncharacteristic restraint and this direct contact may have done much to redeem the Fort Scott commander in his eyes.

More news of a potential relocation from Fort Scott came on June 30th when Major A.A. Massias reached the post and reported that he had spoken to Gen. Daniel Parker in Washington, D.C., and the general had told him to proceed to the fort with haste or he would likely arrive after the departure of the troops. While this news pleased Col. Arbuckle, it also confused him. There had been no official contact since the letter of May 10th telling him to make preparations for the removal of his troops and the colonel was unsure of what to do. He raised this issue in a June 1st letter to Lt. E. Kirby, the acting Adjutant General in Washington, while also reporting that an organized reorganization of the 7th infantry had been completed and as instructed he had detached 150 men forming three companies for transfer to the 4th:

> The quarters and gardens at this post render it much more desirable for troops than Fort Gadsden and I would therefore recommend that the greater portion of the detachment of the 4th (Should the 7th Infantry be removed) be stationed here until October or November. Otherwise I should recommend that the whole force be moved to the Appalachicola Bay except a suitable guard at Fort Gadsden which will necessarily be retained untill the public property is removed. By this arrangement one Physician would be sufficient.[10]

As deadly of a post as Fort Scott was proving to be due to sickness, Fort Gadsden was even worse. A hospital camp similar to Camp Recovery had already been established by an assistant surgeon on the present-site of Apalachicola, but Arbuckle feared disaster if the garrison of the fort was not moved in its entirety to a healthier position by the bay.

The colonel expressed confusion as to whether he should send an officer to New Orleans to arrange for transport ships and further explained that his acting quarter master was completely out of funds having received no new money from the army in many months.[11]

The long awaited orders to evacuate Fort Scott finally came in late July 1821. Col. Arbuckle immediate wrote to the acting assistant quartermaster in New Orleans to make the logistical arrangements for the movement of the troops:

> I have received orders to remove my regiment to the
> Pass Christian and am without a Quarter Master or Funds

and of the opinion that the requisite transports cannot be obtained except at New Orleans, I have therefore to require that you will charter a sufficient number of light vessels to transport seven complete companies of the 7th Infantry with their baggage and stores from the Appalachicola Bay to the Pass Christian or Bay of St. Louis and I have also to require that you will furnish transportation for one hundred and fifty men of the 4th Infantry at this post to be removed to Pensacola. The transport vessels are required to assemble in the Appalachicola Bay between the 1st and 10th of October, and to be well supplied with water casks &c.[12]

Despite – or perhaps because of – the malaria and yellow fever then on the rampage at Fort Scott, Col. Arbuckle worked with great energy to prepare for the evacuation of the post. He reported on August 17th that the cannon, small arms and ammunition stocks at the fort had been removed to Fort St. Marks. He also noted that arrangements had been made to transfer the remaining supplies at Fort Hawkins, which would also be evacuated, to Augusta, Georgia.[13]

As the U.S. occupation of Fort Scott was nearing its end, an unusual situation developed when a mestizo named "Captain Miller" raided a settlement of Black Seminoles near Tampa Bay and brought his captives to Fort Scott. Arbuckle immediately sent them upriver:

We are desired to state, that Col. Arbuckle has forwarded to Governor Jackson a descriptive account and list of negroes taken by Captain Miller, a half breed Indian, near the bay of Tampa. The negroes are now at Fort Mitchell, (Creek Nation) or at the Creek Agency, where they will be kept until called for by their owners. The descriptive list is at the office of Col. Walton, Secretary of West Florida, to whom those interested are advised to apply.[14]

This appears to be a reference to the little known raid by Cowetas on the Maroon or Black Seminole community of Angola. Archaeologists have been searching for remains of this community in South Florida. The survivors of the raid fled down to near Cape Florida from where many of them made their way across to Andros Island in the Bahamas. Some of the original inhabitants of the British Post at Prospect Bluff were among these unfortunates.

The dates set for the final evacuation of Fort Scott were September 27-28, 1821. Col. Arbuckle confirmed this in a letter to the Adjutant General's Office in Washington on the 21st of September and there is no reason to believe that the final departure of the troops did not take place as scheduled.[15]

Arbuckle reported from Apalachicola Bay on October 7th that he arrived there on the 4th with the men from Fort Scott. The transport vessels were riding at anchor, but high winds and heavy rains had prevented him from embarking his men. He hoped to sail on the 9th or 10th of the month. The sick list at the time of the evacuation numbered 154 cases, most of them dysentery, although surgeons lamented that "the whole command was enfeebled by previous disease."[16]

Surgeon Lawson was present during the evacuation and provided a good account in his later writings:

> ...Having descended the Appalachicola, and being encamped near its mouth, the troops were exposed to violent storms of wind and rain, which caused a great augmentation of the sick list. Transportation having at length arrived, the troops embarked for New Orleans in seven sloops and schooners – the sick being stowed away with the other men and the baggage of their companies respectively; and until their arrival at the bayou St. John they were, by this arrangement in most of the vessels, deprived of medical aid. Here the men suffered exceedingly from the quality of the water, which had been put into casks

containing the impure lees of wine. The cases of dysentery were consequently much increased in number, and rendered more fatal."[17]

The number of men who died during the trip downriver or miserable stay on the shores of Apalachicola Bay is not known. The transports sailed as soon as the storm ended and reached New Orleans a short time later via the post at Pass Christian. The troops spent a brief time in the Crescent City before boarding steamboats that would carry them to their new posts. The main body of the 7th headed up the Mississippi River on the steamboat *Tennessee* on November 6, 1821. Their destination was the Arkansas River and ultimately the frontier post of Fort Smith. The rest of the regiment, under Lt. Col. Taylor, left on the same day aboard the steamboat *Courier* for the military post at Natchitoches on the Red River in Louisiana. Col. Arbuckle headed the battalion headed to Fort Smith in person.

Fort Smith offered new scenery and a refreshing change for the officers and men. The post had been established in 1819 on a high bluff overlooking the junction of the Arkansas and Poteau Rivers. The north and south horizons were dominated by the beautiful mountains of the Ouachitas and the Ozarks and to the west was the new frontier and the land that would soon become the home of the Creek, Seminole, Cherokee, Choctaw and Chickasaw people. The Trail of Tears was still in the future when the sick and suffering men from Fort Scott reached their new home on the Arkansas. Instead they saw all of the opportunities and beauty of the new frontier:

> The detachment of the 7th regt. Infantry which passed this place in February last, arrived at Fort Smith on the 26th of that month, and we are happy to learn, that they were left in an improving and much better state of health, than they have enjoyed for several months. The men belonging to that detachment, have been severely afflicted with the dysentery, ever since they left the Mississippi, and a large portion of those attacked have fell victims to the disease. We understand that no new cases of the disease have occurred since their arrival on the Arkansas, but several have been laboring under it for some time, and four men have died since their arrival at the fort. They are now

arrived in comfortable quarters, in a remarkably healthy part of our country, where their wants and necessities can be much better administered to, than they could possibly be in their late disagreeable situation on board of crowded boats, and it is expected that the usual good health of the garrison will soon be restored.

As an evidence of the healthy situation of Fort Smith, it is worthy of remark, that not a solitary death by sickness has occurred among the soldiers under Major Bradford's command, since the establishment of the post, four years ago, until since the late augmentation of the force. The force now consists of 230 soldiers.

There is an excellent farm of about 80 acres belonging to the fort, which is cultivated by the soldiers, and affords them an abundant supply of a great variety of vegetables; and they now have about 1000 bushels of corn remaining of last year's crop. Of stock, there are about 100 head of neat cattle, and about 400 head of hogs.[18]

And so the story of Fort Scott comes to an end. The four men from the 7th Infantry who died after reaching Fort Smith were the first losses of life in the history of that post. Other soldiers had died along the journey from the illnesses they contracted at Fort Scott and behind in the soil of the red clay bluff on the Flint River rested the remains of nearly 100 of their friends, comrades and officers.

A gun monument like the one at Camp Recovery was placed on the site in 1883, but the U.S. Army Corps of Engineers removed it to the site of Fort Hughes in 1953 under the expectation that Fort Scott would be flooded when the Jim Woodruff Dam was completed. The dam was finished and Lake Seminole created in 1958, but the site of the old fort remained about 7 feet above the water level of the reservoir. It remains today overgrown and forgotten with no memorial or reminder of the scores of U.S. soldiers who gave their lives for their country at the post on the Flint and remain buried in its soil.

[1] Samuel Forrey, M.D., late of the United States Army, Thomas Lawson, M.D., Surgeon General, Statistical Report on the Sickness and Mortality in the Army of the United States: Compiled from the Records of the Surgeon General's and Adjutant General's Offices – Embracing a Period of Twenty Years, from January, 1819, to January, 1839, Washington, printed by Jacob Gideon, Jr., 1840, p. 27.

[2] *Ibid.*

[3] *Ibid.*

[4] "Veritas" to the Editor, Arkansas Gazette, February 10, 1821, p. 3.

[5] Fictitious letter from "E-ne-he-Mat-la" dated July 10, 1821, Call Papers, State Archives of Florida.

[6] Samuel Forrey, M.D., late of the United States Army, Thomas Lawson, M.D., Surgeon General, Statistical Report on the Sickness and Mortality in the Army of the United States: Compiled from the Records of the Surgeon General's and Adjutant General's Offices – Embracing a Period of Twenty Years, from January, 1819, to January, 1839, Washington, printed by Jacob Gideon, Jr., 1840, p. 28.

[7] Lt. Col. Matthew Arbuckle to Gen. Henry Atkinson, Adjutant General, June 29, 1821, Adjutant General, Letters Received, NARA.

[8] *Ibid.*

[9] *Ibid.*, p. 29-31.

[10] Col. Matthew Arbuckle to Lt. E. Kirby, Acting Adjutant General, July 1, 1821, Adjutant General, Letter's Received, NARA.

[11] *Ibid.*

[12] Col. Matthew Arbuckle to the acting assistant quartermaster in New Orleans, July 26, 1821, Adjutant General, Letters Received, NARA.

[13] Col. Matthew Arbuckle to Lt. E. Kirby, Acting Adjutant General, August 17, 1821, Adjutant General, Letters Received.

[14] Pensacola *Floridian*, September 1821.

[15] Col. Matthew Arbuckle to Lt. E. Kirby, Acting Adjutant General, September 21, 1821, Adjutant General, Letters Received, NARA.

[16] Col. Matthew Arbuckle to Col. James Gadsden, Adjutant General, October 7, 1821, Adjutant General, Letters Received, NARA.

[17] Samuel Forrey, M.D., late of the United States Army, Thomas Lawson, M.D., Surgeon General, Statistical Report on the Sickness and Mortality in the Army of the United States: Compiled from the Records of the Surgeon General's and Adjutant General's Offices – Embracing a Period of Twenty Years, from January, 1819, to January, 1839, Washington, printed by Jacob Gideon, Jr., 1840, p. 31.

[18] *Arkansas Gazette*, April 22, 1822.

Photographs

Lt. Col. Duncan Lamont Clinch

Clinch as a brigadier general in later life.

Maj. Gen. Edmund Pendleton Gaines

Restored blockhouse at Fort Gaines, Georgia.

Site of Fort Scott, Georgia.

Another view of the site of Fort Scott, Georgia.

Negro Abraham.

Abraham, captured at destruction of the fort at Prospect Bluff.

Moat still surrounding the site of the fort at Prospect Bluff.

Brig. Gen. William McIntosh of Coweta.

U.S. Navy gunboats. The ones involved at Prospect Bluff were similar to the larger two.

Fort Scott was named in honor of Gen. Winfield T. Scott.

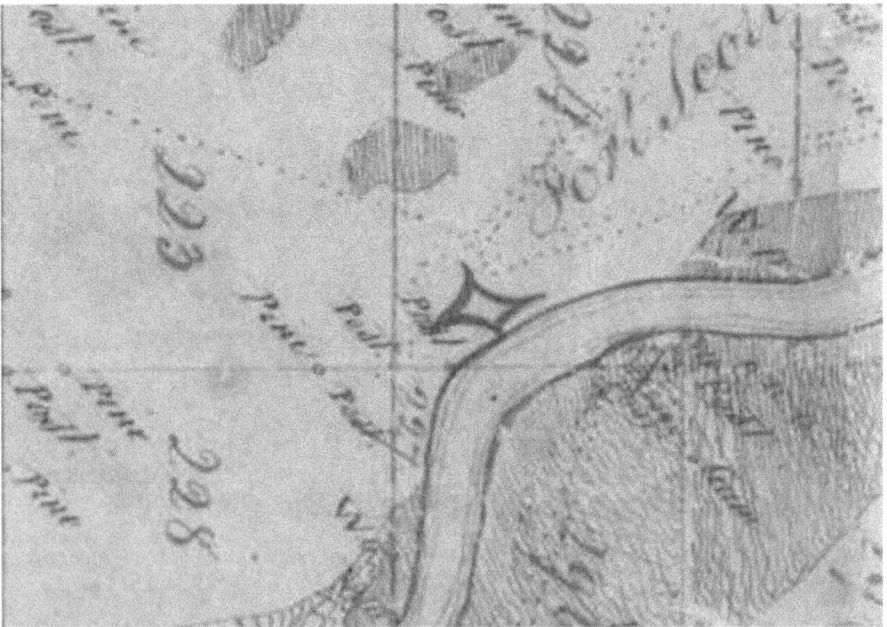

Fort Scott as shown on the 1820 District Surveys.

Ben & Sam Perryman after the Trail of Tears.

The Prophet Josiah Francis (Self-Portrait). Courtesy of the British Museum.

Neamathla (Eneah Emathla), chief of Fowltown.

Maj. David E. Twiggs, 7th U.S. Infantry Regiment.

Lt. Col. Matthew Arbuckle, 7th U.S. Infantry Regiment.

Site of Fowltown in Decatur County, Georgia.

"Indians attacking Scott's party" (19th century sketch).

Site of the Scott Massacre of 1817 at River Landing Park in Chattahoochee, Florida.

Gun monument at site of Fort Hughes in Bainbridge, Georgia.

Flint River at Bainbridge, Georgia.

Earthworks of Fort Gadsden, Florida.

San Marcos de Apalache Historic State Park in St. Marks, Florida.

Osceola in the 1830s.

Dr. Thomas Lawson, surgeon of the 7th U.S. Infantry Regiment.

References

Documents

Adams-Onis Treaty of 1819.

American State Papers, Foreign Relations, Volume IV, Washington, Gales and Seaton, 1834.

American State Papers, Indian Affairs, Volumes I & II. Washington, Gales and Seaton, 1834.

American State Papers, Military Affairs, Volume I, Washington, Gales and Seaton, 1834.

Army and Navy Chronicle, Volume 2 (New Series), 1836.

Andrew Jackson Papers, 1775-1874, Manuscript Reading Room, Library of Congress.

British Foreign and State Papers, Multiple Volumes, Her Majesty's Stationary Office.

Call Papers, State Archives of Florida.

District Plat of Survey for District 12, Early County (now Baker County), Georgia, 1819, State Archives of Georgia

District Plat of Survey for District 14, Early County (now Decatur County), Georgia, 1821, State Archives of Georgia.

Letters Received by the Adjutant General's Office during the period 1805-1821, M566, Record Group 94, National Archives, Washington, D.C.

Records of the Chief of Engineers, 1789-1996, Record Group 77, National Archives, Washington, D.C.

Register of Enlistments in the U.S. Army, 1798-1914, National Archives Microfilm Publication M233, 81 rolls, Records of the Adjutant General's Office, 1780's-1917, Record Group 94, National Archives, Washington, D.C.

References

Survey Book EEE, Office of the County Clerk, Decatur County, Georgia.
"The Indian Frontier in British East Florida: Letters to Governor James
    Grant from British Soldiers and Indian Traders," Florida History
    Online, University of North Florida, Online resource at
    www.unf.edu/floridahistoryonline/Projects/Grant/letters.html
    (transcribed by James Hill).
Territorial Papers of the United States: The Territory of Alabama, 1817-
    1819, Volume XVIII, Compiled and edited by Clarence Carter,
    Government Printing Office, Washington, D.C., 1952.
Topographic Map for Hopeful, Georgia, U.S. Geological Survey,
    Washington, D.C., 1971.

Period Newspapers

Alexandria Gazette
American Beacon
Arkansas Gazette
Augusta Chronicle
Bainbridge Democrat
Baltimore Patriot
Camden Gazette
City Gazette
Easton Gazette
Georgia Journal
Hallowell Gazette
Independent American
London Times
Massachusetts Spy
Milledgeville Reflector
National Advocate
National Standard
Newburyport Herald
New York Daily Advertiser
New York Evening Post

References

New York Gazette
Niles Weekly Register
North Carolina Star
Spooner's Vermont Journal
Salem Gazette

Reports & Articles

Boyd, Mark F., "Historic Sites in and around the Jim Woodruff Reservoir Area, Florida-Georgia," River Basin Survey Papers, No. 13, *Bulletin 169*, Smithsonian Institution, Bureau of American Ethnology, 1958.

Forrey, Samuel, M.D., late of the United States Army, Thomas Lawson, M.D., Surgeon General, *Statistical Report on the Sickness and Mortality in the Army of the United States: Compiled from the Records of the Surgeon General's and Adjutant General's Offices – Embracing a Period of Twenty Years, from January, 1819, to January, 1839*, Washington, printed by Jacob Gideon, Jr., 1840

Doyle, Edmund, "Letters of Edmund Doyle," *Florida Historical Quarterly*, Volume 18, October 1939, No. 2.

Menefee, Samuel P., "Aaron Burr's Arrest," Encyclopedia of Alabama, online article at www.encyclopediaofalabama.org/article/h-2039, February 23, 2009.

Porter, Kenneth, "The Negro Abraham," *Florida Historical Quarterly*, Volume 25, July 1946.

Mark N. Schatz, "Reference Service Report: Monuments on the sites of Fort Scott, Fort Hughes, and Camp Recovery, near Bainbridge, Georgia," National Archives, 1953.

Suarez, Annette McDonald, "The War Path Across Georgia Made By Tennessee Troops in the First Seminole War," *The Georgia Historical Quarterly*, Vol. 38, No. 1, March 1954.

White, Nancy Marie, et. al., "Archaeology at Lake Seminole," Cleveland Museum of Natural History, 1980.

Books

Banks, John, *Diary of John Banks*, privately published, 1936.

Chapman, John Abney, *History of Edgefield County: from the earliest settlements to 1897: biographical and anecdotical, with sketches of the Seminole war, nullification, secession, reconstruction, churches and literature, with rolls of all the companies from Edgefield in the War of Secession, War with Mexico and with the Seminole Indians*, E.H. Aull, 1897,

Cox, Dale, *The Scott Massacre of 1817: A Seminole War Battle in Gadsden County, Florida*, West Gadsden Historical Society, 2013.

Cox, Dale, *Nicolls' Outpost: A War of 1812 Fort at Chattahoochee, Florida*, Old Kitchen Books, 2015.

Cox, Dale, *The Fort at Prospect Bluff*, scheduled for release in the summer of 2016 by Old Kitchen Books.

Charles Martin Gray, *The old soldier's story: autobiography of Charles Martin Gray, Co. A, 7th Regiment, U.S.I., embracing interesting and exciting incidents of army life on the frontier, in the early part of the present century*, Edgefield Advertiser Print.

Heitman, Francis Bernard, *Historical Register and Dictionary of the United States Army*, National Tribune Company, 1890.

Jones, Dixie May, and Mary Elizabeth Scott, *Citizens of Baldwin County, Mississippi Territory, in 1816 as enumerated in Inhabitants of Alabama in 1816*, Broken Arrow Chapter, Daughters of the American Revolution, 1955.

Woodward, Thomas Simpson, *Woodward's reminiscences of the Creek or Muscogee Indians: contained in letters to friends in Georgia and Alabama*, Montgomery, Alabama, 1859.

About the Author

Dale Cox is the author of sixteen books on U.S. history.

He has written extensively about Florida history from the era of Spanish exploration to the troubled times of the 1930s. His books have achieved critical acclaim and rank among the best-selling nonfiction books on history. Cox has been interviewed for hundreds of newspaper and magazine articles, television programs and documentary films. Civil War Books & Authors called him "a skillful constructor of battle narrative" and named his *The Battle of Marianna, Florida* as the best volume in its category.

Active in historic preservation efforts and a popular speaker/story teller, Dale Cox was Jackson County, Florida's "Citizen of the Year" for 2012. He has been inducted into the prestigious Bonnie Blue Society for Southern writers and received the Judah P. Benjamin Award for his work in preserving the history of Florida.

Cox is a descendant of both the American frontiersman Daniel Boone and the Yuchi Creek Indian chief Efau Emathla. He resides near the quaint community of Two Egg, Florida, and is the father of two grown sons, William and Alan. He is often featured on the "off the beaten path" history and travel television station, Two Egg TV (www.twoegg.tv).

Books by Dale Cox

Fort Scott, Fort Hughes & Camp Recovery: Three 19th Century military
        sites in Southwest Georgia
Nicolls' Outpost: A War of 1812 fort at Chattahoochee, Florida
Death at Dozier School
Milly Francis: The Life & Times of the Creek Pocahontas
The Scott Massacre of 1817
The Claude Neal Lynching: The 1934 Murders of Claude Neal and Lola
        Cannady

The Ghost of Bellamy Bridge
The Battle of Natural Bridge, Florida
The Battle of Marianna, Florida
The Battle of Massard Prairie: The Confederate Attacks on Fort Smith,
        Arkansas
Old Parramore: The History of a Florida Ghost Town
The Early History of Gadsden County
The History of Jackson County, Florida: The Early Years
The History of Jackson County, Florida: The Civil War Years
Two Egg, Florida: A Collection of Ghost Stories, Legends & Unusual
        Facts
A Christmas in Two Egg, Florida

All books by Dale Cox are available at www.exploresouthernhistory.com.

Index

Gulf of Mexico, 16, *92*, 154, 185,
194, 208
Hall
Dr., 53
Hambly
William, 12, 20, 24, 32, 72, 107,
126, 128, 150
Hamilton's Brigade, 79
Hancock County (Georgia), *87*
Hardridge
Wiliam, 32
William, 20
Harrison
William Henry, 54
Hartford, 19, 79, *84*, 151, 152, 153,
154, 156, 158, 164, 178
Hawkins
Benjamin, 10, 13, 15, 17, 22, 51,
65, *69*
Samuel, 175
Hayne
A.P., 155, 159, 160, 176
Arthur P., 178
Hillis Hadjo. *See* Josiah Francis
Historic Chattahoochee
Commission, 211
Hitchiti, *65*
Holmes, 159
Homathlemico, 106, 185
Hoskins
J.D.C., 210
Howell
W.B., 51
Hughes
Aaron, *101*, *103*, 118
Huntsville, 152
Ichawaynochaway Creek, 168
Indian Mounds, 26
Indonesia, 120
Irvin
Robert, 134
Irwin's Brigade, 79
J.D. Chason Memorial Park, 118

Jackson
Andrew, 1, 2, 10, 11, 13, 19, 21,
24, 54, 55, 63, *69*, 71, *87*, *93*,
95, 111, 121, 127, 130, 134,
137, 143, 148, 152, 154, 156,
158, 160, 163, 170, 178, 179,
183, 186, 188, 192, 194, 218
Rachel, 180
Jackson County (Florida), 60, 159
Jacob, 51
Jamaica, 46, 51
Jasper County (Georgia), *87*
Jefferson
Thomas, 33, 62
Jefferson County (Florida), 183
Jim Woodruff Dam, 53, 170, 223
Jo, 51
Joe, *68*
John Forbes & Company, 12, 56, *83*
Johnson, 123, 125
Daniel, 2
Milo, *102*
Jones County (Georgia), *87*
Keiser
C., 74
Kenhajo. *See* Cappachimico
Kinchafoonee Creek, 167, 184
King
William, 54, 62, *63*, *69*
Kingsley
Zephaniah, 55, 56
Kinnard
Jack, 158, 184
Noble, 170
Kirby
E., 219
Kolomoki Creek, 197
Lafarka. *See* John Blunt
Lake Blackshear, 165
Lake Miccosukee, 183
Lake Seminole, 16, 26, 27, 53, 80,
170, 223
Lamb, 51

Lawson
  Dr. Thomas, 199, 200, 207, 209,
    213, 217, 221
Lee County (Georgia), 166
Leftwich
  Granville, 195
Leon County (Florida), 183
Lewis
  Kendal, 38
  Mr., 51
Liberty County (Florida), 174
Lincoln
  Abraham, 210
  Robert Todd, 209, 210
Little Ish Spring, 27, 53
Little Prince, 8, 10, 12, 20, 21, 132
Little River, 17
Little River (Oklahoma), 52
Loomis
  Jairus, 33, 34, 36, 41, 43
Lopaz
  John, 37, 38
Lopez
  John. *See* John Lopaz
Louisiana Purchase, 62
Louisiana Volunteers, 12
Lovett
  Billy, 170
Lower Creeks, 12, 34, *65*, *67*, *83*,
  94, 132
Luffborough
  Midshipman, 37, 38, 43
MacGregor
  Gregor, *96*
Mad Tiger, 36, 38
Mad Warrior, 115
Maitland
  Robert, 38
Major Howard, 166
Mann
  John, 158
Margart
  William, 51

Marianna, 175
Marlborough, *101*
Massias
  A.A., 218
McCulloh
  Alexander, 72
McGaskey
  John, 3
McGavock
  Lt., 43
McIntosh
  John N., 118, 119, 120, 121, 173,
    178, 180, 181, 186
  William, 34, 36, 38, 40, 50, *70*,
    71, 80, 133, 137, 142, 158,
    159, 170, 173, 174, 180, 182,
    185
McKeever
  Isaac, 185
McQueen
  Peter, 18, *67*, *68*, *69*, 185
Miccosukee, 1, 20, 39, 56, *65*, *66*,
  67, 80, *83*, *84*, *87*, *94*, 105, 115,
  120, 127, 133, 183
Miccosukee Tribe of Florida, 105
Mico de Coxe, 159
Milledgeville, 33, 55, 61, *88*, 113,
  177
Miller County (Georgia), 163
Milton
  Homer V., 177, 180
Mission
  La Encarnacion a la Santa Cruz
    de Sabacola, 26
Mississippi River, 12, 62, 222
Mitchell
  David, 51
  David B., 55, 56, 61, *63*, *67*, 70,
    131, 132, 134, 155
Mitchell County (Georgia), 157
Mobile, 62, *92*, 153, 186
Mobile Point, 11

www.ingramcontent.com/pod-product-compliance
Lightning Source LLC
Chambersburg PA
CBHW060043100426
42742CB00014B/2684